Penguin Special s245

Immigration and Race in British Politics

Paul Foot was born in Haifa, Palestine in 1937. He had his early education in Jamaica but later went to Shrewsbury and then University College, Oxford, where he was both Editor of *Isis* and President of the Union. After Oxford he went to Glasgow for three years as a feature writer on the Scottish *Daily Record*. He became an active trade unionist in the National Union of Journalists and was a delegate to the Glasgow Trades Council for two years.

After six months working for the *Sun*, Paul Foot now writes for Mandrake of the *Sunday Telegraph*. Politics finds him 'dedicated and militant'.

PAUL FOOT

IMMIGRATION AND RACE IN BRITISH POLITICS

Penguin Books

BALTIMORE · MARYLAND

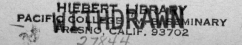

Penguin Books Ltd, Harmondsworth, Middlesex, England
Penguin Books Inc., 3300 Clipper Mill Road, Baltimore 11,
Md, U.S.A.
Penguin Books Pty Ltd, Ringwood, Victoria, Australia

First published 1965

Made and printed in Great Britain by
Cox & Wyman Ltd, London, Reading and Fakenham
Set in Monotype Plantin

Contents

Foreword

I must plead guilty on two counts. First, to living in Hampstead (or rather the Borough of Camden, which houses a large number of immigrants) and to being completely inexperienced about the 'effects' of immigration from a working-class angle. No case is wrong simply because its proponent has not 'lived with' the problem, but for people like me, emotionally and intellectually revolted by anti-immigrant propaganda, there is always the nagging suspicion that some of its less ludicrous aspects may in some respects be justified.

I should therefore like to thank, first, those many people of all colours who have allayed my doubts in this regard: in particular, Mr Jack Morris and Mr Richard Pritchard of Smethwick, both of whom come into close contact, at home and at work, with immigrants; and the Indian and Pakistani workers at the Cortaulds Red Scar rayon mill in Preston, whom I was fortunate enough to meet for several hours while they were on strike in June 1965, and whose courtesy and enthusiasm I shall always remember.

Secondly, more specifically, I have not dealt in any detail with the modern Liberal Party, not because I have any particular quarrel with Liberals, but because their contribution to the immigration discussion has in no major aspect been original. By and large, Liberal policy through the years has corresponded almost exactly with Labour policy.

There is nothing in this book about the personal habits of great men. It is mainly an account of political reactions to immigration, and most of it is on the record. I have, for instance, never met either Mr Peter Griffiths or Mr Gordon Walker, partly through lack of time, but mainly because both have enough on the record to speak for them. I have gone out and interviewed people where they play an important part in the story but have not featured prominently in Press reports.

Anyone who wants to know anything about immigration into Britain must go to the Institute of Race Relations, where they will be given full access to a host of newspaper cuttings and Press summaries on the subject dating back to 1955. I am particularly grateful to Mr Nicholas Deakin who answered a host of frenzied questions with studied patience and good humour.

Others who have helped me considerably are Mr Cedric Thornberry, a law lecturer at London School of Economics and an expert on aliens legislation, and Mr John Shirley, formerly a reporter on the *Middlesex County Times* in Southall (he has since moved to Newcastle). The remarks in the concluding chapter on the beginnings of racial strife in the American South after the Civil War are almost entirely the result of reading the first chapter of Mr Ronald Segal's *The Race War*: a book which bears all the marks of a modern political classic. None of these people, of course, are responsible in any way for the views expressed in this book. I have been lucky, too, in having free access to the Oxford Union library (particularly good for nineteenth century material) and the excellent cuttings library at the *Sun*.

My wife Monica went through the manuscript, and read the proofs. During her three-year association with me she has acquired a remarkable, and for me face-saving, facility for excising unnecessary and emotive adjectives.

PAUL FOOT

May 1965

1. Smethwick: The Background

'More than 50 families have rejoined their menfolk. This is the greatest reunion since the war. There are now about 2,000 coloured people in the town. Smethwick people are being wonderful hosts to them.'

Mr R. J. Kendall, Secretary of the Overseas Institute, Smethwick

19 March 1958   *Birmingham Evening Dispatch*

*

Emigration figures are rising. Of those I have spoken to all have told me that their reason for leaving their homeland is that they could no longer live in a multi-racial community.

There are now 419 lepers in this country . . .

These people could be sitting next to you on the bus, handling the same money as you, and their children could be going to school with your children.

West Indians are prolific breeders. Soon our children will be getting education on a rota system – in the morning one day, in the afternoon the next.

These people do not know the basic principles of hygiene. We have to stand and watch them emptying their noses and throats onto our streets.

Most of them come to batten off the social services . . . we are harbouring one of the biggest fifth columns in the world.

The speaker's heavy Midland accent rose and fell to almost continuous applause. He was rounding off a meeting at Cape Hill School in Smethwick on Tuesday, 25 April 1961.

The meeting had been organized by the newly-formed Smethwick branch of the Birmingham Immigration Control Association to promote the campaign – already well under way in other areas of Birmingham – for a total ban on Commonwealth Immigration to last at least five years, for health checks of immigrants and for the deportation of immigrant criminals. Mr Harry Jones, the speaker, a small wholesaler, had recently been elected secretary of the Association.

This meeting at Cape Hill School started in earnest the process which has now established Smethwick internationally as 'Britain's most colour-conscious town'. Before 25 April 1961, those who had heard of Smethwick knew it as an ordinary industrial borough – its geographic identity long since lost in the huge industrial conurbation of Birmingham and the Black Country. To the chagrin of its inhabitants it is now merely a postal district of Birmingham – the 41st.

Smethwick's industrial history dates back to 1762 when Matthew Boulton and, later, James Watt, the inventor of the steam engine, built one of the first foundries in the country to produce metal castings for other manufacturers.

Today more than ninety factories are crammed tight in this five square miles of county borough – most of them dealing in metal or glass. The huge foundries have been geared to meet the demands of the motor industry in the Midlands: when the motor industry thrives, so does Smethwick. The large Birmid Engineering group has three factories in the town.

Because of this compact wad of industry, the housing situation in Smethwick has always been appalling. Today it is a densely populated county borough – with twenty-seven people to every acre. Before the last war, its housing consisted of old industrial cottages in the centre – particularly around Cape Hill – and several streets of once comfortable, now dishevelled, Victorian villas in which the industrial bourgeoisie of the last century resided. Two new developments have taken place since. A massive council housebuilding programme has cleared away many of the old slums in the centre, and the middle classes have moved from the old Victorian houses to the new comfortable suburbia around Bearwood and Lightwoods Hill. Many of to-day's Smethwick industrialists live even farther afield. Their old houses have been snapped up by workers eager for homes near the factory, and have suffered the fate of their equivalents in every industrial city of Britain – multi-occupation. Many of them now are 'multi-occupied' by Commonwealth immigrants.

The population of Smethwick has steadily decreased since its peak of 84,406 in 1931. In 1951, before Commonwealth immigrants started to arrive in Smethwick, the population was 76,407. Today it is 68,000. Although there is still overcrowding in

Smethwick, there is much less of it now than there was in 1951. There are fewer people and more occupied rooms. The proportion of people per room in 1951 was 0·74. In 1961 it was 0·64. In each of the eight Smethwick wards the number of people per room has decreased substantially over the last ten years.

Nor is overcrowding any worse than in other Midland towns and boroughs. The list below shows the percentage of persons per room in seven areas:

Smethwick:	0·64
Worcester:	0·66
Redditch:	0·68
Droitwich:	0·70
Dudley:	0·72
Birmingham:	0·72
Coventry:	0·72

Towards the end of 1953 a handful of the coloured Commonwealth immigrants who had been settling in Birmingham ever since the end of the war discovered that the massive engineering combine, Birmid Ltd, was straining for unskilled and semi-skilled labour to meet the rise in car production after the 1952–3 recession. There was no mention of immigrant workers in the final 1953 report of the Smethwick Employment Committee but early in 1954 the number of reported cases of Indians before the courts increased alarmingly. Almost all the cases showed an incredible ignorance among lawyers and magistrates of the immigrants' culture and background. For instance one well-intentioned defending counsel told the magistrates that 'Every Indian carries a knife – it is their essential tool'. He was defending a Pakistani.

As the boom strengthened, so the flow of immigrants to Smethwick increased. On 27 August Mr J. E. Sitch the manager of the local Labour Exchange reported:

Shortage of labour is the concern of almost every employer in the town.
A policy of importation is now being pursued. This is a very thorny problem with many attendant difficulties, not the least of which is the all-important one of accommodation.

He added that the gas-works in the town had almost closed

because of the movement of labour into the more lucrative motor-car factories. The gas-works were saved at the last minute by a drastic trip of the employers to Ireland where they hired the first thirty-five unemployed labourers in sight.

There were 641 vacancies and only twenty-two unemployed – most of these last disabled.

Throughout 1955 the labour shortage continued to threaten the stability of Smethwick's industry. The Labour Exchange manager reported happily in April that:

Coloured labour from the Commonwealth is greatly easing the labour shortage. The labour turnover among these immigrant workers is lower than the average, and firms formerly hesitant about employing them are now doing so to a considerable degree.

Nevertheless there were now 920 vacancies and only twenty-three registered unemployed. There were 1,255 coloured men working in Smethwick on the books of the Labour Exchange. Most of them were living without their families in lodging houses and houses bought on expensive mortgages by Indian landlords. By the middle of 1955 there were at least 2,000 coloured immigrants in Smethwick.

Sitch's report went on:

The employers would be very worried if coloured labour were withdrawn. All employers readily pay tribute to the valuable contribution this type of labour is making towards industrial output.

By August of that prosperous summer the number of vacancies had risen to 1,084 – and there were still a mere twenty-three people registered as unemployed. A man who had had both legs amputated, and who had been off work for years, was found work as a press operator. Another, suffering from paraplegia, had taken his place on an assembly line. In five months, noted the Labour Exchange manager with some pride, sixty disabled people had been placed in regular employment. But he remarked also, with alarm: 'The infiltration of coloured workers has slowed to a trickle.'

Yet despite this remarkable contribution, and desperate as Smethwick industry was for this 'type of labour', the new immigrant workers were treated with scant regard once they left the factory. For the most part they lived in dingy hostels, or in rooms let out by their more far-sighted countrymen, usually in conditions of terrible poverty. Most of them worked long hours of overtime in weather conditions to which they were totally unaccustomed. They were loath to move out to shops where men and women spoke a strange language and regarded them with polite suspicion. For food and drink they used anything that came to hand. In a report to the Smethwick Trades Council in December, 1955, Mr Arthur Reed, a patternmaker, described how the Indian workers ate on the premises by making 'chipatties' out of the firm's scrap flour. They rolled them into cakes and cooked them on the furnaces.

Small wonder, then, that the Chief Physician for the town in 1955 reported that the incidence of tuberculosis, which had always been high in Smethwick, had risen yet again, and that a 'special survey had shown that there was a higher rate of TB among immigrants'. Five per cent of available hospital beds had been provided for immigrants. In November, Mr William Kay the Chief Public Health Inspector carried out a special inspection of houses occupied only by coloured people. No less than fifty-nine houses were overcrowded, even under the somewhat liberal terminology of the existing Housing Acts. In these fifty-nine houses were crammed 354 immigrants – almost all of them men.

The 1955 honeymoon with prosperity did not last long. Early in 1956 came the first warning signs of a recession in the motor industry – the life-blood of the industrial Midlands. On 18 May, Dartmouth Auto Castings, a subsidiary of the Birmid Engineering group, sacked 180 men, almost all of them coloured – a move which enabled the rest of the workers to go back to full-time working. There is no evidence of any struggle from the union organizations in Birmid to promote sharing of the work available.

These were not the only redundancies. In three months the number of vacancies on the Labour Exchange dropped from 1,000 to 600 while the number of unemployed rose from twenty-three to 400. The Labour Exchange made it clear that it would be 'difficult to place' the coloured workers.

Then a very strange thing happened. The majority of sacked coloured workers did not turn up at the Labour Exchange for their unemployment money. Of the ninety due to register at the Exchange for their unemployment benefit, only thirty did so. The other sixty were described in the local Press as the 'missing Indians'.

They had gone. They had left Smethwick, to return only when there was work for them to do, and wages and overtime money to be collected. In the meantime, while the motor industry was bogged down in a recession, they would try their luck in the mills of the North or the buses of the South.

The Smethwick Labour Exchange got a few inquiries from its counterparts in towns as far apart as Bradford and Ramsgate. Had they heard of a man called Singh who said that he used to live and work in Smethwick? He's come to work in a catering job, and says that you have his papers.

By the autumn of 1956 the situation was extremely serious. There were 1,151 wholly unemployed or on short time in Smethwick, and only 300 vacancies, most of them for specialized skills. Mr Sitch reported that the coloured workers were flooding out of the town 'as silently as they came'.

The recession had its effect on the Smethwick-born population too. In January 1957, the local newspaper reported that 'hundreds of Smethwick people are being caught up in the nation-wide emigration movement'. No less than 500 Smethwickians had already booked their passages to Canada and a meeting called by the Canadian emigration authorities to explain conditions in Canada was 'sold out' several days before it took place.

By this time the Indian community in Smethwick had been supplemented by a sprinkling of West Indians, and the men of both nationalities were being joined by their wives and families from abroad. This process cleared the men out of the lodging houses and drove them into 'homes' of one or two rooms in Victorian semi-detached villas. The influx of women and children sharpened the pressure of overcrowding, but it had the more vital effect of raising the living standards of the immigrant men.

The women and children rooted their husbands more to their Smethwick homes. The Employment Exchange manager reported desperately in August 1957:

There is virtually no demand now for the services of the Indians . . . our biggest problem by far is to find work for Jamaicans, Indians and

Pakistanis, particularly women, for whom we have absolutely no vacancies.

In March 1958, the Employment Exchange reported that some of the immigrant workers who had moved out of the area were beginning to return, sniffing out the oncoming pre-election 'boom'. Yet the 'boom' was long in coming and for the rest of that year a large proportion of the coloured community in Smethwick lived in congested poverty with the constant threat of long-term unemployment hanging over them.

Yet despite the 'honeypot' of the 1959–60 boom, the 1961 census, held on almost the same day as the inaugural meeting of the Smethwick branch of the Birmingham Immigration Control Association, recorded only 2,901 people in Smethwick born outside the British Isles, of whom 1,546 were from the Commonwealth and 824 from the colonies. Allowing for the inevitable sprinkling of long-standing immigrants from the 'old' white Commonwealth, this reveals a remarkably small number of coloured immigrants.

By October 1961, the Smethwick labour market had shrunk again. There were no jobs for unskilled workers available. There were 364 unemployed or on short time, and the only vacancies were for skilled men. But now the 1957–8 process, whereby immigration into the town stopped and many of the unemployed immigrants left the town, was reversed. The families of the men rooted them to their homes, and – more important – there was widespread talk throughout the country of an Act to halt immigration. There was as yet no accurate indication of what form that Act might take.

Frantic letters to families and relations went from the immigrant community. For the illiterate among them, Ombudsmen were found to communicate the grim news. 'Come at once,' ran the letters. 'Sell everything and get your passage money. This is surely the last chance of ever getting here!'

Whereas such letters had previously contained careful surveys of the jobs and housing situation – 'There is a man displaced in our foundry: I think I can get you in' – now all caution was flung aside. Jobs and houses could be found – sometime. What mattered was to get to the country before the Government barred the door. Even when the Bill was published, excluding from control wives and children of immigrants already in Britain, there was no appreciable slackening in the pressure on these to change their plans and move to Britain at once.

During the next eight months, the trickle increased into a flood. All the reliable sources indicate that the coloured immigrant community in Smethwick doubled during that short time.

There were few enough jobs for the newcomers. By the winter of 1962–3 unemployment had risen to the highest peak in the town's post-war history – 841 wholly unemployed, hundreds more on short time, and only seventy-seven vacancies. Of the 866 unemployed in February, the Employment Committee estimated that more than 300 were Commonwealth immigrants – more than ten per cent of all immigrants insured to work!

Those few Smethwick houses open to the immigrants were bursting at the seams. There were some 400 houses in multi-occupation at the time, most of them inhabited by Commonwealth immigrants, their population split – Indians: 1,550 (250 families and 480 single people); West Indians: 1,350 (320 families and 250 single people); Pakistanis: 300 (twelve families and 240 single people).

Almost the entire West Indian and Pakistani population was living in multi-occupied houses! Only the Indians had managed to break away into relatively spacious accommodation. By the end of 1963 Dr Wilson Russell, chief of the Smethwick Chest Clinic, could say in his official report that 'overcrowding and multi-occupation in immigrant households has been less noticeable in 1963 . . . mainly because of the strong desire of the Indians for normal family lives in separate houses.'

Tuberculosis had risen again among immigrants. Thirty-five of the sixty-three new Smethwick cases were immigrants – twenty-three of them Indians and eight Pakistanis. Dr Russell was in no doubt as to the real reason for this worsening situation:

In the prevention of tuberculosis the abolition of poverty, starvation and poor housing are basic public health measures. Good standards of diet and personal hygiene have been attained in 'the affluent society' but good housing has still not been fully achieved. . . . Many families still live in overcrowded conditions. In my view housing is even more important than schools and hospitals.

Dr Russell also pointed out that 'tuberculosis is comparatively uncommon among West Indians, but is common in Asiatics, who present glandular as well as respiratory disease'.

Dr Russell added his general view of the immigrants in Smethwick:

My impression is that there are more West Indians in the town but fewer Pakistanis and now that the wives and children of Indians have joined their menfolk, the Indians and West Indians have settled down extremely well to lead normal family lives in separate family units, in so far as this is possible in the present housing situation.

In spite of the 1962-3 unemployment, the bad housing, and the rising rate of tuberculosis, there was little doubt that the immigrants were successfully settling into their new environment. Some of the factories – notably Dartmouth Auto Castings Ltd, a subsidiary of the Birmid group, which today draws sixty per cent of its work force from Commonwealth immigrants – had installed special toilets and other facilities for Indians and Pakistanis. Strangely, though, they found that more and more of these coloured workers were adopting English habits. More and more, for instance, were using the ordinary toilets and toilet paper in the factories.

As the British economy moved rather more hesitantly than before into its fourth post-war pre-election boom, so the conditions of the immigrants in Smethwick improved. By the end of 1964 the local paper could carry a front-page headline: ' *A Job For Everyone* – Booming Smethwick has only 159 unemployed.' Of the 159, many were just between jobs, and there were 354 vacancies for them to fill. Although the labour shortage was not as desperate as it had been in 1955 or 1959, the employers and foremen would still welcome a Commonwealth immigrant looking for a job, especially if he could be recommended by a friend or relation already in the factory.

Reactions to the inflow of Commonwealth immigrants over the years had been – until 1960 – on the whole friendly and helpful. There had been a short spate of 'anti-wog' letters in the local paper during 1954 when 'a policy of importation was pursued'. On 30 April of that year Mr T. Brown of 334 St Paul's Road complained:

How much longer are our children likely to remain healthy when Indian workers are allowed to buy houses in the borough and then grossly overcrowd them, thus creating new slums ?

And on 7 May, Mr T. H. Hughes of Forster Street complained:

I can well understand the colour bar operating after having six months as a neighbour, not to a mere houseful but to a colony.

And finally, on 20 August, Disgusted Housewife wrote: 'How much longer have we got to put up with this menace ?'

These were, however, isolated pinpricks of resentment in a general atmosphere of tolerance. Many Smethwick people were irritated by the strangers' curious habits: few actively went to help them find their feet in their new surroundings. But whenever they did come across them, they behaved with the embarrassed hospitality for which British working people are well known.

It was in the foundries and factories that the integration process was most pronounced. Jack Morris, a foreman at Midland Motor Cylinder, described to me his experiences with the several hundred coloured workers in his factory.

I have been with the firm for twenty years. Only once in all that time have I experienced a row between the workers on the shop floor caused by colour. Many of these coloured workers were invaluable when they were taken in – without them it would have been bust for certain sections of the shop. They work hard, and even if they don't understand the language, we never have any trouble communicating with them about what work is needed. They are also prepared to work long hours of overtime, which saves the firm thousands of pounds in insurance money. Indians and Pakistanis prefer to work in gangs. I haven't much experience of West Indians – but they seem to go for the more individual jobs.

Sometimes we have all the immigrants working in a gang – sometimes we find it better to have some white, some black working together. It makes very little difference, because people don't get worked up about colour differences in the factory.

All of them are members of trade unions – and all of them get paid union rates.

Because I defend these workers outside the factories, I get the reputation of being the coloured man's friend. But this silly tag isn't used inside the factory. There is a double standard for what a man thinks at work and at home. He may laugh and joke with the Indians in the foundry, and go home and tell people lurid stories about their toilet habits. People like to take the majority view.

In the schools, too, the immigrant children were very quickly assimilated. In the early years, there was a considerable problem because boys and girls of secondary-school age could not speak a word of English. Now, of the 9,000 children in Smethwick schools, only 600 are immigrants, including Irish and Poles, and less than seventy of these children cannot cope with the language. There is no school with a class where the majority of the immigrant children do not speak English; no class where more than one in four of the children are immigrants. Almost all the immigrants go to four or five schools. Although neighbouring West Bromwich, Bradford and Walsall have introduced schemes to limit the percentage of immigrant children in schools to no more than a third, the Smethwick authorities have rejected such a plan as 'totally unnecessary'.

The early reactions of the general Smethwick public to the immigrants are more difficult to assess. During 1957 and 1958 the local paper ran a series of articles entitled 'Down Your Street' setting out to extol the virtues and merits of the inhabitants of almost all the main streets.

In only two of the streets did the colour problem feature more than temporarily in the articles – South Road and Vicarage Road, which run parallel to each other off the High Street. There were over 100 Indians living in Vicarage Road, and fifty-seven Singhs on the electoral roll.

Despite the extreme views of the local reporter – 'I suspect that it is only the disgruntled dregs of that nation [India] who come here' – the reactions of the white people in these roads were tolerant and cheerful. 'Their behaviour', said one house-wife, 'is perfectly good. They don't interfere with us in the least and they are as quiet as we could wish.' True, two women were 'afraid to go out at night' because of the immigrants. A former mayor complained that the street had 'deteriorated' – apparently because of the new inhabitants.

Yet these were minority views. The general opinion of the residents was that 'these were quiet respectable folk who kept to themselves'. There was, indeed, a mellowing between the years when the immigrants first arrived and 1959. As the menfolk were joined by their wives, and as standards of hygiene rose, so the (to some extent justified) complaints about bad habits and disagreeable manners became rarer. There is little doubt that had events pursued their normal course, this process would have continued despite the increase in the numbers of immigrants entering the town.

*

The Smethwick County Borough Council was slow to react to the problem of Indians and Pakistanis who were entering their area. In June 1954, the Rev. Kenneth Fielding, vicar of St Stephen's church in Sandwell, made a powerful plea for official action to ease the plight of coloured workers.

The condition in which our coloured workers live, [he said] is a challenge to the Christian conscience of the Midlands.

These are men whom we in this country need, whom we have accepted into this country, whose strength we are. They are men – not just transient half-wits in the Ministry of Health lodging-house accommodation schedules. Can we possibly be content to rest quietly while they live in conditions giving them no development but gambling, drink and women ?

It was an appeal, tinged with foresight – yet for a long time the Council, like the Christian conscience of the Midlands, slumbered on. Had the challenge been taken up with half the vicar's enthusiasm and vigour, Smethwick might well have been saved much of its subsequent trouble. Mr Fielding, who has since moved across the Birmingham border to Handsworth, feels that the local authority's failure to respond arose largely from the attitude of the Central Government, which, he believes, answered appeals for help from councils with instructions 'not to bother too much about the Jamaicans and Indians'.

In January 1955, the Labour-controlled Smethwick Council at last stirred a little. The Town Clerk sent letters to all the surrounding local authorities calling a conference that would discuss the problems of immigration and make recommendations to the various Government departments. Wolverhampton Council turned down the invitation, but the offer was accepted by West Bromwich, Dudley, Walsall and the Urban District Councils of Coseley and Wednesfield.

The conference was held on 14 April. In keeping with the tradition of local authorities to hide their deliberations and decisions from the people they represent, no indication was given in the agreed Press statement of the decisions taken.

In fact, the conference decided to call on the Association of Municipal Corporations to approach the appropriate Government departments with requests:

(1) that adequate hostel accommodation be provided for immigrants in local industry;

(2) that immigrants be required to pass a medical examination before entering the country; and

(3) that interpreters be appointed to assist Government departments in their work with immigrants.

The first and third of these suggestions were turned down flat by the Association. Its officers in their reply stated that there was already power under the Housing Acts for local authorities to provide hostels; and that Government responsibility for immigrants' housing would be 'contrary to the general form of housing legislation throughout the years'. In a final spasm of sanctimoniousness they added that the request for hostels 'might well be interpreted as introducing a distinction based on race and colour which would be quite contrary to the present-day view'.

The negative proposal about health checks, however, they considered valid enough to merit a proposal to the Ministry of Health. They therefore formally submitted to the Minister – then Mr Iain Macleod – that those immigrants suffering from tuberculosis, mental illness or any other infectious disease should be barred. Health checks should be carried out at the port of entry.

The Smethwick Council received the Minister's reply on 19 December 1956 – nearly two years after the original conference had been called. It ran:

The Minister appreciated the need to keep the matter under constant review, but on present information he considers that the adoption of measures of control along the lines discussed in the report would necessitate elaborate machinery quite out of proportion to the present danger to the public.

Two features emerge clearly from this exchange. First, the

Association of Municipal Corporations did not even consider the possibility of Government aid to finance facilities for immigrants. The local authorities confronted with social problems as a result of immigration are financed to this day without any regard to the number of immigrants in their area. Yet according to the Association they are still financially responsible for any solution to immigrant problems. The matter did not even merit a discussion with the Ministry of Housing and Local Government.

Secondly, the Conservative Government whose members five years later were to usher in the Immigration Act with spirited 'concern for the health of the nation' had turned down proposals for health checks of immigrants on the familiar grounds that they would cost too much.

The Smethwick education authorities have an excellent record on immigration. The Chief Education Officer had previously taught in India, and had also studied the experience of Australian education authorities in teaching new immigrant children from Guinea. The Australian methods were in the main adopted, new teachers were hired and evening classes in Punjabi were arranged for many of them.

Similarly the health authorities ran special classes for nursing staff – particularly for domiciliary midwives.

In all these activities the Council was assisted by representatives from the Indian and Pakistani High Commissions, and by the Commonwealth Welfare Council. Many homes were visited by such representatives to explain the facts of living in a new community.

In 1961, at the instigation of the Mayor, a Co-ordinating Committee between races was formed from representatives of the three political parties, the Trades Council, the Indian Workers' Association and the churches. A sub-committee was formed in each parish. The committee, however, never really got off the ground, except in St Albans where it was chaired by the Rev. C. F. Wilkinson, a tireless worker in the interests of immigrants.

The Smethwick Council's handling of its immigrant problem, indeed, compares favourably with that of many other British local authorities. Needless to say, some others have moved with more enthusiasm and more determination, notably Bradford and Nottingham. Other committees have been quicker to establish inter-racial coordinating organizations.

Yet the record of Smethwick's Labour Council on this issue between 1953 and 1963 is by no means disgraceful. Smethwick took the initiative over the 1955 health and housing conference. Smethwick's schools had, until 1960, become models of multi-racialism. Many other local authorities, notably Leeds, had written to Smethwick asking for advice and information about enforcing the Housing and Health Acts. Whatever else caused the dramatic events leading up to the General Election upset of 1964, it was not inefficiency or blunders on the part of the local authority.

The truth is that the social structure and the process of immigration in Smethwick are in no way unique. Neighbouring West Bromwich, for instance, a county borough very similar to Smethwick, has a higher percentage of immigrant children in its schools. The same is true of Walsall. Further, Smethwick, unlike many of its neighbouring towns, has been losing population *overall* consistently over the last fifteen years. In these circumstances any talk of an 'unmanageable flood' of immigrants is absurd.

There are areas of Birmingham and London just as large as Smethwick where the immigrant population is much greater. Small Heath, All Saints, Handsworth (in Birmingham); Deptford, Brixton, Southall (in London); Bradford East – these and a number of other constituencies have a far larger proportion of immigrants than has Smethwick.

Although overcrowding in Smethwick is bad, it is mild compared with many areas of London and Glasgow (whether inhabited by immigrants or not). Similarly the town's health facilities are not markedly better or worse than those of most other similar areas.

Immigration into Smethwick industry followed exactly the same pattern as in all other areas of Britain stricken by severe labour shortages. It rose in boom; fell in recession. The only exception to this pattern was in 1961 when the Immigration Act was threatened. Then the number of immigrants entering Britain from overseas, frightened by the prospect of a total bar, rose out of all proportion to industry's capacity to absorb them.

As everywhere else in Britain, they were taken on in foundries and factories and in public transport to do the jobs shunned by local workers; the employers welcomed them because they were ready to obey any order, however harsh, and to work long overtime. The pattern of their housing conditions and social problems is established firmly all over the country.

The working people of Smethwick are no more or less friendly than their counterparts all over Britain. They are warm-hearted and generous people in the main – but suspicious, often savage, if anything threatens their hard-earned and still meagre 'affluence'. They responded to the strangers as did working people everywhere in the country. In the factory they were helpful, if aloof. Outside they were ready to sneer, half humorously, at the strange habits of their neighbours. But the sneers were seldom, if ever, backed by hatred or violence.

Nothing in Smethwick's immigrant problem is in any way unique. An observer at the beginning of 1960 could have assumed with every justification that the town would have followed so many other areas in Britain along the bumpy road towards the assimilation and integration of its dark citizens.

2. Smethwick Politics: The Conservative Party

'I feel that we should keep the white /coloured ratio in true proportion. We must avoid setting up a coloured quarter. We want to see whites in these roads where coloured people are living so that they can set an example to the coloureds, and live free from racial troubles.'

Mr Peter Griffiths,
12 August 1962   *The People*

'My party is against allowing a concentration of coloured people in any particular area. We believe that spreading coloured people through the borough will assist their integration and prevent racial tension.'

Mr Peter Griffiths,
21 December 1962   *Smethwick Telephone*

'An open appeal for the votes of coloured immigrants can indeed bring temporary success but Labour has been paying ever since in Smethwick.'

Mr Peter Griffiths,
12 July 1963   *Smethwick Telephone*

'The socialists are attempting to obtain the coloured vote because they think it will hold Smethwick for them.'

Mr Peter Griffiths,
24 September 1964   *Birmingham Evening Mail*

'I have never, in a public statement or writing, talked about coloured people.'

Mr Peter Griffiths, meeting in Smethwick, reported in the *Birmingham Post*, 29 September 1964

*

'My purpose is to bring about better integration between the coloured and white communities.'

Mr Peter Griffiths,
12 August 1962   *Reynolds News*

'Neither the immigrants nor the white people want integration. I would have thought the word is meaningless.'

Mr Peter Griffiths,
28 June 1963   *Smethwick Telephone*

'I don't like the word integration.'

Mr Peter Griffiths,
Northern Echo

17 November 1964

'The whole object is to help the immigrant by integration – by having white neighbours.'

Mr Peter Griffiths,
Birmingham Evening Mail

5 December 1964

*

In December 1926, shortly after the General Strike, Sir Oswald Mosley was elected Member of Parliament for Smethwick in a tumultuous by-election. During the next four years he played a leading role in the Labour movement, becoming Chancellor of the Duchy of Lancaster in the 1929 Labour Government. His proposed Keynesian remedies for the slump of 1930–31 were defeated by his own party conference, and he withdrew into the political wilderness.

The Smethwick Labour Party, which had cherished their young and brilliant member, were dismayed and overcome at his departure. In the 1931 election their candidate was soundly beaten by a former Assistant District Commissioner in Kenya, Mr A. R. (Roy) Wise – now M.P. for Rugby – who represented Smethwick for the next fourteen years.

The political upheaval of 1945 established Smethwick as one of the safest Labour seats in the Midlands. The beneficiary was a Leeds alderman and boot-workers' union official, Mr A. J. Dobbs; then, the day after the poll, he was killed in a motor accident. The Labour Party looked for a loyal servant to fill the empty seat and they eventually decided upon the Assistant Director of the B.B.C.'s German service, a mild, middle-aged ex-history don called Patrick Gordon Walker.

Gordon Walker increased Dobbs's 10,000 majority by a few hundred votes, and held the seat in 1950, 1951 and 1955 with successively reduced majorities – in line with the swing against Labour throughout the country. In 1951 and 1955 the swing against Labour in Smethwick was slightly less than in other constituencies in Birmingham and the Black Country. He was opposed on the first two occasions by Mr John Fallon, a prominent Smethwick industrialist deeply involved in local politics. In 1955 his opponent was an Old Etonian business executive, Mr John Wells, the present M.P. for Maidstone in Kent, for whom the experience was a 'trial run' before passing on to the safe 'county' seat which was clearly the due of so well-connected a young man. The 1955 General Election was described by the local newspaper as 'the quietest in the town's history'.

Any doubts Gordon Walker may have had about the safeness of his seat could easily have been dispelled by Labour's enormous majority on the local council. Five of the eight wards were apparently impregnable, and in two of the other three, Labour would win as often as not. A typical line-up of the council was twenty Labour councillors and eight aldermen against four Conservatives. In 1954, for instance, Labour won seven council seats to the Tories' one.

The local Tory councillors were content in the main to 'let things ride', to complain every year about the rate increases and write the odd fatuous letter to the Press. These worthies were, however, continually nagged by their Young Conservative branch whose chairman was a keen young school-teacher called Peter Griffiths.

Griffiths was born into a working-class family and had struggled through school with the one aim of becoming a school-teacher. As a grammar-school teenager, he experienced a 'deep sense of shock' when the Labour Government was elected in 1945. Such a rejection of Churchill – the great war-leader – seemed incredible to him. He determined then to pledge himself to the Conservative Party. He was an able speaker, and a diligent organizer. When he was only twenty-one he fought for the Tories in Sandwell Ward collecting a mere handful of votes. He tried again, almost as hopelessly, at Soho in 1953, but finally rode into the Smethwick council on the Conservative wave in 1955, when he was elected for Cape Ward by 230 votes.

Together with a colleague, C. V. Williams, later Mayor of Smethwick, he soon shocked other Tories on the council out of their slumber. Both young councillors complained of being 'shut out' by their older colleagues. Before long Griffiths was moving resolutions attacking the Labour majority for favouritism in the award of contracts, and proposing detailed schemes for allotting council houses in proper priority. The local newspaper dubbed

27

him 'the stormy petrel' of the council, and remarked: 'Young
Councillor Griffiths does more talking than everyone else, or so
it seems.' Before long, inevitably, Griffiths became leader of the
Tories on the council.

On 19 April 1957, the local Conservative Association, by now
almost taken over by the Young Conservatives, adopted Griffiths
as their parliamentary candidate for the 1959 General Election.
At twenty-eight, after a university education, he was deputy
headmaster of Fir Tree Primary School in nearby West Bromwich.

Over the following months his attitudes and views on politics became steadily clearer. He was by instinct a Conservative of the extreme Right – specializing in that brand of reaction that comes not
from the pampered aristocracy but from the man who has fought
all his life to 'make good' and intends to continue doing so. Thus
Griffiths could combine his appeals for more old-age pensions
and higher pay for teachers with stark chauvinism in foreign
affairs, a devoted affection for free enterprise and total opposition
to all forms of penal reform. It is important to appreciate that
Griffiths was no 'middle-of-the-road' young Bow Group Tory
(as he described himself on finally entering Parliament) swept
up by an issue over which he had no control. Griffiths's conduct
during and before the 1964 election campaign was conditioned
not only by opportunism, though this certainly played its part,
but also by an instinctive right-wing approach.

Speaking, for instance, to a Tory tea meeting on 20 October
1961, on the issue of flogging for young criminals, he said:

I completely disagree with the party line on this matter. The only way
to deal with young toughs is to take a tough line with them. It is a
great pity some of these young bullies cannot be caned to get through
to them by a little pain for themselves.

Shortly before his first adoption as Smethwick Conservative
candidate, Griffiths had proposed another remedy to stamp out
crime and moral waywardness among Britain's teenagers. 'What
they need', he said, 'is good, stark outdoor camps' where they
would learn a thing or two.

Griffiths was utterly different from all other Conservative candidates who had ever stood for Smethwick. Wise, Edgar, Fallon,
Wells – all were drawn from conventional Conservative hutches –

from the public schools and the higher echelons of industry. Griffiths could claim to be a 'man of the people'.

Griffiths was a loyal member of the National Union of Teachers, and strongly advocated better rewards for his fellow teachers. Similarly, he made constant demands for better housing, more schools, higher pensions and higher benefits for the unemployed, provided of course that the State did not interfere with 'free' enterprise. He hates 'the State' and all it stands for. He is a great believer in that 'enterprise' which he himself has used to succeed.

This fundamental political contradiction – demanding increased benefits for the poor while requiring the survival of high standards and class superiority for the rich – drove Griffiths time and again into the hideaway of 'the personal approach'. In seeking support from the industrial working class, he was embarrassed by his Party label and was quite prepared to obscure it with mush about 'the people's candidate'.

For instance, in the 1958 municipal elections all the resources of the Smethwick Labour Party were mobilized to defeat Griffiths in Cape Ward. His own election address that year (for the first and last time) did not tell the electors to which political party he belonged. It simply stated that Peter was not a party-man – that he was prepared to help anyone.

I am prepared to argue politics with anyone, but the municipal elections and the town council are neither the right time or the right place.

Possibly on the strength of this 'personal' campaign, he held the ward – by one vote!

He fought in parliamentary elections on the slogan: 'A Smethwick man for Smethwick', and even after his eventual triumph he continued in the same 'personal' vein. During 1964, he wrote: 'The people of Smethwick made it clear that they don't want politics, they want policies.'

No feature in the political make-up of Griffiths is stronger than his chauvinism. In his faith in his country, right or wrong, he follows firmly in the working-class Tory traditions of the West Midlands, which date back to Joseph Chamberlain. He is a chauvinist at home and a chauvinist abroad. The collapse of Empire disturbs him deeply, and when white men hold high the banner of reaction in foreign countries, they can be sure of his support. Thus one of his contemporary heroes is Mr Ian Smith, the Prime Minister of Rhodesia, who ruthlessly promotes a policy of white supremacy. Mr Smith's Government, wrote Griffiths in 1965, has 'shown wise restraint. The British Government should show some initiative and set Rhodesia free.'

When the Colonial Government of Nyasaland imposed a state of emergency in 1959, to imprison some fifty nationalist politicians fighting for independence, Griffiths wrote:

The violence in Nyasaland and Southern Rhodesia are products of race-hatred incited by unscrupulous African politicians. This sort of behaviour destroys the good will between races which has been so laboriously built up over many years.

At that time the people of Smethwick had no idea what Peter Griffiths meant by 'good will between races'.

A common misconception about his attitude towards the coloured immigrant is that he picked up the issue when it appeared to be electorally profitable, and used it to his advantage, although he, personally, had no racial prejudice. This is quite wrong. Instinctively Griffiths favoured strict immigration control before the issue ever dominated Smethwick politics.

In the years from 1954 to 1960, immigration was not regarded as a serious political issue. The influx of immigrants was seen by the local Tories as something slightly unpleasant which was happening everywhere else, and had to be tolerated as an economically profitable evil. As early as 1955, for instance, Mr Harold Jackson, later an alderman and deputy leader of the Conservatives on the Smethwick council, printed his local election address in Urdu and distributed it liberally among the immigrants in Spon Lane ward. The leaflet read:

I am in a position to understand many of your problems as I spent some time in India and Ceylon during the war. You have come to this country because of the prosperity we are enjoying – plenty of jobs and good wages. This has been made possible by a wise Tory Government. We need some Tory guidance in local affairs. . . . Help me to help you!

Mr John Wells, the Conservative parliamentary candidate in that year, also printed his election address in Urdu.

In the 1959 General Election the issue does not appear to have been raised initially by the Labour or the Tory candidates. The *Smethwick Telephone*, the local paper, asked each candidate a set of questions on the important topics of the day. Third on the list was a question about immigration. Griffiths replied in terms many degrees to the right of his party programme.

Immigration into this country should be limited to persons of sound health who have jobs and living accommodation arranged before they enter. Preference should be given to persons holding British passports. Immigrants should not be permitted to remain here without working, nor to overcrowd their housing accommodation.

This statement, in many ways more extreme than others made by Griffiths in later years, was made without provocation, or hope of electoral advantage. There was no evidence that there were any votes in anti-immigration propaganda at that time. In fact the 1959 election, like its predecessor in 1955, was described by the *Telephone* as 'Smethwick's quietest election'. It went on: 'Both candidates speak of each other in terms of almost brotherly affection.' Mr Gordon Walker's majority was cut from 6,495 to 3,544. The swing against Labour in the constituency was 3.5 per cent. In other Black Country seats it was four per cent. Once again, Mr Gordon Walker had done marginally better than his neighbouring Labour candidates.

Immigration first became a political issue in Smethwick during the local elections of 1960, when Mr Fred Thornton, the Conservative candidate for Soho Ward, proposed, as his main policy, the eviction of coloured people from overcrowded houses without council responsibility to rehouse them. Mr Thornton came near to winning this previously safe Labour seat in a year when the Smethwick Tories, on the high tide of their Party's fortunes, gained four seats on the Smethwick Council and for the first time threatened the entrenched Labour majority.

Shortly after Thornton's campaign a series of minor disturbances broke out on the borders of Dudley and Smethwick, to be dubbed 'race riots' by some national newspapers. There then began a spate of letters on immigration in the local newspapers which continued almost unabated until the General Election of 1964.

The *Smethwick Telephone* at the time was an unimpressive local paper – its front page smeared bleakly with advertisements, its news and feature coverage drably written and arbitrarily selected. It has since twice changed its size and format, and is now one of the liveliest and most attractive local papers in the Midlands. It has always been read with great care and loyalty by the people of Smethwick. With a circulation of about 20,000 it reaches some 95 per cent of the Smethwick electorate. It also sells a considerable number of copies over the border in Handsworth, Birmingham, in Oldbury and in Halesowen.

The editor and owner throughout this period was a Miss Katie Billingsley, an outspoken doyen of the local Conservative Party. It is clear that she herself was outraged by the influx of coloured people into her town, and she laid open her letter columns to any amount of racist propaganda. Her only comment editorially – the *Telephone* very rarely stoops to an editorial opinion – was to say in June 1961:

The *Telephone* has no colour prejudice but we recognize that Smethwick does have a colour problem, and that an all-out effort must be made to solve it *now*.

The paper's views on the matter were more sharply exposed in its choice of news coverage. A court case involving an Indian or a Jamaican would get extravagant coverage, often to the total exclusion of cases involving ordinary white criminals. Any amount of column space was available for the slightest hint of sexual malpractice by a coloured immigrant. Miss Billingsley died in December 1962, and the ownership of the paper passed to less interested relations. The 'line' on immigration noticeably softened, but there is still much evidence of doubtful news selection, and only recently has any effort been made by the editors to undo the damage already done.

On 22 July 1960 the paper published the first in a long series of letters by a retired bank official from Manchester called Lawrence Rieper. Rieper himself lived at a comfortable terraced house in Lightwoods Hill where coloured immigrants feared to tread. His first letter to the *Telephone* (he had written many others to Birmingham papers) set the style for his long and devastating campaign:

It is tragic, indeed, to see a fine race destroyed by blood poisoning. These coloured people are bribed to come here by doles, National Assistance and all the amenities of the Welfare State free. Our racial future is at stake.

In the event of war, these coloured people will present a serious menace. Most of them would be useless in the services and white men will have to die to preserve a land fit for every colour but their own to live in.

There followed a three-month correspondence with the prospective Liberal candidate for Smethwick, Mr Michael Watts. Watts attempted point by point to refute the racist ravings of Rieper. All he got in reply were references to 'Mr Watts's coloured friends', and to an 'organized conquest by infiltration in which our womenfolk are being mauled by coloured men'. Watts himself, according to Rieper 'was hell-bent on delivering our money, our houses, our women, our country and our future to anyone coloured, whole or diseased, desirable or otherwise'.

Rieper was joined in the *Telephone*'s correspondence columns by a middle-aged planning engineer called Donald Finney. Finney, unlike Rieper, lived among the working class of Smethwick, in White Road just off the High Street. Like Rieper, he was an immigrant to Smethwick. He had been born at Biddulph in North Staffordshire, son of a miner, and had come to Smethwick at the age of twenty in 1942. Cheerful, simple and much-liked, Finney too showed himself a considerable propagandist. He had been writing many letters to the *Birmingham Evening Dispatch* (since closed) on the subject of immigration. (He says now that the *Evening Dispatch* would print four out of five letters sent: the *Birmingham Mail* only one in ten.) The letters reeked of violent opposition to coloured people. Finney felt then, and feels today, that coloured immigration is nothing short of a menace. It upsets him deeply to see coloured people in the streets and in the houses of his home town. The venom of his language about coloured people, indeed, contrasts strangely with his mild and friendly disposition. Finney had voted four times for Patrick Gordon Walker, but voted Tory in 1959 because he liked Griffiths.

In those still early days Finney's letters and statements were almost identical to those used by neo-Fascists in North Kensington at the time of and following the Notting Hill riots of 1958. Leprosy

T–B   33 was his favourite theme. Writing under a huge, banner headline, 'NOW IS THE TIME TO CONTROL IMMIGRATION', on 24 February 1961, Finney declared:

I wonder how many people realize that in 1951 we had 19 people known to have leprosy and in 1959 the total had jumped to 317 known sufferers in England. In five years' time, at the present rate immigrants are coming into this country, I suppose it will be 1,000 with leprosy.

In 1939 there was no leprosy in England, and tuberculosis had been stamped out. Now our hospitals are full again.

Wherever Finney got these figures it was certainly not from the Ministry of Health. Official figures for known cases of leprosy in 1951–2 and 1959–60 are 105 and 312 respectively. By 1963 the figure had *dropped* to 291. The number of deaths from TB in 1939 was 25,623; in 1961 it was 3,334.

Another development which infuriated Finney was the conversion of an old church in the High Street into a Sikh temple. The church had lost the bulk of its congregation long since, and the Sikhs badly needed a place of worship. The M.P. and the Mayor attended the temple opening, and, in deference to the Sikh religion, took off their shoes and wore garlands round their necks. Finney wrote a violent protest about these 'indignities'. 'This is our town,' wrote the man from Biddulph, 'and I'm sick of standing by and watching it deteriorate as more and more coloured people come and take over.'

On 24 March 1961, Finney announced that he had 'been asked by Councillor Collett to form a branch of the Birmingham Immigration Control Association in Smethwick'. (Collett was a councillor in Birmingham who for many years had been campaigning against coloured immigration.) Following Finney's announcement, a committee of fourteen was immediately formed from a meeting of some forty people in the Red Cow Hotel. Among the applicants were many Labour supporters including senior members of the Smethwick Labour Party.

The committee met in the sitting-room at the house of Mr Peter Beal, a water engineer, who lived at 218 Cheshire Road. The window looked out onto the Town Hall. Today the wall opposite is plastered, somewhat symbolically, with huge white lettering reading 'ALL NIGGERES ...' (*sic*). The daubers had obviously been interrupted in their work.

Finney was chairman of the branch, Rieper vice-chairman. Their long and effective partnership had started in the columns of the *Smethwick Telephone*. The other twelve were almost all working-class people who were known around the town as people who 'do things'. Mrs Mansell, the secretary, had done some work for the National Savings Movement, for the Co-operative Women's Guild and for the local Labour Party ward committee. She was used to committee work, and went forward to 'do her bit' on this one. The same was true of the vast majority of the others. They were not racialists: four of the seven interviewed by the author (many have left the town, including Rieper, who has bought a castle in the Isle of Man, 'where', he tells me, 'they keep out the blacks') agreed that they would be quite happy to serve on a multi-racial body to help the immigrants already in the town. But they were also interested in stopping any more from arriving. Of the fourteen, only Rieper and one other were life-long Tory voters, and most of them had voted Labour all their lives.

The committee organized the meeting whose proceedings are recorded at the beginning of this book, inviting Jones and Collett from the Birmingham Association because they were the most effective speakers available. Its own propagandists were relied on to make local points from the floor. The first meeting was, however, 'spoiled' for the committee by the intervention of a retired commercial artist from Bearwood, Mr John Jackson, who insisted on going up to the platform to debate the issue with Collett. Jackson could hardly speak for cries of 'Nigger-lover!'

The meeting was attended by some 300 people, and in the week following the branch signed on more than 500 members. Three more meetings were arranged during the summer – at Waterloo Road on 15 May, at Oldbury Road on 5 June and at Crocketts Lane on 11 July. All of them were attended by more than 200 people and all were addressed by Mr Harry Jones. The branch also organized a petition calling for immigration control, collected several thousand signatures, and sent it to Sir Cyril Osborne, M.P. for Louth, who was then organizing similar petitions on a national scale. The branch furthermore busied itself in distributing several hundred thousand leaflets put out by its parent organization calling on people to 'wake up' and not sell their jobs and their heritage to the immigrant invasion.

The feeling among Smethwick people about the work of the branch was not unlike general attitudes towards the National Society for the Prevention of Cruelty to Children. It was a 'good thing' – naturally. It was an organization doing something to help the town.

This almost unanimous popularity, with the remarkable good will which greeted the branch's canvassers as they hawked their propaganda around the town, is hugely important in any consideration of what happened in Smethwick later. The people of Smethwick were disturbed by immigration. Mrs Mansell, the secretary – a working-class housewife – explained in interesting terms the popularity of the branch.

Edgbaston Road used to be a *lovely* road . . . you used to have nannies up that way, you know. Really good class people used to live there, and it was a pleasure to walk in that area. Now *they've* taken over, and the place is a slum. It's horrible.

I've nothing whatever against the black people. My husband once objected in one of the pubs when they refused to serve a coloured man. I work in the schools, and I know how well most of the children are looked after.

But these people are ruining our town . . . the houses are falling apart, and they have a very high rate of TB.

Their habits are pretty terrible. They use the front garden as a rubbish dump, and heaven knows what they do in the toilets.

My husband and I joined this committee because we wanted to do something about it.

There were quite a lot of good speakers on the committee. That Mr Rieper was very good, and so was Don Finney. They seemed to have a lot of facts about leprosy and TB and such. They were good to listen to because they had the facts. We gave them all our support because we realized that through people like that we could get ourselves heard.

What worried Mrs Mansell and hundreds of other housewives like her in Smethwick were the habits and behaviour of the strangers, the irrepressible feeling that they were being surrounded by men and women with whom they had nothing, in many cases not even language, in common. Smethwick, it seemed to them, was being taken over by these people.

There are problems – of housing, health, social assimilation – which worry any responsible person in an immigrant area. Yet these problems can be very easily exploited beyond the reasonable, merged with unrealities and fantasies by men who feel strongly about race. This is what happened at Smethwick. The 'facts' which Finney, Rieper, Collett and Jones presented were more often than not laced with insidious racial propaganda ... Immigration was a 'Communist plot', the 'black battalions' said to have fought in the war were no more than 'phantom legions', intermarriage 'weakened the race', etc.

The average working man and woman in Smethwick could not tell the difference between fact and fantasy, between the real and the racial. The more Finney and Company abused the blacks, the more they cheered. Here, to them, was a man who was out to 'clean up' the town. The more grotesque the lies of Rieper, the more they sat spellbound. 'Was that really true? Were they really as bad as that? They must be. We must get rid of them.'

This merging of the real and the fantastic was at once the easiest and the most crucial of all the processes which led to the upheavals at Smethwick. There is no clear line between saying that Asian immigrants are more prone to tuberculosis than natives of Britain (the truth) and castigating all 'blacks' as spreaders of lurid disease. The fact that immigrants live largely in multi-occupied rat-infested homes merges easily with the myth that they 'live like cattle'. A single case of a black man's accosting a white woman can easily be enlarged into tales of countless ultra-virile black monsters combing the streets for the innocent womenfolk of Smethwick whites. The clusters of bemused immigrants seeking work and shelter turn at the flick of a phrase into a band of invaders, inspired by International Communism, ready to take all that has been so carefully and preciously won by others.

Throughout that summer of 1961, Finney and Company were helped in their work by three events, all of which brought Smethwick and Colour into the national headlines. The first was the eviction of a 'Korean war veteran' (he was almost always described as such), Mr Fred Jones, from a house owned and occupied by Indians. Finney and Rieper organized a petition of protest (signed by only 150 people) declaring (with some justification) that the war veteran had been victimized by the Indian landlady because he was white.

Secondly, in July one of the largest youth clubs in Smethwick,

Sandwell Youth Club, announced a colour bar. The President – Mr Ken Bunch, a former Labour councillor – championed his 'members' right to do what they wish '.

The following week came the decision of the Labour-controlled council to allot a council house to a Pakistani who had been living in Smethwick slums for many years. His house had been demolished by slum clearance, and legally the council was obliged to rehouse him. The outcry, however, was extravagant. The council tenants in Price Street threatened a rent strike if the Pakistani was allowed into the estate. The corporation was backed by the Tory Opposition and by the *Telephone* in its insistence on rehousing the Pakistani, and their firmness soon smashed the attempts by only a handful of the tenants affected to withhold rent. The man who organized the Price Street petition was Mr Fred Thornton, Tory municipal candidate for Soho, who was the next year to win his seat on the council and later to be elected chairman of the Estates Committee.

These three events provided ample 'incitement' for correspondents to the *Smethwick Telephone*. Hardly a week passed without the familiar cluster of letters under headlines such as: '*The Growing Colour Problem*'; 'Why should people integrate if they don't want to ?'; 'The face of the Midlands is fast being known as the Black Hole of Calcutta'; 'The poor whites have been utterly defeated by their own council'; and finally, by way of light relief, Finney's masterpiece: 'I know of women who lock their doors early at night because they are afraid to leave their homes.'

Politics gradually infiltrated the mounting hysteria. On 5 May Fred Thornton sent a letter to the Cabinet protesting at their refusal to control immigration. He himself refused to make the text public. At the same time all the Smethwick Tory councillors, led by Griffiths, sent a letter to Harold Gurden, M.P. for Birmingham, Selly Oak, supporting his demands for immigration control. This is the first evidence of Griffiths's own interest in immigration as a political issue. During the municipal campaign in 1961, in which he himself had been re-elected for Cape, he had not mentioned it.

At the municipal by-election for the Labour stronghold of Victoria in late June, all the candidates agreed that immigration was the key issue. The Labour candidate, Mr Ron Badham, promised to 'raise a petition asking the Government to ban immigration for two years'. He won the seat with an increased majority, but no one in Smethwick can remember having heard anything more about Badham's petition.

Until the late summer, the Smethwick branch of B.I.C.A. had avoided party politics. Its policy towards political parties was ably summed up by its vice-chairman in a strong letter:

Disregard the jibberings of fanatics bent on fouling their own nest. The Socialists snatch at any vote, however black. The Liberals live in a dream world with a kind of Christian hangover. The Conservatives are jellyfish . . . *don't vote.*

Yet as the summer of 1961 wore on, it became clear that the Smethwick Conservatives were not acting in the least like 'jellyfish'. On 28 July Finney wrote: 'I demand an *en bloc* Labour resignation so that we can get Smethwick run by councillors who are servants of the people of Smethwick.' This letter caused Gordon Walker to refuse an invitation to speak at a branch meeting of the British Immigration Control Association – because, he wrote, 'Your leaders are obviously connected with the Conservative Party'.

On 25 August Finney demonstrated his close connexion with the Conservative Party by declaring, long before any definite statement had been made on an Immigration Bill: 'This autumn the Government will introduce a Bill to control immigration'. And sure enough, at the October Tory conference Mr Butler did promise such a Bill. Finney held a celebration dinner for the officers of his Association, although they all felt that the promised Bill did not go far enough.

Gordon Walker's leading Commons speech that November in opposition to the Immigration Bill infuriated the Association's members, who produced a torrent of letters abusing their Member of Parliament. When this provoked two young gentlemen from the British National Party to come down from Birmingham and smear the walls of Smethwick with slogans reading: *Gordon Walker Traitor, Niggers Out, Long Live England,* Finney 'deplored' the action.

On 6 March 1962, Finney wound up his Immigration Control Association and handed over the funds – about £16 – to a children's home. In a spasm of hypocrisy, he told the Press: 'We have never sought to discriminate at any time. We did not seek to make it a colour issue.' (Two weeks earlier in one of his more juicy letters he had written of a critic: 'If he prefers blacks to his own people, he should go to Kenya where Jomo Kenyatta would soon teach him a thing or two.')

Yet this was not the end of Finney's career – far from it. Mr Peter Griffiths, leader of the Conservatives on the council, had been watching his progress with interest and admiration. Small wonder that when he was again adopted as prospective parliamentary candidate for Smethwick on 23 March, he should have announced immediately: 'Being a councillor I have been able to keep in touch with the people, particularly on special matters such as immigration.'

There was little time to lose. A single week later Donald Finney joined the Conservative Party, and was adopted as the prospective candidate for Spon Lane, his home ward, which in the previous two years had been won by the Tories.

The manner in which Finney joined the Conservative Party, and so quickly rose to such eminence within it, is not clear. Interviewed by the author in November 1964 Finney said:

After we wound up the Association I was approached by one or two Conservative councillors, among them Alderman Griffiths who was then leader of the council's Conservatives.

They suggested that my work would be more effective if I was a Conservative councillor.

Mr Harold Jackson, now deputy-leader of the Smethwick Tories, in an interview on the same day agreed that he and Griffiths had been the first to 'put it to Finney that he join the Conservative Party'.

When this information was later used in the House of Commons, it was vigorously denied by Finney, Griffiths and the Conservative agent, Mr Charles Dickens. Griffiths said (interestingly enough) that he 'only became responsible' for Finney after the latter had joined the council. Finney's denial was less categorical. Whatever the desire of Griffiths and his agent to disown Finney, however, it is clear that the man whose name was associated throughout the town with the campaign against coloured immigration was absorbed into the Tory Party as a councillor.

The consequences were obvious. The anti-immigrant feeling whipped up by such disreputable means now became associated clearly and directly with the Conservative Party. Any lingering doubts about the campaign must have been instantly dispelled. The Conservative Party, with its standing as the party of government in the country, had given it its approval.

It is scarcely surprising, therefore, that in the 1962 municipal elections the results at Smethwick shocked the psephologists. Against a sharp national swing to Labour, the Tories won three seats and lost none. Finney was elected for Spon Lane with the biggest Tory majority the ward had seen since the war – 549 votes. Throughout the whole of the West Midlands only five seats had been gained by the Tories – and three of them were in Smethwick.

During 1962 Finney and Griffiths closely synchronized their activities. For the first time in Griffiths's short political history he started to use the immigration question in his weekly political columns (the *Telephone* gives weekly space to party candidates or their agents):

After reading the last issue of *Combat* I advise them [house-owners in Vicarage Road] to ask Mr Gordon Walker how to treat this take-over bid for their property. *Combat* reports that in the rich Hampstead Garden Suburb the Hampstead Garden Protection Society has won a High Court case to prevent a take-over of their property.
20 July 1962   Finney
(*Combat* is the monthly organ of the British National Party.)

How easy to support uncontrolled immigration when one lives in a garden suburb.
3 August 1962   Griffiths
(Mr Gordon Walker was then living in Hampstead Garden Suburb.)

The Housing Committee should purchase houses in Vicarage Road – and to stop this road being turned into another Varna Road.
20 July 1962   Finney

We do not want another Varna Road in Smethwick.
20 July 1962   Griffiths
(Varna Road, Birmingham, is known for its prostitutes.)

41

If we don't do something immediately, there will be race riots. . . .
27 July 1962   Finney

The Conservative leader, Councillor Peter Griffiths, told the
Telephone yesterday that one single incident could spark off race riots
similar to those in Dudley.
3 August 1962

As our M.P. you've been a dead loss – but no doubt you'll get a medal
from the West Indies.
7 September 1962   Finney

Smethwick's M.P. was the architect of Labour's 'let-em-all-come'
policy. He speaks very differently here in Smethwick away from his
intellectual friends – mind you knowing the temper of the Smethwick
people, I don't blame him!
14 September 1962   Griffiths

For a brief moment at the end of 1962 Griffiths relaxed his anti-
immigration propaganda. In the last week of November, he and
senior officers of the Smethwick Tories met the officials of the
Birmingham Indian Workers' Association.

What a valuable meeting it was! [exclaimed Griffiths] Personal contact
has been very slight . . . There has been much misunderstanding as a
result.
    The Indian leaders expressed their confidence in the Tory Party's
policy of developing the Commonwealth into a multi-racial society,
especially in Africa. The petty pinpricks of prejudice in some shops and
public places are entirely alien to the British spirit . . .
    We hoped that Indian boys would be able to become apprentices . . .
    We agreed to meet again!

The next week Griffiths's young, attractive wife, Jeannette, gave
tea to the wives of the president and secretary of the Indian
Workers' Association, Mr J. S. Rai and Mr Avtar Jouhl. The
session only lasted half an hour but Mrs Jouhl, who does not speak
English, says that it was a most friendly and hospitable affair.
Griffiths wrote that 'it is no use two communities complaining
about each other unless they get together'. The Indians promised
to return the invitation.
    A fortnight later, Griffiths led the Conservatives on the council
in vetoing a plan to grant a house mortgage to a Pakistani, on the

grounds that such action would lead to a 'ghetto' policy. The man, who was perfectly entitled to his loan, would have to go on living in multi-occupied slums because Mr Griffiths and his friends held strong views on ghettos.

Mrs Rai and Mrs Jouhl decided not to send their invitation to the two Tory wives. The women never corresponded again. Further, despite Griffiths's promise, the Conservative Association never again met the Indian Workers' Association for a general friendly discussion. The next time Griffiths mentioned a 'multi-racial' society, it was in very different circumstances.

Why this brief excursion into multi-racial chivalry? Perhaps Griffiths had realized the electoral importance of the immigrant vote? Maybe he had a flash of regret at his own headlong stampede into 'Finney' tactics. More relevant, possibly, is the comment of a Birmingham organizer for the British National Party, Mr Norman Smith: 'I've never been too sure about Griffiths. He had those blacks in his house for a tea party you know. That didn't go down at all well, I can tell you.'

The year 1963 opened with the usual flood of weekly letters to the *Telephone*. In early April, Griffiths coolly sidetracked the nation-wide resentment against the Government caused by the highest unemployment figures since the war. As leader of the Conservative councillors he wrote to the Home Secretary, urging him to deport all immigrants who had been unemployed for six months. The suggestion brought Griffiths 'the heaviest post of my political career – and an overwhelming number of letters are in support'.

In May 1963, Donald Finney instituted 'Vigilante Patrols' in Spon Lane Ward. The 'patrols', which consisted of two cars, cruised through the area looking for 'vice'. Finney explained:

Women who live in the area are ashamed and bitterly angry at these outsiders. Some mothers have told me they are afraid of allowing their teenage daughters to be out after dark for fear of being molested.

The *Smethwick Telephone* detailed a special investigator to probe Finney's allegations. He found during an evening's close observation that no one entered the house which, according to Finney, was 'constantly visited by white girls'. The house from which 'a young woman had fled crying chased by a West Indian'

43

was quiet – and was occupied by a highly respectable Indian. The three couples knotted against the walls were all white. The investigator found 'as much vice as one would find at a vicarage tea party'.

Finney submitted a 'dossier' on vice in Spon Lane to the Watch Committee of the council on 29 May. The Watch Committee set up its own detailed examination of the 'problem'. It reported that there was no evidence of soliciting by white girls, no evidence of molestation, no evidence of indecent behaviour, no evidence of violence or of knife fights. Finney's dossier, significantly, was never published. The secretary of the Indian Workers' Association called on the Tories to get rid of Finney for such blatantly inflammatory and unjustified activities. This appeal elicited from Finney himself the following, savage reply: 'This kind of attitude by you in my country will do you and your people more damage than anything ever printed and can lead to race riots: or is this what you want?' Don Finney is not a man who takes criticism kindly.

Griffiths had by now openly discarded any idea he may have had of wooing the immigrant vote. Writing of the 1963 Deptford by-election, he pointed out: 'An open appeal for the votes of coloured immigrants can indeed bring temporary success, but Labour has been paying ever since in Smethwick.'

In July 1963, Gordon Walker announced that at the municipal elections in May (where the Tories, right against the national swing, gained another seat from Labour), gangs of children had been organized to chant, 'If you want a nigger neighbour, vote Labour.' Griffiths wrote, in reply:

We can't stop children reflecting the views of their parents. The people of Smethwick certainly don't want integration.

To the Midland correspondent of *The Times*, Griffiths said of the 'nigger-neighbour' slogan: 'I would not condemn anyone who said that. I regard it as a manifestation of popular feeling.'

The Indian and West Indian leaders immediately asserted that integration was their main aim.

By now immigration was an almost constant theme in Griffiths's weekly *Telephone* column. On 20 September, for instance, he started the lie, repeated often since, that the Labour Party was responsible in the first place for the Commonwealth right of free entry to Britain. 'Immigrants', he wrote, 'come here from the Commonwealth under the provisions of the British Nationality Act. This Act was passed by a Labour Government.'

The British Nationality Act merely rationalized the existing law about British citizenship after Indian independence. It was supported by all parties in the House. The right of free entry for Commonwealth citizens dates back to the start of the British Empire.

On 25 October Griffiths recorded that he had personally seen white girls entering houses owned by Indians. He urged all head-mistresses in the town to warn their schoolgirls against such behaviour. 'The girls', wrote this guardian of the public con-science, 'are in moral danger.'

An Indian, Dr A. Vetta, followed up the matter. He discovered that the 'girls' whom Griffiths had seen entering the multi-occupied houses were in fact social workers. There was ab-solutely no evidence whatever that schoolgirls of any kind had gone into these houses. He challenged Griffiths to substantiate his statement or withdraw. Griffiths did neither.

On 29 November Griffiths wrote to the Ministry of Housing, suggesting, again on behalf of the Smethwick Tory councillors, that there should be a ten-year residential qualification for im-migrants displaced from their homes by slum clearance. 'If immigrants start to get a lot of council flats,' wrote Griffiths, 'there will be a riot.'

The Indian Workers' Association in desperation called on their members to vote against the Conservatives at the next election. Griffiths pounced on the appeal:

This is an attempt to thwart the interests of the town by outsiders who are abusing the hospitality given to them in this country. I can't see it having any effect on our chances. In fact, it could have the reverse effect.

It could indeed. And Peter Griffiths redoubled his activities to ensure that 'the reverse effect' obtained. His columns in the *Telephone* referred frequently to 'Labour's immigrant friends', and, on 17 January 1964, he wrote:

The biggest political joke for some time in Smethwick was a passage in

Gordon Walker's column last week. He said: 'I wish the Conservative leaders in Smethwick could get their minds off the racial issue.' I'll say he does. But they won't. . . .

Apparently the plight of English children held back by the presence of non-English speaking children in a class doesn't bother the immigrant leaders. Well, it bothers the Smethwick Tories and our kids are going to get a square deal in spite of the combined opposition of the Socialists and their immigrant friends.

This drivel (the Indian children had a remarkable record in Smethwick schools – many of them, once having mastered the language, proving just as able, if not more so, than their English schoolfellows) revolted the Smethwick teaching community. Yet the slander took hold of the Smethwick imagination. Remorselessly, Griffiths continued his propaganda until the municipal elections of 1964, when the Tories finally seized control of the local council.

Still he was not satisfied. His description of the election was inflammatory:

There were the voters in their turbans and saris, and the babel of many tongues as the Indian Workers' Association gave instructions to non-English-speaking voters. . . . Undoubtedly the immigrant vote was significant and Smethwick people who stayed at home should ask themselves just whom they wish to decide Smethwick's future. . . . It is fair to assume that more than a quarter of Labour's voters could not speak English. . . . To fail to vote now is tragic.

In June 1964, Griffiths gave his complete support to a petition organized from Bradford calling for a complete ban on immigration for at least five years. 6,000 signatures were collected in Smethwick, and Griffiths was not slow to comment: 'This is stronger action than the Parliamentary Party has taken, but it is what Smethwick Tories want.'

By this time he was confident of victory in the General Election. The local election results, the reports of canvassers, even the opinion polls, all were in his favour. 'I do not wish to win by a majority of only two or three thousand,' he wrote on 3 July. 'There will be so much to do in the years ahead. Smethwick rejects the idea of being a multi-racial society. The Government must be told this.'

On 31 July he delivered himself of perhaps the most nauseating of all his utterances on this subject. Gordon Walker had been saying for many months that the real immigration problem was caused by the housing shortage, and that more houses would solve the greater part of it. This was a dangerous argument, and Griffiths answered it savagely:

Will more houses end the nuisance and filth. . . . Would more houses end the knife fights? Would more houses make the streets safe for women and girls? There are 300,000 immigrants in India and Pakistan waiting to come here if restrictions are lifted. Would Labour house all these too? . . .

The man who, on his own admission, had been fighting on the immigrant issue for two and a half years ended: 'If Labour wishes to fight on the immigrant issue, so be it. I will not be silent.'

As the election campaign began in earnest Griffiths and Finney flung themselves all the more desperately into the fight over this single issue. On 11 September, Finney wrote:

The Conservative candidate Alderman Peter Griffiths fights seven days a week for a cleaner and better Smethwick. He is always fighting our housing and other problems forced on the Smethwick people because of the huge influx of coloured people.

And his hero suitably responded:

The same gentleman [Gordon Walker] tells us that immigration will not be a major issue at the coming election. How out of touch can you get? Over half the town it is *the* issue now, and the threat hangs over all.

Far more in line was a letter from Don Finney. Speaking of immigrants he said 'They fought for their freedom and we should not deny them the right to go and enjoy it'. There's a lot in that.

Griffiths held only three meetings during the campaign. At one of them a scuffle broke out between some Birmingham University students and his most loyal supporters. At another, on 2 October, Griffiths spoke for about half an hour on conventional Tory policy. Mrs Dorrie Crow, a member of the British National Party with violent views on the immigrants, interrupted half-way through:

'What about immigration? That's what we've come to hear about.' He replied: 'Later Madam.' At question time, she rose again: 'To bring in a lot of people where there is not enough room is wicked and breeds hatred. I want immigration stopped at once, otherwise in twenty years' time we shall be ruled by them.'

Griffiths leapt to his feet and shouted back:

This lady has put over the kind of thing that for years I have heard on hundreds of thousands of doorsteps. Without fear or favour I will put forward what I hear because I believe that is the duty of an M.P. I do not care who this does not suit. If it suits the people of Smethwick, I will say it.

He was asked again: 'Do you personally accept the idea of a multi-racial society?'

He replied:

I am not going to decide. The mass of the people of Smethwick will decide. If this [a complete ban on immigration] is endorsed on October 15, then what more do you want than that I should go on supporting it?

It was the final seal. If anyone in Smethwick had had any doubts, they could reasonably have them no longer. Griffiths had pledged himself to fight in Parliament on *the* issue – that of immigration. He pledged himself to speak out against a multi-racial society, and for a complete and immediate ban on immigration.

In his 'personal message' to the electors in his election address, Griffiths included two paragraphs in bold type, spaced out to catch the reader's eye. One of them repeated the 'Smethwick man for Smethwick' theme. The other ran:

I shall press for the strictest possible control of immigration. We British must decide who shall or shall not enter our country. So vital a matter cannot be left to other Governments. Overcrowding and dirty conditions must be ended. There must be no entry permits for criminals, the unhealthy or those unwilling to work. Our streets must once again be safe at night.

The police reported that Smethwick streets were no less safe than any others in Britain.

Shortly before polling day the Conservatives issued another

last-minute leaflet. This time they did not bother with the subsidiary issue. A copy of the leaflet is reprinted on p. 255. Suitably, the leaflet and the election address were printed by the Smethwick Telephone Company Limited.

Particularly remarkable was the whispering campaign against Gordon Walker himself. Canvassers from both opposition parties were met constantly with the weirdest of rumours. Gordon Walker had sold his house in Smethwick to the blacks. Gordon Walker went out to the West Indies to recruit blacks for Smethwick industry. Gordon Walker's wife was a black. So was Gordon Walker.

Maurice Foley, M.P. for neighbouring West Bromwich, reports that, at a work-gate election meeting where he and Gordon Walker spoke, all these allegations were flung at the sitting M.P. by Smethwick workers. Mr Graham Greene, Gordon Walker's son-in-law, was surprised to hear from a Smethwick housewife he was canvassing that, 'All Gordon Walker's daughters married black men'. It was only after proving his identity to her that he convinced her this was incorrect.

Of all the other rumours the most popular was that many immigrants were lepers, particularly the children, and that two leper hospitals were being built, secretly, in the town.

That such slander gained wide credence is hardly surprising in view of the invasion of Smethwick during the final campaign by every known extremist right-wing organization. Inspired by what they described as Griffiths's 'forthright' campaign, they came in droves to help him. The British National Party threw its meagre resources into the campaign. Even Colin Jordan sent as many of his storm-troopers as he could muster, not to seek the headlines with lurid antics (as at Leyton, later) but to work in enthusiastic, undramatic dedication on the doorsteps and in the streets. Mr Tom Jones, a well-known Birmingham admirer of Sir Oswald Mosley, who believes that the Jews are ultimately responsible for coloured immigration, rang Griffiths personally and asked if he could come and help him. Griffiths assented willingly, having discovered that Jones was not an official member of any other political organization.

In a speech to the Young Conservatives of London on 25 November 1964, Griffiths said:

I want to give you a categorical assurance: that no one worked for me other than the Smethwick Conservative Association or personal friends of mine who I can vouch have no political associations whatever. I give you that as a firm and categorical assurance.

26 November, 1964   *Guardian.*

On 15 October the people of Smethwick voted. Griffiths won. His vote remained almost exactly the same as in 1959, despite a sharp drop in the electorate. Gordon Walker's vote dropped from 20,670 to 14,916 and David Hugill, the Liberal candidate, a young research chemist who had come into the field late and fought bravely with meagre resources, collected just over 3,000. The swing away from Labour to the Conservatives was 7·2 per cent, compared with a national swing towards Labour of 3·5 per cent. In the Midlands the swing to Labour was lower than the national average, but still substantial – just over two per cent.

As Gordon Walker left the Town Hall after the count and the result, he was followed all the way to the car by a crowd of dancing, gleeful, blue-rosetted fanatics. Their chants were stereotyped, consistent:

  'Where are your Niggers now, Walker?'
  'Take your Niggers away!'
  'Up the Tories!'

It was a fitting epitaph on Mr Peter Griffiths's two-year campaign.

The result shocked many people in Britain who had refused to believe that such things could happen on this side of the Atlantic. To those who knew something of politics in Smethwick since 1960 the only surprise was that the majority was so low. The jubilation of the Smethwick Conservatives was tempered by complaints all over the country from political leaders. Ten clergymen in Smethwick, many of them Conservatives, issued a statement deploring the use of the race issue during the election. Even stronger statements came from the leaders of the Labour and Liberal Parties.

Yet far more remarkable than these reactions was the sudden dramatic change which came over Peter Griffiths, the new Member of Parliament.

*

The man who had promised to reproduce 'without fear or favour' the plea that immigration must be stopped 'because in twenty years we will be ruled by them', the man who had refused to join a multi-racial committee, and had opposed a council grant to the Midlands Commonwealth Welfare Council, could tell the House of Commons in his maiden speech that, 'I have on every occasion called for the most active cooperation between the members of all races in the town'.

The man who, just before polling day, had demanded that non-English speaking voters should produce passports to prove their identity could write to Smethwick teachers eight days later: 'You know that I personally am in favour of complete equality as between the different races.'

On 19 September he had told the *Birmingham Evening Mail* that 'the only possible solution is coexistence. The word integration is not one we would want to find in this town.' On 5 December he could say to the same paper (on the council plan to sell houses to whites only): 'The whole object is to help the immigrant by integration – by having white neighbours.'

Before the election Griffiths had scorned the idea (of his opponents) that housing was at the root of the immigrant problem. 'Would more housing end the nuisance and filth?' he had asked. 'Will more housing make the streets safe for women and girls?'

Yet by 14 November he was telling a reporter from the *Birmingham Post*:

I think that when we have solved such problems as overcrowding in houses, large classes in schools and other similar ones, we shall have solved the problem of race relations.

Constantly, before the election, Griffiths had complained about the past Labour policy of re-housing immigrants displaced by slum clearance. On 24 September he had said:

Councillor Lowry, the leader of the Socialist group in Smethwick, is saying that people who live in slum clearance areas should be rehoused. To me this indicates a policy of providing for new homes for immigrants without the seven-year qualifying period that the ordinary people of Smethwick have to face. There would be an explosion, an outcry, a demonstration and angry protest and I would certainly lead it.

On 15 January 1965, the Conservative chairman of the Smethwick Housing Management Committee, Councillor E. Gould, made a public announcement to the *Smethwick Telephone*:

Coloured families from slum clearance and redevelopment areas will be rehoused in council flats anywhere and at any time.

Despite signs of the 'explosion' which Griffiths had so accurately forecast and inspired, the Alderman M.P., who still sat on the council benches, led no protest. On the contrary, he gave the impression of complete approval.

The Alderman who had urged Gordon Walker in November 1963 to 'forget the immigrants' votes and speak up for Smethwick in favour of keeping immigration control' could tell Mr Luther Thomas, leader of the West Indian Smethwick community, that, 'I am as much an M.P. for the immigrants in Smethwick as I am for local people.'

Finally, perhaps most ludicrously, the man who had stomped the streets of Smethwick for nearly three years blowing up the 'horrors' of the immigration invasion; the man who had not scrupled to emphasize the more salubrious aspects of anti-immigration propaganda; the man who promised that 'Smethwick was not to become a dumping ground for criminals, the chronic sick and those who have no intention of working' – the same man could turn to the two reporters from the *Northern Echo* in mid-November with a gentle smile, and say:

At no time, in any article, speech or leaflet have we sought to raise emotion. I can say quite categorically that none of us has ever played on prejudice.

As Griffiths tries in vain to soothe the racialist tiger on which he rode so shamelessly to Westminster, such contradictions will, no doubt, multiply.

3. Smethwick Politics: The Labour Party

'This is a British country with British standards of behaviour. The British must come first.'

Mr Patrick Gordon Walker,

31 August 1962   *Smethwick Telephone*

One of the most ironic aspects of the three-year racist campaign by the Smethwick Conservatives was its target. The man who bore the brunt of their attack, the man they painted in the most lurid colours was perhaps the most conventional and reactionary of all Labour's old guard – the Right Honourable Patrick Gordon Walker, P.C.

Gordon Walker was born in Worthing, but spent most of his early childhood in the Punjab, where his father was a judge of the Supreme Court at Lahore. His grandfather too had spent his life in Imperial India – as Lieutenant-General of the Punjab. Gordon Walker inherited from his father that brand of Fabian socialism whose main characteristic is patronage. It is the form of 'socialism' which inspires the present Lord Longford, for example, to say Good Morning to a black man every day on the tube, in order to impress on the foreigner that people wish him well.

While his grandfather administered kind and wise government, and his father dispensed divine British justice, Patrick Gordon Walker was brought up in a political atmosphere where crude generalizations like 'all men are brothers' were replaced by the realistic view that the British are parents and all other men are their truculent sons. Like sons they must be treated with gentleness, sympathy, but, when the need arises, with firmness and even force.

These solid ideals were reinforced at Wellington School and at Christ Church, Oxford. At Oxford, Gordon Walker revitalized his Fabianism with some solid performances in the scrum of the University 2nd XV.

He joined Cripps's Socialist League, which stood well to the Left of the Official Party, only to leave it when it sanctioned the Popular Front against Fascism in 1936. In the meanwhile he had fought the 1935 election as Labour candidate for Oxford, and lost by some 6,000 votes.

In 1938, he was again adopted by the Oxford Labour Party to fight a by-election caused by the death of the Conservative member. The by-election came to be regarded as a political comment on Chamberlain's negotiations at Munich, and the opposition parties were invited to drop their choices and combine to elect Mr A. D. Lindsay, Master of Balliol, as an anti-Munich candidate.

Gordon Walker adamantly refused to stand down and, when the local party withdrew its official support from him, he publicly proclaimed his disapproval of such a policy. In a letter to the then powerful *Daily Herald* he wrote:

The flag of socialism must be kept flying. It is specially at a moment of crisis like the present that Labour must bring before the people its full working class and democratic policy both for foreign and domestic affairs.

He was in Germany for the 1945 election, but when Mr Dobbs, the boot and shoe union official, died he was recommended by Attlee and others for the safe seat of Smethwick, which he gladly accepted.

When the Labour Government was re-elected with a majority of six in 1950, Gordon Walker found himself in the Cabinet as Secretary of State for Commonwealth Relations.

Gordon Walker had long since hauled down the 'flag of socialism' and phrases like 'working-class policy' now stuck in his throat. He was already firmly established on the extreme right wing of the Labour Party, from which no traveller has ever returned.

In 1957, after six years on the back benches, he was appointed to the Shadow Cabinet where he became a strong supporter of Mr Hugh Gaitskell – particularly during the internal party struggle that followed the 1959 General Election. He spoke for the Opposition on Home Affairs, and after Gaitskell's death he was regarded by the new Leader, Mr Harold Wilson, as a vital link with the Gaitskell past. Although Gordon Walker had never even been mentioned as a contestant in the leadership battle, he soon found himself in the lofty position of Shadow Foreign Secretary.

His rise to such eminence was almost an accident. Among his political associates he appeared unexceptional. He was a tedious speaker, even by parliamentary standards. He lacked George Brown's enthusiasm, James Callaghan's cosy familiarity. He lacked the cold intellect of Jay or Jenkins, and Gaitskell's passionate adherence to principle. Even on minor issues of law reform and civil rights, on which his associates were without exception committed, Gordon Walker took the conventional, reactionary view.

He was, for example, prepared to support capital punishment right up to 1955, abstaining in the Commons on the issue as late as February ('The abolition of capital punishment would lead to criminals carrying guns,' he wrote).

Almost his first job as Commonwealth Secretary, in 1950, was to inform the Commons that Seretse Khama, Chief of the Bamangwato tribe in Bechuanaland, was to be banned from returning to his country because he had married a white woman. Seretse's marriage had originally shocked his tribe into rejecting him, but they had reconsidered their decision and accepted him finally without recrimination by a vote of about 5,000 to fifty. He had then come to London for 'talks' without being informed that he could not return. The only recognizable reason for the Labour Government's behaviour was that Dr Malan, racist Prime Minister of South Africa, had strongly protested against such a blatant example of multi-racialism on his doorstep. Labour, in true socialist tradition, was loath to offend such a loyal Commonwealth ally.

Walker stuck to his line throughout a hectic Commons row on the Seretse Khama affair, and savagely remonstrated with several of his own Labour supporters, who threatened to vote against their party on the issue. The rebels, led by the Rev. Reginald Sorensen, M.P. for Leyton, finally agreed to support the Government, and Gordon Walker survived.

Explaining his attitude to a school of Labour students on 2 April 1950, the Commonwealth Secretary declared:

The right of mixed marriages has never been challenged, and never will be. But what we had to decide was whether a particular mixed marriage of a man who has to rule a country was in the interests of that country.

'We' had to decide in 'their' interests, regardless of 'their' express wishes and demands. The words floated down like ghosts from the bench of the Supreme Court at Lahore.

The next year, 1951, Gordon Walker and James Griffiths, the Colonial Secretary, dreamed up that unhappy political union, the Central African Federation, and Gordon Walker himself stuck to the concept of Federation long after African opinion had declared itself resolutely opposed. In 1954, he was one of the eleven Labour M.P.s who abstained on a Labour motion criticizing the Conservative Government for not giving the Africans enough say in the Federation's political structure. Informing his constituents of his abstention, he wrote:

I felt that the safeguards for African interests were adequate . . . I felt that the only way of preventing South African rule over all these territories was to build a strong British State in Central Africa.

Once again the answer to a problem was 'to build a strong British State'. The natives were not capable of acting for themselves. Further, their legitimate demands for safeguards, which later, with Gordon Walker's assent, smashed the entire Federation, were in his opinion unjustified. On this occasion, incidentally, when British Rule was at stake in Central Africa, it was quite legitimate to abstain against the party whip.

Mr Patrick Gordon Walker was one of the first men in Britain to advocate control of Commonwealth immigration. At a meeting in Smethwick on 12 November 1954, he addressed a meeting of some 100 of his constituents on the problem:

I don't think any country has a moral obligation to import a racial problem, but at the same time I would not support any immigration policy based on colour. I am a great believer in Commonwealth unity, but I cannot see that there will be any danger to it if Britain takes powers over immigration. Every other country regulates immigration from other parts of the Commonwealth, including Britain.

Almost exactly seven years later Gordon Walker made the best Commons speech of his life in opposing the second reading of a Bill which 'removes from Commonwealth citizens the long-standing right of free entry to Britain, and is thus calculated to undermine the unity and strength of the Commonwealth'. One of the points in this powerful speech was that 'in India there is complete reciprocity. A Briton can go to India as easily as an Indian can come here. He can go there, stay there and work there.' Mr Gordon Walker, not for the first time in his career, had changed his mind and his facts.

In March 1955, the landlord of the Red Cow, a popular Smethwick pub, instituted a colour bar in his Men Only smoke-room. The decision created a furore in Smethwick, and Gordon Walker was eventually forced to comment: 'I can see nothing to be gained by changing the well-established law of this country which leaves the question of licensing to the local licensing justices.'

This attitude infuriated the Birmingham Liberal Party, whose Press Officer, Mr Bernard Prendergast, wrote to Gordon Walker demanding support for legislation banning a colour bar in public houses. Prendergast commented: 'It now seems that Mr Gordon Walker has no time for his coloured constituents.' Gordon Walker replied three weeks later:

I am of course against any form of discrimination on grounds of race, colour or religion. I am, however, doubtful whether the remedy in this case you mention would be new legislation. We have a long-established law concerning the rights of licencees – and the enforcement of this law is in the hands of the local justices. The operation of this well-established law has given us very good administration of public houses throughout the country for many years. I have no reason to doubt that the licensing justices who know local conditions will continue to keep up this excellent record.

Prendergast replied, with every justification, that 'It is well-known that the existing law is not sufficiently strong to deal with cases of discrimination at the Red Cow hotel'.

Gordon Walker's faith in the licensing justices can be measured against the fact that the colour bar in the Red Cow's Men Only room, at the time of writing, persists (as it has in at least ten other Smethwick pubs) and that his own party has promised legislation to make discrimination on grounds of colour in public places illegal.

It is clear that, as the campaign against immigration in Smethwick gathered momentum, Patrick Gordon Walker was incompetent to fight it properly.

His first reaction was simply to ignore the problem. He had enormous advantages over his adversaries. He had space in the

Smethwick Telephone, which was granted to his political opponents only after they had been officially adopted. Further, he had the prestige and influence that attaches to the sitting M.P. Right through 1960 and 1961 he used neither of these weapons. On 8 September 1961 he spoke in West Bromwich on the issue, saying that there 'is no case for immigration control yet'. His only other recorded reaction in the tumultuous year of 1961 was to say, when the Immigration Bill was mooted in the Queen's Speech that November:

One proposal is on control of Commonwealth immigration. This Bill is complicated and I have not yet had time to study it. At first glance there are many things I don't like about it. But I must reserve comment until I have fully studied it.

During the next week or so he studied hard, and it was his loyalty to Gaitskell rather than any political principle which probably drove him to oppose the Immigration Bill in such powerful terms.

Having taken this stand, he tried to explain it to his Smethwick constituents, who were furious. He started by explaining patiently that the Act would not solve the real problems, the overcrowding, the high incidence of tuberculosis, the exploitation.

But he had waited too long before intervening effectively against the rising racial hysteria in the town. Letter after letter appeared in the *Telephone* attacking him personally for his stand on the Bill. He tried with desperate obstinacy to maintain his line on the issue: it was basically a housing problem. Immigration should, like industry, be planned to avoid clotting. Yet in the face of the campaign (and his own instinctive reactions towards foreigners) he was bound to retreat.

Not until the Smethwick Labour Party was forced to produce a final election leaflet, was this retreat turned into a rout. Gordon Walker always referred to the housing problem and the need to plan industrial location. He almost always blamed the Rent Act. However, all too easily, he sabotaged his position. Indeed, as early as 31 August 1962, he delivered himself of one of the most reactionary remarks ever made by a leading Labour spokesman on this issue: 'This is a British country,' he wrote, 'with British standards of behaviour. The British must come first.'

And the immigrants second. Peter Griffiths must have envied the phraseology.

During 1964 Gordon Walker referred to the problem usually to dismiss it as irrelevant to the town. On 14 February he said: 'People will soon get bored with the immigration question.' On 17 April: 'Immigration has lost that hysterical note which was being so successfully played on some time ago.' On 4 September: 'Immigration is not the main issue in this election. As we get nearer the election and bigger issues come up, I think the immigrant problem will become less and less prominent.'

Another theme used constantly by the Shadow Foreign Secretary was that most of the immigrants had arrived under the Conservative Government. On 13 March, for instance, he wrote: 'The whole wave of immigration has occurred since 1951 whilst the Conservatives have been in power. It is false and unfair to blame the Labour Party for immigration.'

And in the personal message attached to his election address he wrote:

The lie has been spread about in Smethwick that I was in some way personally responsible for the coming of Commonwealth immigrants to Britain. Anyone who thinks for a moment knows that that is sheer nonsense. How could any one man be responsible? In any case, the main flow of immigrants happened to come in the thirteen years during which the Conservatives were in office.

Finally, just before the poll, the Labour Party issued a special election leaflet on Gordon Walker's behalf. It was headed, absurdly, *Urgent Stop Press*. It carried the following message from the Labour candidate on immigration:

Be fair:
 Immigrants only arrived in Smethwick in large numbers during the past ten years – while the Tory Government was in power. You can't blame Labour or Gordon Walker for that.
 Labour favours continued control of immigration, stricter health checks and deportation of those convicted of criminal offences. Labour will give local authorities greater power to help overcrowding. Labour will provide new and better housing.

Gordon Walker had been in favour of immigration control in

1954 and against it in 1961, and now he was in favour of it again in 1964!

Canvassers who came to help in Smethwick from outside report that Gordon Walker's personal advice to them was to avoid the immigration issue if possible, but if it arose to point out, 'in all fairness' (*sic*), that the immigrants had come to Britain under the Tories.

That the immigration problem arose under the Tories, who refused to construct a social policy to deal with it, is of course true. It is, however, dishonest and morally distracted to place the blame for the *influx* of immigrants into the country on the Conservative Party, particularly after the Labour Party had rejected legislation to control that influx. Such an argument implies that the Labour Party, in power, would never have tolerated such an influx, though they tolerated it in opposition. It lays the candidate open to ridicule and contempt. Gordon Walker never hesitated to use it.

Gordon Walker's five meetings during the campaign were rowdy affairs. He could not speak for long on any one issue without a shout from the hall, 'What about Immigration?' Donald Finney and other Tory councillors attended his meetings to make sure that the issue was raised. They could have saved themselves the trouble. Gordon Walker would carefully repeat his theme – 'they' came in under the Tories. It was a housing problem, and industry would have to be more equably distributed. He himself was opposed to discrimination against the immigrants – a comment which was howled down in fury by the rabble.

At one meeting Mrs Gordon Walker added fuel to the flames by describing in some detail all the 'lovely places in the Commonwealth' which she and her husband had visited.

Early in the campaign Gordon Walker had written to Sir Alec Douglas Home asking him to repudiate Griffiths on the basis of Home's remark in a television programme the night before. Asked about the statement by Griffiths that 'Smethwick rejects a multi-racial society', Home had said that, 'We should not indulge in statements of that kind'.

Home completely evaded the issue by saying that, 'Alderman Griffiths finds himself in entire agreement with what I said'. He went on to say that every immigrant in the country should be treated 'like one of us'. It is worth comparing this last statement with Gordon Walker's assertion that 'the British should come first'.

Patrick Gordon Walker's retreat from a principled stand on the immigrant issue into opportunism was largely his own decision. But he was helped by his supporters in the local Labour Party.

The local Labour Party had been rotting away for many years, corrupted from within by those who had joined it not from political principle or purpose, but with their main sights fixed firmly on local power and prestige. Hardly a year had gone by when a prominent local Labour councillor had not resigned, either from the council or from a position in the party, through some petty personal dispute.

One highly relevant resignation was that in November 1960 of Councillor Ken Bunch. Bunch, who ran the 'colour bar' Sandwell Youth Club, has since played a leading role in the town's anti-immigration campaign, collecting some 20,000 signatures for a petition demanding a total immigration ban for at least five years. Similarly, the doyen of the Labour Group, Alderman Fred Perry, found himself in complete agreement with the boys and girls of Sandwell Youth Club when they imposed a colour bar. He remarked, fatuously, 'It would not matter so much if the club members were all males.'

Several other Labour councillors were, at one time or another, responsible for remarks on immigration which were quite out of keeping with their party's (or their unions') official line. Even Mr Ron Badham, now secretary of the Labour Party, had fought a municipal by-election on the platform of a complete ban on immigration.

There are, of course, many worthy exceptions. Successive Mayors like Mr Robert Pritchard and Mr Les Morris went out of their way, at considerable personal cost, to help and encourage the immigrant communities. And there are signs that the present party leadership is progressive and constructive on this problem. But no one in Smethwick would deny that, even if Gordon Walker had wanted to fight the campaign in a principled and forthright manner, he would have encountered considerable opposition from his own supporters and councillors.

Would Gordon Walker have done better with such a campaign? Would he, for instance, have held his seat? The answer, almost certainly, is no. So vicious and long-standing was the anti-immigrant campaign in Smethwick, so shameless the Conservative association with its activities that the most brilliant orator and debater in the world would probably have lost Smethwick for Labour.

Yet Gordon Walker could not gain even the luxury of silence by his prevarication. A Birmingham M.P. for an area seriously affected by immigration, arguing with the author that the immigration issue should be 'played down', said: 'Look at Patrick. He never left the subject alone. You couldn't open a local paper without reading what he had said about immigration.'

Gordon Walker would shake his head mournfully over these words. If anyone tried his best to play the subject down, it was he. On every conceivable occasion he sought to divert attention from immigration. It was all in vain. The Tories, the Press and at least half his constituents were interested in only one issue – immigration.

Without gaining more than a handful of votes, Labour's tactics at Smethwick lost what was far more important – a hard core of principled opposition to racialist propaganda.

If the Labour candidate in any such area enthusiastically welcomes immigrant workers, if he demands for them council houses, health facilities, smaller school classes, with exactly the same vigour as he makes the demands for indigenous workers; if the Labour candidate urges the trade unionists in his area to accept the immigrant workers gladly, while insisting on trade-union membership, trade-union wages and conditions in every case; if he faces the subject without fear or evasion, appealing constantly to the decency and solidarity of the working class – if he does all this, he may not win many votes. He may even lose some. But he plants the seed of principle which will grow. The alternative is to allow anti-immigrant slander to gain credence and respectability *by default*.

Patrick Gordon Walker and his supporters prevaricated, apologized, dissociated and, as a result, the opposition to Griffiths and his followers became confused and disarrayed. The racial bitterness stirred up in Smethwick over the last four years could well continue for a generation. For this, Patrick Gordon Walker must take his share of responsibility.

4. Smethwick: Aftermath and Lessons

'I have had no adverse comment from any of the Conservative leaders either on my campaign or on my politics.'

Mr Peter Griffiths,
Birmingham Post

5 October 1964

'I am in receipt of the Conservative Party whip and have been more than welcomed by members of the Conservative Party.'

Mr Peter Griffiths,
Birmingham Post

4 November 1964

'At least twenty seats in London, the West Midlands and elsewhere can be won if the Conservatives take a firm line on immigration.'

Mr Peter Griffiths, speech to the London Young Conservatives
24 November 1964

Mr Peter Griffiths has done his best since his election to persuade people that race was not the issue which produced Smethwick's sharp swing to the Conservatives in a Labour year.

His main target has been Patrick Gordon Walker himself. Gordon Walker's own personal deficiencies, his home in Hampstead Garden Suburb, his awkwardness with industrial workers and his coolness towards his constituency were, said Mr Griffiths, the real reasons for the Tory victory. In this propaganda he was heavily assisted by the remarkable by-election at Leyton in January 1965 when Gordon Walker lost the seat in an eight per cent swing against Labour. Griffiths did not watch the result on television. The *Birmingham Post* woke him at one in the morning, and asked him his view. 'It shows', said Griffiths, 'that Gordon Walker would have lost anywhere.'

The short answer to that is that Gordon Walker won Smethwick five times in fifteen years. His majority was reduced each time – as was that of nearly every other Labour candidate in England.

It is true that voters at Smethwick had become, apparently

63

for the first time, angry and sour about their M.P.'s abilities. 'I'm not a racialist, but it's high time we got rid of Gordon Walker', was a common attitude among Smethwick voters before polling day.

Yet this resentment against the sitting member was linked with the immigration issue and its exploitation by the Smethwick Conservatives.

The fact that Gordon Walker led the Labour Party in Parliament against the Immigration Bill in 1961 made it easier for his opponents to smear him as a 'friend of the blacks'. Yet other Labour members from immigrant areas who spoke strongly against the Bill, notably Mr Dennis Howell of Small Heath, Birmingham, experienced none of the antagonism engendered in Smethwick against Mr Gordon Walker.

Griffiths's comparison of Smethwick with Leyton is ludicrous. In Smethwick there had been a sharp swing (7·2 per cent) to the Conservatives, while there had been a general swing throughout the country (3·5 per cent) towards Labour. At Leyton the eight per cent swing against Labour can be compared with a five per cent swing the same way at the Nuneaton by-election held on the same day demonstrating a swing against Labour overall. Leyton was a by-election in a Labour stronghold, with Labour voters less likely to vote than in a General Election. At Leyton, moreover, Gordon Walker was a totally new candidate replacing a man who had represented the constituency for decades. At Smethwick Gordon Walker had been the sitting M.P. for nineteen years. Both Leyton and Smethwick have a large proportion of old-age pensioners in their areas. Yet when Gordon Walker fought the Leyton campaign the Labour Government had delayed an increase in pensions while agreeing to back-date a pay-rise for M.P.s. At Smethwick Gordon Walker had been able to hold out rosy promises of large pension increases if his party was elected.

Without the race issue, Gordon Walker had been set fair to increase his majority in Smethwick, or at worst, to see it slightly reduced. At Leyton he was up against countless difficulties – irrelevant to the Smethwick campaign – which, on all estimates, accounted for the greater part of the swing against him.

The race issue was, nevertheless, relevant to the remarkable Leyton result, although not, at any rate for the last three weeks of the campaign, exploited by the Conservative Party. What Griffiths and his friends had done to Gordon Walker took root in the minds of many working-class people worried by immigration. The stone thrown into the pool at Smethwick brought ripples of racialism to Leyton. Gordon Walker could not shake off the stigma of 'nigger-lover', and at Leyton as at Smethwick, he refused to face the issue. Certainly, had it not been for Smethwick, the race issue would never have been thought relevant by the Leyton electorate.

Mr Leslie Stone, who acted as Labour Party Press Officer in Smethwick during the election campaign, has written that 'Griffiths rode to Westminster by the skilful manipulation of a single issue'. Mr Michael Hartley Brewer who covered the campaign, thoroughly and in detail, for the Institute of Race Relations, has written: 'It seems clear that Alderman Griffiths's victory was due to the immigration issue.' (Smethwick was the only constituency where the Institute was not afforded full facilities by the Conservative Party.) Despite the efforts of many, often enlightened commentators, to explain the Smethwick result in other ways, this remains the only accurate diagnosis.

When Gordon Walker returned from his defeat to Hampstead Garden Suburb, he no doubt discussed the election with his neighbour the new Prime Minister, Mr Harold Wilson. The character of the campaign which Griffiths had mounted was described in detail. Wilson, who had already commented on the result in strong terms, was shocked. He determined to pay the Conservatives back in kind for their Smethwick victory. Thus, in the middle of his opening address on the Queen's Speech, Wilson broke off in a passage about foreign affairs:

'I am sorry', he said, 'that the Foreign Secretary cannot be here today.'

The remark produced exactly the embarrassed snigger which Wilson had expected.

I am surprised, [he went on, looking up] that they should laugh at that.

Is the Leader of the Opposition proud of his hon. friend the Member for Smethwick ? Does he now intend to take him to his bosom ? Will the Conservative whip be extended to him, because if he does accept him as a colleague he will make this clear: he will betray the principles which not only his party but also his nation have hitherto had the right to proclaim. And if he does not, if he takes what I think is the right course, and what, I am sure the country will think is the right course, the Smethwick Conservatives [Interruption] – Hon. Members will have to listen now – if, as I say, the right hon. gentleman takes what I am sure the country would regard as the right course, the Smethwick Conservatives can have the satisfaction of having topped the poll, and of having sent here as their Member one who until a further General Election restores him to oblivion, will serve his term here as a Parliamentary leper.

There was immediate uproar. Some twenty-five Conservatives led by the leader of the Birmingham Tories, Mr Geoffrey Lloyd, stormed out of the Chamber. Wilson refused to retract the remark, and the Speaker said that he deplored 'the use of language of that kind'. A motion 'regretting' Wilson's remarks was tabled by some fifty Conservatives led by Geoffrey Lloyd, Sir Lionel Heald, Mr Nigel Birch, Mr Robin Turton, Sir Richard Nugent and Mr David Renton (knighted January 1965).

The motion was countered by one from the Labour benches reproving the Prime Minister for insulting lepers with his comment about the new Member for Smethwick. This served only to fan the flames of Tory fury.

Most Conservative M.P.s regarded the comment as disgraceful. Mr Robin Turton, on a visit to the Oxford Union a few weeks later, remarked that he 'did not know Griffiths from Adam'. He thought that there was 'something fishy' about Smethwick and he 'couldn't care less about Griffiths. But I thought it was very rude of Wilson and a breach of the forms of the House.'

This was probably a typical reaction among Conservative M.P.s. Griffiths appeared to his seniors as a tousle-headed, beaming fourth-former who had just won a race in a bad athletics year. Maybe he really *did* break the rules. And that sort of thing is bad for the name of the school and regiment. But the point was that he had won. And he was on the Right Side.

This feeling of solidarity with Griffiths was strengthened by Griffiths's own reaction to the leper comment. Interviewed by the *Birmingham Post* on 3 November he said:

It is most unfortunate that the Prime Minister should make comments which indicate that he is very ill-informed about the situation. I am amused and delighted by the incident and delighted by the response from Conservative M.P.s.

In a masterly maiden speech during the first week of parliament Griffiths strengthened the impression among Conservative M.P.s that Wilson's attack was cheap and unfounded. Not a vestige remained of the frenzied enthusiasm with which he had excited his constituents. His speech was a parliamentary model, calm, reasoned, bland.

I want to make it quite clear that there is no resentment at all in Smethwick on the grounds of race or colour. I can assure Hon. Members that the people in my constituency are as warm and welcoming towards strangers as are those of any other community in the British Isles. . . . It is essential that all those who seek to represent people or to speak for them should be honest and face up to these problems and discuss them rationally . . .

I have on every occasion called for the most active cooperation between the members of all races in the town.

I ask the House to judge the people of Smethwick and their Member on first-hand knowledge of the Member and the town, rather than on second-hand reporting which is so often exaggerated. I know of no cause for shame arising from the Smethwick election.

May I respectfully suggest that we in this honourable House address ourselves, without personal rancour and without animosity, to the real tasks which face us.

Griffiths was cheered to the echo by the Conservatives in the chamber. Lingering doubts about the 'fishiness' of the Smethwick campaign were cheerfully discarded. After all, here was the Member for Smethwick, 'on first-hand knowledge'. He seemed a decent enough bloke. Respectful too. Bit of an accent of course, but he couldn't help that. As he said himself, a lot of this reporting was exaggerated.

Yet it was precisely the 'reporting' to which Griffiths referred so scathingly which more than any other single factor enabled him to settle down so comfortably among his fellow M.P.s.

The fact is that before the General Election result was announced, despite the constant references to Smethwick in the news, only one national paper had sponsored a serious feature investigation of what was going on at Smethwick. Even the Institute of Race Relations *Newsletter* had not carried quotations from the *Smethwick Telephone* in its monthly round-up of newspaper cuttings.

Here had been a clear and simple subject; there had been no danger of libel, since most of the information had already appeared in print. For 'popular' papers with a supposedly 'radical' bias like the *Daily Mirror*, the *Daily Herald* (now extinct), the *Sunday Mirror*, or *The People*, such an investigation would have been politically legitimate.

Yet on the occasions before the election when national newspapermen had visited Smethwick they had busied themselves with trivialities. For instance, who had printed the 'nigger neighbour' slogan ? Could the printing and distribution be pinned to the Smethwick Conservatives ? Did Donald Finney know Colin Jordan ? Were they friendly ?

Such questions had been easy enough to parry or deflect. The real business of describing the campaign in some detail had been scrupulously avoided. Articles by Lewis Chester in the *Sunday Times* and by Dennis Barker in the *Guardian* had come nowhere near to describing the grim realities behind the campaign of Smethwick Conservatives. The whizz-kids of the *Sunday Times* Insight Column had never gone near Smethwick. As so often when a real scandal exists, the Big Bold British Press had run away from it.

The single exception among national newspapers had been *The Times*, with the reports of its Midlands Correspondent, Mr Brian Priestley. Priestley knows the Midlands and its politics as well as anyone in Britain. Throughout his journalist's career he had always recognized the strength in the 'opposite view' and had always felt compelled, perhaps overmuch, to give that opposite view an airing. The Conservative campaign at Smethwick had been the first exception to Priestley's rule. He had clearly been horrified by it.

Priestley had written two devastating dispatches from Smethwick which were published in *The Times* on 9 March (eight months before the election) and on 13 October, two days before the poll. He had gone to the Smethwick Public Library and measured the number of column inches which the *Smethwick Telephone* had devoted to immigration in 1963 (not the worst year). (The total, which he had published, had been 1,650 including headlines.) He had described the role of the *Telephone* ('a local newspaper quite remarkably interested in the immigrant problem') as 'unconstructive'.

He had recounted in his March article the activities of the Finney–Thornton syndrome, and publicized the fact that Griffiths had opposed the appointing of a Smethwick council delegate to the Midlands Commonwealth Welfare Council. He had been the first to ask Griffiths – not whether he had printed or distributed the 'nigger neighbour' slogan, but *what he thought about it*. Griffiths had then made his famous reply that it was a 'manifestation of popular feeling' and that he 'would not condemn anyone who said that'. Priestley had also elicited from him the assertion that 'the party was acting as a safety valve – a function that might otherwise be undertaken by right-wing groups'. Priestley had ended his article:

The point is, perhaps, that if Smethwick Conservatives are right, then a good many Midland Conservatives outside Smethwick are wrong. These people have tried with a good deal of success to keep the emotional temperature low in immigrant areas. They have attempted to reconcile people. They have not shouted 'Vice' in the streets but talked to police superintendents and medical officers of health. They have often been aided by newspapers, which have refused to print letters with an obvious racialist complexion to them. These Conservatives have not been winning seats lately. And some of them would by no means celebrate if Mr Gordon Walker were to lose his.

Despite the complete lack of support from other national newspapers, Priestley had continued in the same vein in his second article:

Smethwick at last has come to this – that the great issues of the day are all twisted and perverted by the question of colour and that slanders and verminous untruths which might be dismissed in a second elsewhere are here a considerable factor in the campaign . . .

In the creation of this electoral atmosphere, the Conservative Party at Smethwick has played a leading role. The evidence is there in black and white in the files of the local newspaper. It is plain and undeniable. Over a period of years if Smethwick has ever been in danger of forgetting the immigrant problem, the Conservatives have not scrupled to remind people of it.

After Griffiths made his maiden speech in the Commons, *The Times* printed a report from its Parliamentary Correspondent. Under the sub-heading: *Judge First-Hand*, the report ran:

The Smethwick Conservative Party and the electors were convinced that control of immigration was vital to racial harmony. Judge them, Mr Griffiths said, on first-hand knowledge – not on second-hand and often exaggerated reporting.

Members murmured approval . . .

Whatever may or may not have happened in Smethwick it was still a brave speech to make. Mr Griffiths had a quiet hearing and a warm chorus at the end.

But the House of Commons is a place where personal courage and integrity rank highly, and on this initial test Mr Griffiths emerged with credit.

If, as he should have done, *The Times*'s Parliamentary Correspondent had read his colleague's earlier dispatches from the Midlands he would have known better than to use a word like 'courage' in this context. Moreover, the implied approval of the comment by Griffiths on second-hand reporting was nothing less than a slap in the face of the Correspondent's own colleague.

The local Press had kept strict silence on the important aspects of the Smethwick campaign. True, most *Birmingham Post* reporters had predicted that Gordon Walker would lose and one of them – David Talbot – admitted that he would lose because of the race issue. True, the *Post* had lectured Griffiths in the nanny-like prose of Conservative provincial dailies. But neither the *Post* nor the *Birmingham Evening Mail*, the only surviving evening paper in Birmingham, had ever come near to unveiling the full strength of Griffiths's resources. Moreover, both papers during the election campaign had taken an almost exclusive interest in the immigration issue at Smethwick. Leslie Stone, Gordon Walker's Press Officer at Smethwick, says that it had been impossible to get anything about the Labour campaign in the Birmingham newspapers outside of the immigration debate. The papers had used all the gossip about immigration without ever attempting to find the real story. The sole exception had been John Horrocks's article in the *Sunday Mercury*, which won a Hannen Swaffer award.

The *Birmingham Evening Mail* had had less scruples than the *Birmingham Post*. On the day of the election the paper had carried a story headed '*Smethwick's Immigrants Flock to Polls*', in which the impression was given of foreign herds being driven by left-wing shepherds to vote on issues that they could not understand. On the next day, after the result was announced, an article appeared over the name of A. J. McIlroy – in eulogy of the 'schoolmaster who packs a punch, a political punch'.

So incompetent had the newspapers been in telling the real story that politicians and commentators everywhere displayed a remarkable ignorance about Smethwick.

Making his maiden speech on the continuance of the Immigration Act on 17 November 1964 Mr Norman St John Stevas said:

One argument which I trust will not be put forward in this Committee tonight . . . is that there should be stricter control of immigration because the crime rate and the prevalence of disease is higher amongst immigrants than amongst other sections of the population. . . . I feel it is the duty of members not only to refrain from presenting it themselves as an issue but to repudiate those who for electoral gain put it forward on their behalf. I do not think one can stand by on this issue like Pontius Pilate washing, or wringing one's hands. I think one has a positive duty to dissociate oneself from that kind of support.

Surely an attack on Griffiths! Surely now the issue would come out into the open! But Mr St John Stevas went on, at once:

I am not referring to the situation in Smethwick in particular, because I do not know what went on there at the time: I was busy in my own constituency. I mention it as a matter of principle.

He did not know because he had not been told.

Many such politicians, even Labour Members, were frankly in the dark about Smethwick. Yet many others took refuge behind the lack of publicity to avoid or even applaud the consequences of Smethwick.

Mr Quintin Hogg, for instance, said on television on election night that he 'did not know anything about Smethwick'. He had been busy in his constituency. Yet Hogg had paid a visit to the Midlands during the campaign, and had spoken in Oldbury and Halesowen, a constituency bordering on Smethwick. There he had repeated the fantasy that there would be 300,000 more immigrants in the country were it not for the Immigration Act. It is unlikely that the discordant echoes of the Smethwick campaign had not reached Mr Hogg's sharp ears.

Nor was there any excuse for idiotic argument. Mr Roy Wise, moving the debate on the continuance of the Immigration Bill on 17 November said:

They [the Smethwick electors] rejected a member whose majority had been over four elections progressively reduced from 12,000 to losing the seat. Who can blame them if they had come to the conclusion that they wanted a Member with more local knowledge and a great deal more local interest than their previous member had shown?

Gordon Walker's majority had never been more than 10,000. The argument that his majority had been reduced in four elections is utterly irrelevant to its having been wiped out in a year when his party succeeded all over the country. The 'local knowledge' and 'local interest' arguments have already been exploded.

Similarly Mr Geoffrey Lloyd, who led the walk-out when Wilson made the 'leper' comment, must as leader of the Midland Conservatives have known about Griffiths's campaign. From Lloyd's other speeches and his record on this issue, it would be no surprise if he approved.

The Leader of the Opposition, Sir Alec Douglas Home, remained silent in the House when challenged to comment on Griffiths's campaign and refused support from his front bench for the censure motion against Wilson. He knew too much about it for any public comment. He knew only too well what kind of consequences a full-scale Commons debate on the Griffiths affair might have for him.

Yet as time went on, Home and his cohorts gained confidence. In a speech to the Conservative Association of Cambridge University on 20 November he spoke of the Foreign Secretary 'crawling back from Geneva'. He went on: 'I wish I was an elector at Leyton. I would do exactly the same as the electors did at Smethwick.' In fact, Sir Alec's party drafted two special agents into Leyton to make sure that the candidate there did not 'do exactly the same as the candidate had done at Smethwick'. Sir Alec could boast about Smethwick – but he knew too much about it to let his boasting get out of hand.

Perhaps the most remarkable of all the attacks made upon Wilson for the 'leper' statement came from Mr Iain Macleod.

Macleod, who is for some inexplicable reason associated with the radical wing of the Conservative Party, rounded on Wilson in the editorial columns of the *Spectator*:

The opening day of the New Parliament was completely overshadowed by one vulgar and venomous phrase from the Prime Minister. The House of Commons guards its traditions jealously, not least that which affords protection to a new member until he has made a maiden speech. That Mr Wilson in a carefully-scripted part of his own maiden speech should have used the words 'Parliamentary leper' infuriated the whole of the Conservative Party and dismayed many of his supporters. However long this Parliament lasts those two words will not be forgotten or forgiven.

Mr Macleod certainly could not plead ignorance about the Smethwick Conservatives' four year exploitation of the immigration problem. Twice during 1963 he, as joint chairman of the Conservative Party, had received letters from the Birmingham Co-ordinating Committee against Racial Discrimination complaining about the stand of Griffiths and his fellows on separate classes for schools, a residential qualification for council houses, and the repatriation of unskilled immigrants. In April 1963, for instance, the Committee had written:

We feel the Conservatives in Smethwick are not only damaging the Conservative Party, but far more seriously are pursuing a policy which will ultimately result in a second Notting Hill.

On both occasions Macleod had brushed aside the Committee's requests that the Conservative Party should disown Griffiths. 'The Local Conservative Associations', he had written, 'are autonomous.'

Maybe. But at any rate Macleod knew the whole story. Perhaps he was proud of what had been accomplished at Smethwick. Certainly when the Prime Minister 'insulted' the town's new Member he was beside himself with rage. While 'forgiving and forgetting' all that he had heard about the Smethwick campaign, he could neither forgive nor forget a breach of Parliamentary politeness. In a speech at Leyton in December 1964 Macleod went even further by attributing the Smethwick result to Gordon Walker's personal inadequacies.

The general ignorance and doubt about the reality of Smethwick rubbed off on the Labour Party. Wilson himself had clearly heard the story direct from Gordon Walker himself, and had taken considerable interest in Smethwick since Griffiths had threatened to sue him for libel eighteen months earlier.

His backbenchers had no real knowledge of what exactly had happened in Smethwick. Many of them were appalled at so forthright an attack. Two days after the speech, the Whips were urging the backbenchers not to boycott Griffiths and to afford him 'every courtesy'. The speeches which followed Griffiths's maiden contribution on the Queen's Speech were models of decorum. Similarly, during the debate in the middle of November on continuing the Immigration Act, only one Labour member directly challenged Sir Alec Douglas Home to commit himself on Griffiths and Smethwick (predictably without success). The others treated the issue with nervous politeness. Sir Frank Soskice and Mr Ray Gunter, for instance, the two main speakers from the Government bench, fell over themselves to appear 'reasonable and responsible' Thus it was that Wilson's famous 'leper' statement, designed to split the opposition and embarrass its leaders, united them in attacking him.

Smethwick itself rarely kept out of the headlines. The revelation that the town's Labour Club maintained a colour bar received more publicity than it deserved, since most people in Smethwick had known about it for at least three years. A decision by the local Conservative-controlled council to attempt to buy houses in Marshall Street for sale to white people only provoked another rash of comment about 'Britain's most colour-conscious town'.

Griffiths himself, as usual supported by Finney, defended the decision strongly. He quoted Martin Luther King on the dangers of 'black ghettoes' in the areas of immigration, suggesting that the 'white sale only' plan of the council would prevent such ghettoes. Indeed he had himself proposed such a policy in the Smethwick council in 1962 – with reference at that time to Vicarage Road.

Buying houses for white people only without making similar arrangements for coloured people is a racialist policy. Griffiths has never yet answered the counter-proposal, made among others by the *Birmingham Post*, that the council should also buy houses for immigrants in otherwise 'white' areas. He could not countenance such a proposal, yet without it his own policy was naked discrimination.

The town continued to be besieged long after the election, first by 'probes and inquiries' (for which I must take some share of responsibility) and by racialist organizations. For instance a copy of Colin Jordan's paper (the *National Socialist*) was pushed through letter-boxes in Marshall Street, and the White Vigilantes League, a Keep Britain White organization, distributed literature and asked (unsuccessfully) for Griffiths's support.

The Oxford University magazine *Isis* packed fifty undergraduates into a bus and took them to Smethwick to examine the problem on the ground. The result was by far the best journalistic analysis of Smethwick that has yet appeared.

The *Isis* team interviewed some hundreds of Smethwick people in the street. As many as thirty-three per cent were 'bigoted in their prejudices' against the immigrants and only thirty-one per cent offered any reasonable comments on the immigrants – their contribution to society and so on. Some of the remarks picked up by the undergraduates are worth re-quoting:

Black, dirty sods . . . I hate their guts. They stink, cause trouble, stab people up South Road. (A milkman, aged twenty-one.)
They ought to do to the niggers what they did to the Jews. (Young married woman.)
Pakistanis are – well – shit aren't they? Ignorant and dirty – the real rubbish.

This was countered by a few sane remarks about the need to 'help them with their problems'.

Griffiths found himself in great demand after the election. The Young Conservatives in particular were keen to hear so distinguished a former member, and he addressed them in London, Carshalton and Liverpool. He scored a tumultuous victory at the Cambridge Union where a motion – supported by Griffiths – deploring the Labour Party's hypocritical line on immigration was carried by an enormous majority. Griffiths's able oratory and mild approach won him many friends and supporters. His mastery of the *volte face* has, indeed, charmed thousands of liberal conservatives. He has succeeded in fooling almost all of the people all of the time.

There are strong signs that Griffiths, together with his fellow

Smethwick Conservatives, have since the election striven hard to extricate themselves from the racialist mess they created. Griffiths himself has on many occasions, to the best of his ability, qualified the extreme statements he made before the election. He has described the immigrant problem as 'purely and simply a housing problem' and has said that immigrants should be treated 'exactly like everyone else'.

Perhaps most interesting in this regard has been the resignation from the council of Don Finney. Finney had at the time of his resignation built up a reputation in Smethwick second only to that of Griffiths. He was well known throughout the town as a campaigner against immigration, and was also a studious councillor in ordinary day-to-day matters affecting his constituents. Yet early in 1965 he announced his probable retirement, on the grounds that he could not get enough time off from work. Sure enough, when nomination time came around, a new name was submitted by the Conservatives for the Spon Lane candidature. Griffiths and C. V. Williams, the Mayor, had already shown signs of cooling in their attitude towards Finney. When Finney threatened to stand in West Bromwich Griffiths declared that he 'would be delighted to help Don Finney' if he were chosen to fight West Bromwich, but 'it would be a pity if he were to stand only on the immigration issue'.

Yet the job of calming down tempers is not an easy one. The Marshall Street episode, started by Finney, with its clear racialist undertones, demonstrates that time and again the Smethwick Conservatives will be forced by the weight of the public opinion they have helped form to adopt policies which even to them will appear obviously discriminatory. Backsliding on the immigrant issue will do the Smethwick Tories no good.

Many of Griffiths's closest colleagues and supporters will be urging him on; indeed these people may well take the matter into their own hands if Griffiths tries to cool the atmosphere down. When Mr Fred Thornton – the man who started the immigration band-wagon running in Smethwick – was adopted as Conservative Party candidate for Stoke-on-Trent South, in May 1965 he launched at once into his favourite subject:

I am a bit different, [he said] from Peter Griffiths in that I speak more firmly on immigration. I want a ban on immigration immediately so that we can set about educating those immigrants we have here. By that I mean education in hygiene and education in overcrowding as well as academic education.

Man must work to eat. These people are not aware of this. When they get off the boat or plane they are given a card bearing the phone number of the National Assistance Board. . . . I don't know whether you are aware of the type of person we are talking about.

They are the lowest of the low as far as the working class are concerned. They have no intention of working. They struggle up to the unemployment exchange and want the British people to support them.

7 June 1965   *Smethwick Telephone*

This form of language was enthusiastically endorsed by the Tories of Stoke-on-Trent South – an area with no Commonwealth immigrants whatever. It was the direct, inevitable result of the Conservative campaign at Smethwick.

The balancing act between appearing liberal to outside observers and pacifying sentiments at home in Smethwick has been made much easier for Griffiths by the general stampede of the Tory Party and the Labour Government towards his election policies.

Statements from Sir Alec Douglas Home and Sir Frank Soskice, each trying to outbid the other in their 'firmness' over immigration, have enabled Griffiths to turn to his constituents and say, with every justification, that the powers that be, regardless of party, were coming round to his point of view.

I have dealt at some length with politics in Smethwick over the years 1960–64, and with the General Election at Smethwick, not only because the record has to be put right, but also because they constitute a milestone in British politics. Before Smethwick no Conservative Association in the country had dared to associate itself unambiguously with anti-immigrant propaganda. The multitude of Conservative statements about the need for multi-racialism deterred them. Before Smethwick the Conservative Party had not found any political formula to remove their stubborn electoral stumbling-block – the loyalty of the industrial working class to Labour.

This class loyalty is undeniable. At every election since 1945, some 12,000,000 people have voted Labour. There are large areas of Britain, such as South Wales, Durham, Clydeside and

Merseyside, where people seldom think of voting any other way. It is true that modern 'affluence' has corroded this loyalty – but it has done less to destroy it than 1930's poverty.

Griffiths, Finney and their friends, helped by their own working-class origins, found a formula at Smethwick which dynamited that loyalty. They may in so doing have alienated some middle-class supporters who prefer a more liberal line on the immigration issue. But in towns like Smethwick, liberalism is largely irrelevant. Griffiths and his cohorts understood well that working-class people are more affected than any other group by the influx of immigrants. They used the issue to the utmost to obtain the working-class votes they needed for success and power. Indeed, the truly remarkable feature of the entire Smethwick campaign is that Griffiths's majority was so small. In spite of a long and devastating campaign on this inflammable issue more than 14,000 people clung, limpet-like, to traditional voting patterns.

Yet now the dynamite has blown away a whole section of the obstacle, and, unless the repair men get busy soon, other vital sections are in danger of collapse. What happened at Smethwick is relevant far outside the boundaries of the town itself. From the moment that the election result was announced just before midnight on 15 October, it was clear that a campaign of Smethwick proportions would no longer be necessary in other, similar constituencies. The same electoral effect could now be achieved with less effort.

In a very real sense, Griffiths did the work of many Conservative candidates for them. He laid the charges. All that is needed now is to light the fuse.

Smethwick was unique for three closely-interwoven reasons. First a powerful and aggressive anti-immigrant organization, independent of party and of extremist right-wing splinter groups, had been in the field some three years before the count, had built up a substantial membership and put out an enormous weight of propaganda. Secondly, the leaders of this group were assisted by the local paper which showed, in the words of *The Times*, a 'remarkable interest' in their activities. Thirdly, and most important, their policies and propaganda were absorbed by the local Conservative Association. To these three factors must be added a fourth, less exceptional – the inability of the local Labour Party, corroded as it was by anti-immigrant sentiments, to hit back in a determined and principled way.

In no other constituency in Britain did these factors interact as they did at Smethwick. The closest parallels were at Southall and at Birmingham, Perry Barr. Yet at Southall the issue was confused by the nomination as a parliamentary candidate of a member of the British National Party, whose supporters had worked hard in the area, and which had scored considerable success in the local elections. Although the Conservative candidate at Perry Barr was happy to use the issue as it suited him, and although he was assisted during the election by officers and members of the Birmingham Immigration Control Association, there had been in the constituency none of the tough spade work done which had marked out the Griffiths campaign in Smethwick. These conflicting factors explain, in the main, why Mr George Pargiter retained his seat at Southall and why Mr Charles Howell, despite the absence of the 1959 Liberal candidate, lost Perry Barr by only a handful of votes.

The four-year campaign at Smethwick had placed post-war coloured immigration in the centre of the party political stage. This was not the first time that the foreigner had disturbed the isolationist calm of British politics.

5. Politics and the Alien, 1886 – 1914

It is a familiar belief that Britain is not a country of immigration.
Yet it is true only in the negative sense that emigration from industrial Britain since the beginning of the last century has been
much greater than immigration. From 1871 to 1931, for instance,
Britain lost a net outflow through migration, mostly to her Empire,
of well over 3,000,000 people.*

What is wrong is the implication that the inhabitants of the
British Isles have through the centuries avoided the influx of
people from other countries. The history of Britain is a long story
of immigration – the immigration of Angles, Saxons, Normans,
Danes, Dutchmen, Belgians and many other people from different
parts of the world. In 1540, for instance, as a result of immigration
from the Low Countries, a third of all those who paid subsidy in
London to the king were aliens, and in the St Martin's-
Le-Grand Ward there were six Englishmen to 207 foreigners
among the taxpayers. Indeed London became so overcrowded
with Protestant refugees that an Order in Council was passed
dispatching them to surrounding towns. Canterbury, Colchester,
Norwich and Yarmouth were inundated with waves of immigrants, and by 1569, for instance, there were 3,993 resident
Walloons in Norwich alone. This deliberate dispersion of
immigrants, incidentally, is the only example in British history
of Government action to avoid 'clotting' in special areas.

In 1685, Louis XIV revoked the Edict of Nantes, so removing
from the French Huguenots the last vestige of protection from
political and religious persecution. Some 80,000 of these Huguenots came to Britain, again under the friendly auspices of the
English Government. Later, in the reign of Anne, some 10,000
Palatines were admitted to Britain from the Continent.

The nineteenth century saw the largest yet flow of immigration
into Britain consisting almost entirely of Irishmen. Hundreds of
thousands of Irish crossed the sea from their homeland to serve

* Royal Commission on Population, 1949.

as factory-fodder for an expanding capitalism, with the numbers increasing spectacularly after the Irish potato famine in 1851.

Through all these waves of immigration which profoundly affected the pattern of life in Britain, there were two sharply different attitudes within the host community. First, there was considerable hostility towards the immigrants among the people who had to deal with them. The Huguenots, Palatines and Walloons, whose praises were sung so vociferously by Protestant champions, arrived destitute. They were foreign in their ways and their language. They were not, as later panegyrics attempted to describe them, hardy well-dressed artisans who commended themselves immediately to their new hosts. On the contrary. Among the people with whom they had to deal on entry, they encountered resentment and bitterness.

This was even more true of the Irish. In Scotland and in the West of England, the Irish met with a hostility more vicious than anything met by any immigrant wave before or since. In Scotland particularly, where the bulk of Irish immigrants first settled, racial and religious riots between Scots and Irish were a common feature in the ironworks of the Clyde valley or the mining villages of Lanarkshire. In Glasgow, the local population staged an annual demonstration against the Irish immigrant – which ended with a charming game called 'Hunting the Barney': an Irishman would be hunted out in the narrow closes of the Trongate, and near-murdered for sport.

Much of the resentment against the Irish was religious, but the terms in which the religious bigots rationalized their resentment were as familiar as those which racial bigots use in the 1960s. The Irish were all diseased, ran the propaganda; they were nearly all criminals, and they were certainly all lazy. A continual stream of pamphlets and speeches, often from the worthiest of doctors, ministers and lawyers, spread lies to nourish this religious discord.

There was slender evidence to back the charges. Doctors commented on how fit the Irish managed to remain, despite their appalling living conditions; chief constables could find no marked tendency to crime among the Irish; and the poor law was so jealously guarded by the British ratepayer that any chance of living 'off the cheap' for the immigrant was out of the question.

Yet the charges continued, loyally supported by the Press. *The Times*, for instance, kept up a constant barrage of racist abuse throughout the 1840s. One typical leader was headed: '*Indolent Preference of Relief to Labour*', and went on:

It is the national character, the national thoughtlessness, the national indolence. . . . The Government provided work for a people that love it not. . . . Alas! The Irish peasant has tasted of famine and found that it was good. When the Celts once cease to be potatophagi, they must become carniverous. With the taste of meats will grow the appetite for them; with the appetite the readiness to earn them.

Such abuse found favour not only in middle-class circles where *The Times* was popular. The bullied, battered working class, sunk in drudgery at the height of Britain's industrial prosperity, objected strongly when the Irishman was imported by his employer specifically to smash his embryonic trade-union organizations. Frederick Engels, champion of the working classes and their revolutionary role, wrote disparagingly about the English working class in 1844. He called them 'a physically degenerate race, reduced morally and physically to bestiality', but he still believed that they held the seeds of future revolution. But to Engels the Irish immigrant could not possibly be regarded as a potential revolutionary, since 'his crudity places him little above the savage'. Engels was as wrong as the other anti-immigrant propagandists of the time. For after only a generation the Irishman not only integrated himself in the British Labour movement, but became an essential and valuable part of it.

Whole books have been written on the racial savagery between Irishman, Englishman, and Scot during the last century. They make all the more remarkable the second main characteristic of the host community's attitudes to immigration – the almost total indifference of the politicians.

In the eighty years from 1825 to 1905 not a single immigrant of any nationality was deported by order of the central political authorities. Moreover, despite the considerable feeling within the host community against immigrants – particularly the Irish – this feeling never in all that time translated itself into a coherent political demand for control of immigration, in Parliament or anywhere else.

Indeed even before 1825, immigration control into Britain was rare and slack. Apart from a Royal Prerogative to expel any aliens who did not please the monarch, there were few Acts of Parliament giving powers to keep out or deport the foreigner. In the period of the French Revolution and the Napoleonic Wars several Aliens Acts were passed with the purpose of keeping out the alien in war-time. These Acts, culminating in the Aliens Act of 1793, were harsh enough, but when the wars came to an end and peace became customary, opposition to the Acts in the Commons grew in intensity and they were eventually removed from the statute book altogether. They were replaced by the Aliens Act of 1826, and the Aliens Registration Act of 1836, which provided, not for control over entry, or for deportation, but simply for registration. Even these registration provisions were very soon abandoned.

In general, then, the words of Erskine May in his voluminous Constitutional History are a fair summary of the law until the beginning of this century:

It has been a proud tradition for England to afford an inviolable asylum to men of every rank and condition, seeking refuge on her shores, from persecution and danger in their own lands. . . . Through civil wars and revolutions, a disputed succession and treasonable plots against the State, no foreigners had been disturbed. If guilty of crimes, they were punished: but otherwise enjoyed the full protection of the law.

The sonorous words of Erskine May are relevant not only to the fact of no control, but to the reasons for it. The 'free' approach to immigration flourished in the hey-day of free trade and of British industry's expansion to the four corners of the globe. Booming, bourgeois Britain – the pioneer of industrial revolution – was 'the workshop of the world'. Her future competitors trailed far behind in the development of those techniques which shaped the new capitalist society. As victor in the international trade race, Britain could well afford to lay herself open to free competition and free trade. Corn Laws and tariff barriers were repugnant to the world's leading industrial nation and commodities were encouraged to flow freely across national boundaries.

With the free movement of trade went the free movement of labour. The British countryside, with the Corn Laws repealed, could not supply the labour necessary for Britain's fast-expanding industry.

James Handley in his book *The Irish in Scotland* states that 'in the half-dozen decades before 1845 the Irish immigrant was an indigent labourer meeting the demand created by the expansion of industrial and agricultural Scotland', and the same was true of all the immigrants whether or not the motive for their immigration was persecution. The industrial revolution in the boom years lapped up labour insatiably, only to throw the workers into even greater dejection in the seemingly inevitable slumps. Immigration control, like protection, was irrelevant, unnecessary – a symbol of national decline.

The stark economic case for ignoring pleas that control be introduced was, as ever, cloaked in the woolly idealism of Victorian Liberalism. British politicians of both parties, particularly the Liberals, regarded themselves with some pleasure as champions of the right of political asylum. Persecuted foreigners could come to Britain without hindrance. Such was the slogan of men like Gladstone, who could then justify his grandiloquent speeches about 'the savage, as we call him' having a right to live as much as anyone. Such idealism was bred partly from the fact that British politicians regarded themselves with every justification as leaders of world revolution against feudalism and reaction. Their friends, therefore, were men like Mazzini and Garibaldi who were fighting the same struggle in other countries. Such men were welcomed with open arms.

But the unchallenged supremacy of the British ruling class could not last forever. New industrial nations, some conceived by British emigrants, quickly rose to challenge Britain in the world markets, and the politicians tasted real economic crisis for the first time in their country's industrial history. People started to talk about 'protection' as the solution to the rising status of Britain's competitors. Moreover, the political struggles in these countries, as well as in Britain, were no longer clearly defined as between revolutionaries and feudalists. In many industrial centres throughout Europe and North America, a new class of revolutionary was emerging – not confined this time to saving his country from the evils of Popish feudalism, but concerned to attack all capitalist authority everywhere. Under the rules devised for people like Mazzini, Karl Marx could live in Britain as a political exile for thirty-four years, though his political purpose was enormously different.

There was another type of awkward revolutionary too, a revolutionary opposed not so much to capitalism as to imperialism – the patriot who wanted to rid his country of foreign power and influence. Such people presented Victorian politicians with a dilemma. Palmerston could compel Portugal to amnesty her political offenders in 1847 and Gladstone with all the humanitarian oratory at his command could expose the shocking treatment of 20,000 political prisoners in Naples. Yet at almost the same time (1848) the Young Ireland State trials were being held at Clonmel and the convicted prisoners deported (by the same administrators) to Tasmania. The attitude of the Liberals was one of understandable cynicism. They favoured all political offenders with whose politics they agreed.

It was around the issue of the 'nihilist' – as the anarchist, socialist or anti-imperialist was contemptuously known at Westminster – that Parliamentary opposition to unrestricted immigration first arose.

Britain did not sign the agreement among other European nations to refuse entry to foreigners wanted by other countries for revolutionary crimes, but the politicians had a close watch kept on the ports and unofficially exchanged information about 'nihilists'. The Extradition Act of 1870 gave the Government powers to deport criminals wanted by other countries with whom Britain had signed an Extradition treaty. Although the Act was hedged around with exceptions which in theory kept the right of political asylum alive, it marked the beginning of the end for uncontrolled immigration into Britain. The anarchist with his 'general war against the laws and institutions of organized societies' (Lord Granville in the House of Lords) was the first butt of the new protectors, imperialists and controllers who were tightening their grip on the Tory Party.

The second more vulnerable target was the Jew. The Jews had been emigrating in small numbers from Europe and Russia for decades. By the beginning of the 1880s the latent anti-Semitism in Russia and Rumania had turned into systematic persecution. The Russian May Laws of 1888 and the subsequent

85

pogroms drove the Russian Jews back into their already over-crowded and under-employed Pale. All the considerable resources of Tzarist despotism were deployed against the defenceless and impoverished Jew. Small wonder that the victims turned desper-ately to emigration and streamed across the boundaries, almost all headed for America.

Throughout the 1890s this stream of emigration remained steady and relatively controlled at source. The tidy mind of the Jew, even when persecuted, organized emigration so that the flow at no stage grew unmanageable. Until the end of the 1890s, each year about 2,500 Jews, on the way to America, decided to stay in Britain. Then the hysterical outburst of anti-semitism at the turn of the century turned the orderly exodus into a rout. The Rumanian exodus (1900), the series of intensified pogroms, the vicious chauvinism of the Russo-Japanese War (1904) threw the emigration into total confusion. Between 1899 and 1902 figures for immigration into Britain trebled. In all, between the years 1875 and 1914 some 120,000 Jews came to Britain, and almost all of them settled automatically in the hovels of East London.

In 1889 a Select Committee of the House of Commons investi-gated the immigration question. The Committee concluded that the number of aliens was 'not large enough to cause alarm', that their health was good but that they were clotted in specific areas which had unreasonably to deal with too large a problem, and that they disobeyed the sanitation by-laws. The Committee was not prepared to recommend control legislation, but added that it 'contemplated the possibility of such legislation becoming neces-sary in the future'.

The sober arguments of the Committee did not halt the mount-ing campaign against the foreigners, being well received in High Tory circles. In 1892, the Conservatives declared their intention of bringing in control legislation, but were defeated before they could do anything about it. The incoming Liberal Government found no trace of any research work on control in the Home Office. The Marquess of Salisbury, in fact, introduced a Bill in the Lords in 1894 to control immigration, and was somewhat embarrassed when, four years later, under his Premiership, Lord Hardwicke re-introduced almost the same Bill and asked for the

Prime Minister's support. Lord Hardwicke reinforced his argument with a dose of lukewarm racism:

It would be a very serious matter if the type of population which is now to be found in many districts of the East End, where there is a strong alien element, were to become at all a common type in the poorer districts of our large cities. It would mean, my Lords, that these classes would become to a great extent non-English in character, and that, both in physique and in moral and social customs, they had fallen below our present by no means elevated standard.
23 May, 1898

Salisbury accepted the Bill with relish, but regretted that there was no room for it at present in the Commons. He mused at length on the miseries of the English ratepayer, forced to fork out money for the destitute and worthless Jew, and was delighted when the Bill's Second Reading was carried in the Lords by eighty-one to nineteen. The Bill went through all its stages in the Lords and stopped there.

The Bill was, however, the signal for the formation of a powerful and dedicated anti-alien lobby in the House of Commons which made it its aim to push similar legislation through the House of Commons in the shortest possible time. The pace was set by the Honourable Member for Sheffield, Sir Howard Vincent. Vincent was a formidable figure in the Conservative Party, becoming chairman of the National Union of Conservative and Unionist Associations in 1895, and vice-chairman of the Primrose League in 1901. He was also an ex-A.D.C. to the King and British delegate at the anti-anarchist Conference in Rome in 1898.

Vincent's interest in the question of aliens was not inspired by demands from his constituents. In 1902 for instance there were twenty-one aliens in the whole of Sheffield and by 1904 the figure had swollen to twenty-four. Vincent explained that his passionate interest in the alien problem arose from his associations with aliens in his past job as Chief Director of Criminal Investigation for the Metropolitan Police. He described himself as 'concerned about [the] effect on the British working man'. His statements, however, while always denying any personal animosity towards Jews or any other group of foreigners, were crammed with humdrum anti-alien propaganda which had little relevance to the facts.

Vincent's main assistant in this campaign was the Tory Member for Stepney, Major William Evans Gordon. Evans Gordon had some considerable interest in the problem since his constituency bore the brunt of Jewish immigration. Yet his speeches, like Vincent's, are stamped with the marks of an irrational hatred of aliens.

These two and a small group of acolytes pressed every possible Minister with questions and demands about the possibility of quick, strict immigration control. The Tory Ministers were embarrassed by the fact that Salisbury had already committed himself on the matter, and that there were strong doubts within the party over whether legislation of this kind should be introduced – particularly under pressure from such patently disagreeable quarters. When Vincent demanded control in a question to the President of the Board of Trade on 5 July 1900, the harassed Mr Ritchie could only say that he 'supposed no steps have been taken because the House has been engaged on other business'.

On 29 January 1902 Evans Gordon moved an amendment to the Queen's Speech demanding immediate immigrant control. For those who believe that Britain's first taste of anti-alien propaganda started in the 1950s it is worth quoting from his speech:

Not a day passes but English families are ruthlessly turned out to make room for foreign invaders. Out they go to make room for Rumanians, Russians and Poles. Rents are raised 50 to 100 per cent and a house which formerly contained a couple of families living in comparative decency is made to contain four or five families living under conditions which baffle description. . . . It is only a matter of time before the population becomes entirely foreign. . . . The rates are burdened with the education of thousands of children of foreign parents. . . . Among the thousands who came here there is a considerable proportion of bad characters, and the competition with home industries extends to burglary and other cognate crimes. I should have thought we had enough criminals of our own. . . .

These are the haunts of foreign prostitutes and *souteneurs* of gambling dens and disorderly houses. A band of Italians, every one with a knife, which he is too ready to use, is at this moment causing great anxiety to the County Council. . . . The working classes know that new buildings are erected not for them but for strangers from abroad; they see notices that no English need apply placarded on vacant rooms; they see the schools crowded with foreign children and the very posters and advertisements on the walls in a foreign tongue; they see themselves deprived of their Sunday for that too is gone, and it is no longer within the power of an English working man in many parts of East London to enjoy his day of rest. . . . A storm is brewing which, if it be allowed to burst, will have deplorable results.

Deplorable as the results of such a storm might have been, Evans Gordon did his best both inside and outside Parliament to provoke it. He had formed a militant, racist organization called the 'British Brothers' League'. Only a week before his speech he had led 6,000 shouting East-Enders to a mass meeting in the People's Palace, Tower Hamlets, where he had bawled abuse against the foreigner. The Borough Council of Tower Hamlets, under his guidance, had passed a resolution calling for control legislation. Despite the Government's promise, after his speech, to appoint a Royal Commission on the Aliens Question, and even include Evans Gordon as a member, he and his friends in Parliament agreed to step up their campaign.

Before the Commission reported, Vincent moved another amendment to the Queen's Speech of January 1903, in which he likened Jewish immigration to the entry of diseased store cattle from Canada. He himself asked six questions on the issue in the first three months of 1903, making every possible allegation of crime, disease and moral decay against the immigrants. He was delighted to receive some support from the Liberal benches. Mr Cathcart Wason for instance, Liberal M.P. for Orkney and Shetland, an area not known for immigration problems, asked on 18 February:

What is the use of spending thousands of pounds on building beautiful workmen's dwellings if the places of our own workpeople, the backbone of the country, are to be taken over by the refuse and scum of other nations?

In the summer of 1903, the Royal Commission reported. It had heard a mountain of evidence, and addressed itself in the first part of its report to an examination of the charges made by the anti-alien lobby over the previous few years. In effect, this examination dismissed all the charges as wild and inaccurate. The number of immigrants was found to be still very small compared with countries abroad. No more than 0·69 per cent of the British population were aliens while comparable figures for other countries were: Germany 1·38; France 2·66; Austria 1·98; and Switzerland 9·58. To the charge that the Jews were taking people's jobs, the Commission found that 'alien labour is only or chiefly employed in doing work for which the native workman is unsuited or which he is unwilling to perform'. Less than four per cent of the aliens were living on poor relief – a much lower proportion than that for the native population – while only 1·16 per cent of the aliens had been sentenced to imprisonment at some time in their life (a higher proportion than for the native population, but a very small figure overall). The Commissioners accepted the view of Dr Herbert Williams, the Medical Officer of Health for the Port of London, who told them, 'I cannot say that much infectious disease has come into this country among these people', and they agreed that the aliens lived as cleanly and healthily as their hosts, particularly in view of their appalling housing conditions. They also rejected out of hand the theory that overcrowding had been caused or even heightened by the influx of immigrants. They pointed out that the highest overcrowding in London was in the wards of St Margaret and St John where there were no aliens, and that in the City of Westminster Ward, where many aliens lived, overcrowding had in fact decreased during the previous ten years. The Commissioners commented warmly on the progress of alien children in the schools, where, they said, once the language problems had been overcome, the children adapted remarkably well and integrated quickly with English children.

The Commission found terrible housing conditions and appalling exploitation. Out of 686 housing cases investigated, 347 had produced evidence of 'key money' having had to be paid, for a total of £3,757.

It also found that 'the industrial conditions under which a large number of aliens work in London fall below the standard which ought, alike in the interests of the workman and the community at large, to be maintained'.

The Commission commented too on the extraordinary clusters of immigrant aliens in Britain. Out of the total 286,925 aliens, 135,377 lived in London, and of these 54,310 lived in the Borough of Stepney. Further, despite the considerable increase in the number of people living in Stepney, the number of houses there had diminished because of the unscrupulous building plans of greedy factory-owners.

The first part of the Commission report, in short, constituted a monumental refutation of the anti-alien propaganda waged by Vincent, Evans Gordon, their parliamentary protégés and the considerable army of hacks throughout the country who were eagerly mouthing their slogans. Yet when it came to remedial action, the Commission was in an appalling dilemma. For the terms of reference referred exclusively to control. Social legislation to cope with overcrowding and new laws against scurrilous land-lords; new methods of town planning to stop the building of factories without adequate housing for workers – such obvious solutions were outside the remit of the Commission, and it was forced to apply itself to the question: control or no control. As a result, although the Jewish immigrant was acquitted of the charges against him, and although the case for control was refuted by the Commission's own findings, the recommendations in the second half of the report supported control of a very stringent nature. Major Evans Gordon's views had – against all the facts – triumphed.

The main recommendations were that 'undesirable' aliens should be kept out of the country, with the decision on undesirability taken by immigration officers after questioning immigrants at the ports; that aliens convicted of criminal offences should be liable to deportation; that overcrowded areas should become prohibited to new immigrants; and that 'undesirable aliens' should include those without visible or probable means of support. Since, on the Commission's own findings, some forty per cent of the immigrants coming into Britain at the time had less than 10s. in ready cash each, this last recommendation was crucial.

These recommendations were signed by five of the seven members. A minority dissenting report was signed by Major Kenelm Digby, Permanent Secretary at the Home Office, and Lord Rothschild. Digby's own contribution is a masterpiece of bitter logic. Since it had been found, he said, that there were hardly any criminals and there was practically no disease – what on earth was the point of establishing this monstrous bureaucracy to keep the criminals and the diseased out in the future ? Digby also pointed out that it was quite impossible to ascertain bad character by means of a few hurried inquiries. He said that the idea of prohibited areas was ludicrous and inhumane, and that a lot of the problem would be solved by enforcement of the local by-laws which had lapsed into obsolescence.

Rothschild, himself a Jew, quietly concurred.

> I am opposed [he wrote] to the adoption of restrictive measures because even if they are directly aimed at the so-called undesirables, they would certainly affect deserving and hard-working men, whose impecunious position on their arrival would be no criterion of their incapacity to attain to independence.

Despite this substantial minority report, the Tories around Vincent and Evans Gordon were jubilant. They could pass over the first part of the report and the bulk of the evidence. Their demands for rigid control of immigration were no longer merely the outpourings of a reactionary Tory rump, but were now written into the recommendations of a full-blooded Royal Commission. Vincent stepped up his campaign, organizing his small cohort well at Question Time, and driving the Government into submission.

Indeed, Balfour's Government was not by this time particularly worried about the aliens lobby. The Conservatives, who had been in power, almost without interruption, for twenty years were punch-drunk, politically bankrupt. The Boer War which, with much drum-beating, had won them the 1900 election, had petered out to no apparent advantage, while the Irish problem appeared to them as insoluble as ever. Torn internally by the powerful protection lobby centring around Chamberlain in the West Midlands; savaged by the Liberals over their cheap-labour policies in South Africa; stubborn in their opposition to any social reform for the working class, the Tories were, as Churchill put it, 'adamant in drift'. What new legislation could they introduce in their last two years of office which would please all the warring factions of their own party ? Had not Vincent and Evans Gordon, despite their obvious deficiencies as policy-makers, supplied the answer ? Immigration control would not only please the protectionists in Birmingham. It would appease most sections of the party who were militantly 'anti-anarchist'. There was the added advantage of winning a few cheap votes around the East End.

Thus the King's Speech of 1904 announced a Bill to deal with 'the evils consequent on the entry of destitute aliens'. Sir H. Campbell Bannerman, Leader of the Opposition, said that his party would have to see the Bill before commenting; but he could not resist noting that it had been introduced 'to the great delight of the Honourable Member for Sheffield'. Another Liberal remarked caustically that 'the Honourable Member for Sheffield ought to be Prime Minister'.

The Liberal Party then went into discussion over its attitude to the Bill. The matter was crucial, for this was clearly one of the major pieces of new legislation to be introduced in the 1904 session, and the election was not more than two years away. Immediately, the representatives of the Liberal tradition – champions not only of free trade but also of free political asylum – found themselves in the majority. The case for outright opposition to the Bill was put most powerfully by the ageing Sir Charles Dilke, by now a supporter of the Labour movement, though still nominally Liberal M.P. for the Forest of Dean.

Yet opposition to Dilke's demands was strong enough to give the Liberal leaders pause. Mr H. Norman, a front-bencher and the Member for Wolverhampton South East, announced his intention of supporting the Bill. Sydney Buxton, one of the few Liberal Members in the East End of London (M.P. for Poplar) desperately urged the party not to favour the 'open door'. There were valuable votes to be lost, he urged. He himself would undoubtedly lose his seat, and any hope of gains in East London would be out of the question. At the First Reading, when the Bill included the Royal Commission's recommendations about undesirable aliens, the Liberals – while rejecting their proposals for prohibited areas – still had not made up their minds, and did not divide the House. But by the Second Reading on 25 April, Dilke and his supporters had gained the day.

The Liberal Party proposed an amendment as follows:

That this House, holding that the evils of low-priced alien labour can best be met by legislation to prevent sweating, desires to assure itself before assenting to the Aliens Bill that sufficient regard is had in the proposed measure to the retention of the principle of asylum for the victims of persecution.

Meanwhile the yellow Press had been whipping up support for the Tories. Feature articles in the popular papers and numerous pamphlets appeared about the evils of undesirable aliens. Their titles were familiar: 'The Invasion of Destitute Aliens' (1892); 'Foreign Undesirables' (1901); 'The Alien and the Empire' (September, 1903); and so forth.

Arnold White, whose writings wove a strange pattern of nascent anti-Semitism and demands for social reform, wrote in praise of Russian anti-Semitic persecutions in his book *The Modern Jew*.

The intellect of the Jew is masterful [wrote White]. His assiduity, his deadly resolve to get on, his self-denial and ambition surmount all natural obstacles. If all careers in the Russian Empire were thrown open to a Russian Jew, not a decade would go by before the whole Russian administration from Port Arthur to Eydtkuhnen and from Archangel to Yalta must pass into Hebraic hands. . . . The Russian nature is self-indulgent, impulsive, kind-hearted, generous and passionate. Russia would have no chance of survival against the cold determination of a people that exists only when living as a parasite growth on another race. . . . This is precisely what is involved in the antidotes of education and equality so glibly prescribed by Anglo-Saxon doctrinaires who condemn Russia without understanding the difficulties with which she has to deal and who do not treat their own racial problems on abstract principles.

Such views gained currency, particularly in the East End where outbursts of violence against the Jews became the norm rather than the exception. The campaign instigated by Sir Howard Vincent, and taken up by Balfour, excited what before had been no real racial problem in the East End of London. On the morning of the Second Reading debate, one of the more unscrupulous of the daily newspapers announced in its leader column: 'It is hoped that every London newspaper under British control will publish a list of the traitors in Parliament who vote against this measure.' Another proclaimed: 'The small-pox epidemic was attributed to the scum washed on our shores from dirty water coming from foreign drain-pipes.'

In this atmosphere Sir Charles Dilke rose in the House to move his amendment. Dilke was still one of the finest speakers in the House, and in this speech he combined his attachment to the Labour movement and the working class with the logic and attention to detail which had marked him out for so many years. He started his speech by warning the Tories 'that they have raised a devil which they will find it difficult to lay'. He proceeded coolly to shatter the core of the Conservative argument – showing that immigration in 1902 had in fact decreased from the 1901 figure, and quoting from the House of Lords Committee on Sweating in 1888 which had found that 'undue stress has been laid on foreign immigration, inasmuch as we find that the evils complained of obtain in trades not affected by immigration'. He declared that the cheap labour of women and girls was a far more serious matter for the trade unions than was the influx of immigrant labour.

Dilke dwelt at length on the past history of immigration into Britain pointing out that each wave had initially met with hostility, yet after a generation or two had become accepted and even praised. 'Honourable Members,' he said, 'are always inclined to give away the past. They are always inclined to say that alien immigration was a benefit in its day.'

Dilke ended his extraordinary speech with a peroration which visibly shook the Tory benches, and flung his own backbenchers who supported the Bill into considerable confusion.

I am afraid that in this country, though not in this House, there has been an agitation kindled and fanned and that an anti-Jewish feeling has been aroused. Those who read the newspapers which support this Bill cannot help seeing what their tone is. The faults which are set down against the Jews are caused by persecution in the past – the historical growth of the persecution of that race.

The principle of the right of asylum, strong as it is, in the case of Jews ought to apply with double strength to every one holding Christian principles, as a proper exchange for the hateful and shameful system of persecution. Before you change those principles in this matter an overwhelming case ought to be made out. I have examined the figures, numbers and proportion alleged by the Hon. and gallant Member (Evans Gordon) and I ask the House to say whether any overwhelming necessity has been established for this Bill.

Dilke was followed immediately by a young Liberal – Charles

Trevelyan – who made up in enthusiasm what he lacked in Dilke's experience and eloquence. Yet the House had to wait until the end of the debate for the most powerful attack of all. It came from John Burns, the old socialist from Battersea who had turned Liberal in 1900. Something about the Tory case for the Bill must have stirred the dying embers of Burns's class consciousness. His speech, although falling fatally into blatant anti-Semitism when attacking 'the Rich Jew' ('The Conservative Party has made the Stock Exchange a new Jerusalem and Park Lane a new Mount Pisgah'), came closer than Dilke, Trevelyan or Asquith (who also spoke in opposition to the Bill) to underlining the real motives and cures for the Tory campaign.

From the fourteenth century to the eighteenth there were the Howard Vincents of those particular days who made equally ridiculous statements and advocated equally ridiculous and futile legislative oppression. The fact was that every fifteen or twenty years some tariff reformer in disguise, some full-blown protectionist, some grand Imperialist set up a crusade against the poor foreigner. . . .

If we would put an end to the evil, let us establish fair-rent courts, extend the powers of the local authorities, facilitate communications, stop the doing of work at home, abolish sub-contracting and the like. There are other methods. We should kill home work altogether; make it impossible to have work carried out in tenements where people eat and sleep; we should totally abolish sub-contracting, do away with child labour, and, above all, we should make each employer in the East End give their workers one day's rest a week.

The combination of Dilke, Trevelyan and Burns had two immediate effects. It reduced the Conservative case to shreds, and the Home Secretary, Mr Aretas Ackers-Douglas, unhappy in any event about his party's collapse before Vincent, flannelled his way through a miserable speech. Even Vincent was not at his best, despite his personal triumph. But the second main effect was more important. The speeches galvanized the vast majority of Liberal Members into outright and vigorous opposition to the measure. The Tory majority at the Second Reading was 124 – only slightly less than the overall majority at the 1900 election. But the Liberals opposed the Bill with all the fierceness at their command. A decision to 'send the Bill upstairs' (to Committee) was carried by a majority of only ninety, and in the first six days of the Standing Committee the Government got through three lines of the Bill. On 11 July the Prime Minister was forced to tell the House that the Bill had 'received treatment which would make it impossible to carry the Bill into law in the present session'. The Bill was immediately withdrawn, which led Winston Churchill to conclude that, 'The Government did not desire to pass the Bill', and that it was simply a measure to waste parliamentary time and keep the Conservative Party's extremists happy.

Churchill may have been right. If he was, the pattern of events in the country through that autumn and winter of 1904 changed the Conservative leaders' minds. The Birmingham protectionist clique kept up the pressure on the party to continue its anti-alien propaganda and legislation. At the Stalybridge by-election of January, 1905, the Conservative Central Office put out an official leaflet, distributed to all electors:

'Let them all come' is the radical cry. The radicals by their obstruction to the Aliens Bill are evidently glad to see all foreigners who are criminals, who suffer from loathsome diseases, who are turned out in disgrace by their fellow-countrymen, who are paupers who fill the streets with profligacy and disorder. The radicals welcome them all.

At the by-election at Mile End, in the same month, Tory shop-keepers sported pictures in their window of the Jewish Liberal candidate, Mr Straus, robbing poor English workers.

The Tories who had held Stalybridge by eighty-one votes in 1900 lost it by 951 to the Liberals, and Mile End was also a Liberal gain, but the Birmingham clique was quick to point out that, without the anti-alien propaganda, even more votes would have been lost in the rising tide of Liberalism. Thus on 14 February 1905, the King's Speech promised another Bill to deal with alien immigration, one which, when published, was seen to be a considerably watered-down version of the 1904 Bill; it proclaimed the perennial right of asylum and applied controls only to 'undesirable aliens' who came into Britain on 'immigrant ships' carrying more than twenty third-class passengers.

Three factors distinguished political reaction to this measure from the year before. First, the Liberals could not make up their minds. Although Dilke and Trevelyan divided the House on

T – D

2 May, they could muster only fifty-nine votes to 211 for the Tories. Asquith and Campbell Bannerman abstained. Yet as the parliamentary battle developed, so Liberal opposition strengthened.

There were almost 150 amendments to the Bill, and some fifty divisions. Crucial clauses were carried in committee by majorities of only 20 to 30, and at the Third Reading, when Asquith and Campbell Bannerman voted against the Bill, the Government's Second Reading majority was halved.

Furthermore the Tory cause had degenerated still further. Typical of the speeches from the Government side of the House was that of Mr W. Hayes Fisher, the Member for Fulham:

> Just as one river could carry a certain amount of sewage, but not the sewage of the whole Kingdom, so one portion of London cannot carry the whole of the pauper and diseased alien immigrants who come into the country.

For the first time in the controversy, Joseph Chamberlain, Member for Birmingham West, came out into the open. Chamberlain had already had some experience in controlling immigration into the colonies. As Colonial Secretary, for instance, he had helped to formulate the Australian Immigration Restriction Act of 1901. In the spirit of his own Fair Wages Resolution, Chamberlain addressed himself to the working classes:

'It is on the unskilled labourer that this immigrant produces the greatest mischief.' So strong was Chamberlain's commitment to the Bill, that the Prime Minister himself was forced to sum up in the important debates.

The attitude of the more genuine representatives of the working class, the Labour Party, showed the third important change since 1904. In that year, no Labour Member had spoken on the issue, and only three of the Labour Members had voted against the Bill (the others abstained). Yet now, goaded possibly by Chamberlain's hypocrisy, they rallied in stern opposition. Their leader, James Keir Hardie, said that he supported the deportation of criminals and diseased but regarded the Aliens Bill as 'fraudulent, deceitful and dishonourable'. He rounded on Chamberlain, perhaps the worst enemy of the Labour movement at the time, and asked what possible relevance Birmingham had to the alien problem. He pointed out that in 1902 Birmingham suffered from the 'plight' of 121 aliens in the city, while by 1904 the figure had gone *down* to eighty-nine. He said that this miserable legislation should have been replaced by an Unemployed Workmen's Bill, and alleged that 'there is no demand for this Bill from the working classes'.

Nevertheless by the end of August the Bill had become law. Major Evans Gordon was knighted. But the Tories only had six months to administer the Bill before they went to the country in January 1906 and were given the biggest trouncing in British political history. There is some evidence that their anti-alien campaign had won a few votes. Evans Gordon and Vincent retained their seats, and Mr Claude Hay, a prominent campaigner for control, considerably increased his majority in Shoreditch, right against the national 'swing'. Yet many other prominent members of the anti-alien lobby lost their seats, and a Jew, Mr Straus, retained the London East End seat of Mile End. Not all Jews, incidentally, were in favour of the unrestricted entry of their fellows. Sir Bernard Cohen, Jewish Tory M.P. for Islington, had voted for the Aliens Act and had been awarded a baronetcy soon afterwards.

The only legal change which the Tories made to the Act they had passed was to cut the maximum number of immigrants on an 'immigrant ship' from twenty to twelve.

Mr Herbert Gladstone, the Home Secretary in the new Liberal Government, was faced with the unenviable task of carrying out an Act which he himself and his party had opposed. He decided not to repeal the Act but made immediate concessions to the radicals in his own party and on the Labour benches by lifting the minimum number on an immigrant ship to twenty. He also issued new instructions to immigration officers that from the incoming of the new Government the benefit of doubt as to the right of political asylum should rest with the immigrant and not, as under the Tories, with the immigration officer.

For this relief, Gladstone faced a barrage of protest from the remainder of the anti-alien Tories. The cry of Evasion went up. The Act was being evaded! In the first year of the Act 6,567 aliens came in on ships with less than twenty third-class passengers – thus totally evading the law. There were, complained Evans

Gordon, only twenty-one deportations in 1906. On the whole, Gladstone dealt with such remarks and questions firmly. He complained that he was 'in the unhappy position of knowing that whatever I do or say on this subject will draw fire on me from all quarters of the House'. He refused to cut the numbers on an immigrant ship, and refused, when asked by a Northern Irish M.P., to repatriate unemployed immigrants. On 25 February 1909 Claude Hay moved an amendment to the King's Speech to include tighter control of immigration. He wanted it to apply to all ships, and to all classes of passengers. He pointed to the recent murders of policemen in Tottenham by a foreigner, and called for stricter control of foreign criminals. Gladstone coolly replied that the number of immigrants had dropped sharply, as had the number of immigrant criminals, and any amendment to the existing Act would be absurd. He hotly denied Hay's allegation that there had been a 'virtual suspension of the Act', though in many ways Hay was right. Gladstone's attitude had been: we will go through with the machinery of the Act, but the more foreigners who slip through, the better. Short of repealing the Act, it was, for someone who opposed the whole principle, the most honest approach.

Hay's amendment was defeated by 208 to eighty-two, but the protests against evasion persisted through the next three years. Hardly a parliamentary month went past without one of the anti-alien lobby complaining about the evils caused by alien immigration.

In January 1911, a new Home Secretary, Mr Winston Churchill, went to Sydney Street to take charge of a police operation against a Russian anarchist, called Peter the Painter, and his associates. The house in which the fugitives were hiding caught fire and Churchill gave the order to leave the fire to burn. Considerably moved by this heroic exploit Churchill, who until that date had been as liberal as Gladstone on the aliens issue, decided that something had to be done to keep out aliens more effectively than the Aliens Act. After all, Peter the Painter and most of the 'anarchists' who were making his job so difficult were foreigners. When asked by another Irish M.P., on 9 February 1911, what the Government were doing to tighten up the regulations, he said, to the surprise and delight of the anti-alien lobby: 'The Government has legislation in contemplation on the subject – legislation which will not involve registration of aliens.'

The 'contemplation' of such legislation appears, however, to have been superseded by matters of greater political importance, for little more about aliens legislation was mentioned either in the House or out of it before 1914. It appears that the Liberal Party, after its slender victory of December 1910, was prepared to concede to the Opposition certain aspects of tighter immigration control, particularly as the 'anarchist' threat seemed to both parties now a reality. But events in Europe were moving too fast for such legislative trivia to take up the minds of leading politicians.

Suddenly, on 5 August 1914, all the liberal arguments, all the 'traditions of asylum', all the high-blown talk about the free haven of Britain, all the long, tumultuous opposition of Liberals and socialists to strict immigration control were washed away by a single Act passed through all its parliamentary stages on a single day. The Home Secretary, Mr Reginald McKenna, asked leave of the Commons to introduce the Aliens Restriction Act. The purpose of the Act was 'in time of war or imminent national danger or great emergency to impose restrictions on aliens'. McKenna explained that the country was on the brink of war and more and more German spies were being captured. His Bill would empower the Home Secretary absolutely to prohibit immigrants from landing and to deport them. He also required all aliens in the country to register with the police.

The House was disposed to pass automatically to next business and to allow this emergency Act to go through without comment, but it was all a little much for Sir William Byles, the Labour M.P. for Salford North. He had to ask whether there was any time limit on this 'dangerous power' which the House was giving to the Home Secretary. He was greeted with cries of 'Sit down' from the chauvinists on all sides of the House, and the cold assurance from McKenna that of course the Order would cease to have effect as soon as the war or a state of national danger had passed. Sir William shut up at once. Yet his was the only voice raised even to question this dangerous power, which was to last in substance for more than fifty years. The entire discussion covered eight columns of Hansard.

*

A Tory Government, bankrupt after long years of war and mis-rule, was forced by pressure from its extreme right wing to introduce an Act to control immigration. What problems that immigration brought could only have been solved by a degree of social planning and social reform. Neither of these were proposed by the Tories. Their remedy was control. This remedy went against the grain of many within their own party, but for lack of anything else to do, and in the hope of picking up cheap votes, the Tory leaders gave way to the reactionary and racialist right.

The move flung the Liberal opposition into confusion. After some strong argument they agreed to oppose the measure, and the opposition grew out of uncertainty into prolonged and principled resistance. Eventually the Tories were forced to use the 'guillotine', and the Act was passed after a bitter battle, seriously mangled by Amendments.

Almost immediately the Liberals came to power and were forced to administer the Act. They were bombarded with cries that the Act had been evaded, and eventually gave in to the pressure. Finally the whole process was ended in the holocaust of war.

Outside parliament the effect of the Tory manoeuvre was to associate the more sordid outbursts against the foreigners with the respectability of the Conservative Party. Racial violence and incitement, hitherto a discreditable, back-street activity, acquired virtual Tory sponsorship during elections. The cry of control – irrelevant as it was to solving the problems – was taken up by the racialists in common with the Tories.

No one can doubt that the net result of the process was seriously detrimental. The so-called 'advantage' to Britain of control legislation – marginally fewer immigrants – must be set against the racial feelings stirred up by the campaign for control. After control, the Jews in East London lived in as squalid conditions as they had done before it. The only difference was increasing hostility from people and politicians who had previously borne them no grudge. Anti-Semitism in Britain starts with the adoption by the Tories of the views of their own extremists. From that date it assumes political significance.

6. Politics and the Alien, 1914 – 65

War and the threat of war breed racialism. And when – as in 1914–18 – the war is demonstrably futile, the politicians must beat the racist drum as hard as they can to keep the enthusiasm alive.

In 1914 there were about 75,000 men and women of German or Austrian birth in Britain, and when war was declared, the Liberal Government embarked on a stringent policy of internment and repatriation. By early 1916, some 21,000 had been repatriated and 32,000 interned in huge, prison-like camps. In May 1915, Asquith, the Prime Minister, decided to intern all aliens of military age, and set up Advisory Committees to investigate the possibility of interning the others. The committees were instructed to assume that the enemy alien should be interned unless he could show overriding reasons why he should not be.

As the futility and huge cost of the war became increasingly obvious, so the chauvinism of the British who did not go to the front intensified. Each person wanted to demonstrate that he was 'doing his bit' for king and country, and the best method of proof was to show hostility towards strikers, socialists and, most of all, the enemy alien.

The isolated case of genuine spying was enlarged out of all proportion by the yellow Press, and the myth spread that the 'hidden hand' of Germany was clutching Britain's throat. German wives of British husbands were scrupulously boycotted by shopkeepers, and many of them almost starved for months at a time. D. H. Lawrence has described how he and his German wife, Frieda, were persecuted in their Cornish home. Dachshunds were found murdered and disembowelled in the streets. By 1917 one and a half million people had signed a petition calling for the internment of all enemy aliens.

The racist fever caught on quickly among politicians of all parties – though particularly among the Tories. William Joynson Hicks, the Member for Brentford, who was later to be Home

Secretary under Baldwin, used particularly venomous language in his insistence on indiscriminate internment. On 17 December 1917 he spoke of the 'terrible danger' of 6,700 enemy aliens not yet interned. 'They are not a nation' he said about Germany 'we want to treat with either before or after the war. . . . Would you grasp their bloody hands?'

The Home Secretary, Sir Herbert Samuel, tried desperately to stem the tide with some semblance of reason and humanity. The following exchange is typical of the parliamentary struggles he fought with the chauvinists:

SAMUEL: Another case is that of a German, sixty-six years of age, who had a British-born wife. He has been here forty-three years and is nearly blind. Does my hon. and gallant friend say that man, in accordance with his general rule, should be interned?

BRIGADIER-GENERAL HENRY PAGE CROFT: There should be no exception. You cannot make exceptions. We are at war, and exceptions cannot be made on ground of sentiment.

SAMUEL: Why can they not?

CROFT: It is folly.

This xenophobic fever continued through 1918 – even after the war was over. At a big meeting three nights before polling day, Mr David Lloyd George presented his miserable programme to a delighted crowd. Interrupted about the 'Germans in this country' he replied:

Oh, they will not be long in this country. They are going to be fired out [*Cheers*]. You cannot go to men who have been spying, plotting and intriguing against the country which has entertained them and say: 'Come back gentlemen; we are glad to see you; make yourselves at home'.

One of the first Bills introduced by the Lloyd George coalition Government after the war was the Aliens Restriction Bill. The Bill's main aim was 'to continue and extend the provisions of the Aliens Restriction Act, 1914' – the Act which was passed in one day without opposition on the understanding that such enormous and arbitrary powers would only last in wartime or in time of national emergency.

Mr Edward Short, the new Home Secretary, was careful to explain that the new Act would only last for two years of peace.

In his view the country was still in a state of emergency. Yet he found that he had to make out a case for the entry of *any* aliens, in the face of speeches which showed only too clearly that the anti-alien, anti-Semitic feelings of 1904 were very far from dead. For example:

SIR ERNEST WYLDE (West Ham): An enormous amount of the work of our courts is caused by the aliens and their crimes. Vice! Why they are at the bottom of at least one half of the vice of the Metropolis and of this country. . . . The white slave traffic, unnatural vice, the brothel-keepers who are too clever to be caught; the people with gambling hells who lead young men to destruction and who bring in doping and unnatural offences – that is the sort of atmosphere that is being introduced into this country by these people.

MR NOEL BILLING (Hertford): Why not have badges? Why not badge these aliens? So that at least people might say, 'This fellow is a German; I will have nothing to do with him.'

All that is clean in the British character has been debased by the type of alien that has invaded us. They have debased our morals in the higher standard and have debased our morals in the lower standard, and I make bold to say that they have debased the Treasury bench.

15 April 1919   Hansard

All this, and much more besides, was said, in spite of the fact that the Lloyd George Government had already repatriated 19,000 Germans, and 5,160 were still interned. There were in addition to these, including women and children, only about 14,000 aliens in the country who had the remotest connexion with Germany or Austria. Crazed abuse on the above pattern was totally unconnected with the influx of aliens; moreover it overlapped, inevitably, with abuse against all foreigners, particularly Jews.

Indeed the anti-alien lobby, now very much bigger than ever before and spurred on by the willingness of Lloyd George and others to meet its demands, started tabling amendments to the original Bill. One such allowed for the deportation of all former aliens. On 27 October Lloyd George received a deputation of the nine leaders of the anti-aliens lobby and agreed with them to let the clause through.

Opposition to the Bill came only from the Labour Party, and in particular from Josiah Wedgwood. Wedgwood – a member of the

Staffordshire china family – had entered Parliament as a Liberal in 1905, but had changed over to the Labour Party in April 1919. He was by then a dedicated Socialist, greatly influenced by Henry George, and hated attacks on foreigners perhaps more than any other of the reactionary utterances from Tory and Liberal front benches. Wedgwood begged the Government 'to consider the alternative of dropping the Bill and allowing the Jew-baiters to yap'. In a debate on the Bill in Committee on 22 October 1919, Wedgwood made a speech which applies as well to 1965 as it did to 1919:

Generally speaking, aliens are always hated by the people of this country. Usually speaking, there has been a mob which has been opposed to them, but that mob has always had leaders in high places. The Flemings were persecuted and hunted, and the Lombards were hunted down by the London mob. Then it was the turn of the French Protestants. I think that the same feeling holds good on this subject today. You always have a mob of entirely uneducated people who will hunt down foreigners, and you always have people who will make use of the passions of the mob in order to get their own ends politically. There is behind this amendment a real party movement and a desire to show on the hustings and platforms what has been done. Members will come forward and tell the people: 'I voted against these foreigners and I voted to keep them out.'

We believe that the interests of the working classes everywhere are the same, and these gentlemen will find it difficult to spread a spirit of racial hatred amongst these people who realize that the brotherhood of man and the international spirit of the workers is not merely a phrase but a reality. We know that the whole of this Bill is devised in order to satisfy the meanest political spirit of the age.

That Wedgwood's view was not an isolated one in the Labour Party is shown by the united vote against the Bill's third reading. Yet four subsequent Labour Governments have administered the Bill almost without changing it.

The general principles of the 1919 Act have been embodied in Orders in Council which have been made for aliens since then (the latest and most relevant being those for 1953 and 1960). They are, that any alien can be refused entry into the United Kingdom at the discretion of an immigration officer; that, in general, he shall not be allowed into this country for more than three months unless he holds a Ministry of Labour permit for work or has visible means of financial support; and that any alien can be deported either by the courts or by the Home Secretary when 'he deems it conducive to the public good'. Against such decisions there is no right of appeal before any normally-constituted court of law. (Since 1956 the alien has been able to be heard at a magistrates' court, but the court's recommendations can be overruled by the Home Secretary.) There is also the general exception that anyone likely to be persecuted on his return to his own country should be granted political asylum. To this exception the most accurate comment (not written into the law) is Balfour's in 1904 – that Britain is always ready to extend political asylum to those with whose politics her governing party agrees.

During the twenties and thirties the numbers of aliens settling in this country diminished sharply. Up to 1926 more aliens left the country than entered it, and the annual average entry of aliens throughout the decade 1921–30 was a mere 732 – compared with 21,000 from 1906 to 1914. The figures then rose in the first half of the thirties – from 1930 to 1935 the annual average net entry was 5,000 – and from 1935 to 1940 rose again to 18,000 a year.

All these figures – particularly for the period 1920–35 – are remarkably small compared with the period before the 1914–18 war or after the 1939–45 war. The explanation can be found in the collapse of traditional capitalism in the inter-war period. During the 1930s particularly, a figure of one and a half million unemployed in Britain or eighteen million unemployed in America was regarded as a sign of economic upsurge. In that situation the migration of labour *internationally* automatically decreased. In conditions of overall hopeless slump, there is no drive, no motive for mass migration.

Indeed Britain had, for the first time in her history, to pay the penalty for her own policy of uncontrolled, indeed encouraged, emigration of the past sixty years. For the slump hit hardest at the primary producing countries, and the farmers of Canada and Australia demanded immigration control. British emigrants were met with a stony reception and indeed many emigrants who had already settled down were forced to return through what amounted to a boycott of their business in favour of native endeavour. Thus of the 3,300,000 who had left Britain mainly for the 'white

Commonwealth' from 1871 to 1931, some 500,000 returned during the thirties.

This was a constant source of disquiet to the Tory M.P.s who still lived in the grand imperial past. On 18 December 1935, for instance, a Captain Macnamara introduced a Private Member's Bill asserting that:

The time has arrived when immediate steps should be taken to survey possibilities for restarting migration within the Empire, and urges His Majesty's Government to set up at an early date an Empire Settlement Board with a view to examining all schemes for organized settlement, and to recommend to Parliament any means which will assist the redistribution of population within the Empire.

The Government could point out with every justification that considerable machinery already existed to encourage workers to go abroad to the Empire. The Bill was violently opposed by Aneurin Bevan who spoke of the idiocy of 'deporting the unemployed to other countries where they are still to be unemployed'. Yet, with Government support, the Bill and the Settlement Boards won acceptance.

Nothing more clearly demonstrates the hypocrisy and chauvinism in the attitude of British politicians to immigration than their approach to emigration within the Empire. Their view was that the immigration process was fine provided that British people were immigrating to another country. When people from other countries tried to come to Britain, however, they were to be stopped.

Most of the labour permits issued to foreign workers during the inter-war years were for domestic servants. During a debate in the House of Lords on 5 May 1927, the Earl of Mayo spoke up bravely for allowing qualified domestic servants into the country. 'I am not very fond of foreigners,' he said, proudly, 'yet I do not want to see specially qualified persons turned out of the country. Not only can you get most excellent cooks from Sweden, but you can also get most excellent governesses.' In a similar vein, nine years later in the House of Commons the Member for Lanark, Lord Dunglass, or Sir Alec Douglas Home as he is more generally known today, grappled with the problem of mass unemployment in his mining constituency. His keen eye had perceived a 'very definite and extensive demand for a certain type of labour covered by the term "domestic service of every kind".' He reckoned that there was room for some '2,000–3,000 families giving this sort of service in Kent, Surrey and Sussex alone'. He therefore proposed the forced migration of miners and steelworkers with their families from Lanarkshire to live in camps built by the Government and secure work as maids, butlers, cooks and gardeners for his noble friends who found such labour in short supply. This suggestion was inspired, no doubt, by Sir Alec's oft-proclaimed personal knowledge of miners and his sharp common sense which sees a shortage of labour in Kent as an immediate answer to unemployment in Lanarkshire. But Sir Alec had not spoken carefully enough to his friends. They did not want miners from Lanarkshire as butlers. They wanted maids from France, cooks from Sweden, governesses from Germany and serving girls from Switzerland. It is a strange comment on Britain's class society that in a decade when unemployment was running at a minimum of 1,500,000 the Ministry of Labour saw fit to issue labour permits to 20,000 women from France and Switzerland – almost all of whom came to serve as hand-maidens in the houses of Europe's richest ruling class.

Although the total flow of aliens in the inter-war period was small, and although it was largely confined to supplying domestic labour for the very class they represented, members of the Tory right-wing never once let slip their consistent and unrepentant anti-alien propaganda. Backbenchers went to ludicrous lengths to raise 'the aliens question'. One asked why so many foreign jockeys were entering the country; another, if the Home Secretary would tighten up on the number of onion-sellers coming over from France to the detriment of British merchants. Violent complaints were made about thirty-one sugar-beet workers from abroad. The wartime scourge of the foreigner, Sir W. Joynson Hicks, was appointed by Baldwin as Home Secretary in 1925, and even he was bound to dismiss the more absurd claims of the anti-alien lobby.

As inter-war anti-Semitism began to take root, so the language of Tory M.P.s became more and more racist. As early as 1923 Mr Charles Crook, Tory M.P. for East Ham, while moving a Private Member's Bill for stricter immigration control, asserted:

These four limbs of the race – Saxon, Norman, Dane and Celt – have given the nation the power that it is today by the mingling of their strength. I am content to maintain our stock as nearly as possible from these four races.

And Mr W. P. C. Greene (Worcester), who was born in Australia, said:

The Americans have noticed, owing to indiscriminate immigration and the great fecundity of these undesirable aliens, that the whole type of race in the United States has tremendously altered in the last 50 to 100 years. The old Nordic type is absolutely changing, and becoming what may be called the Alpine or Mediterranean type – a type far inferior to the fine old original English and Scottish colonist type. It is absolutely essential to preserve the purity of our race and to prevent contamination with the riff-raff of Eastern Europe, the stiffs of the Mediterranean and the dead beats of the world.

11 February 1925

The specifically anti-Semitic streak in the anti-alien lobby did not crystallize until the early thirties when Mr Edward Doran, Tory M.P. for Tottenham, initiated a series of questions about refugee Jews from Germany. In the view of Mr Doran and his friends, German Jews were better off in concentration camps than they were in Britain. Thus on 9 March 1933, he asked:

Will the Home Secretary take steps to prevent any alien Jews entering this country from Germany? Hundreds of thousands of Jews are now leaving Germany and scurrying from there to this country, now that other countries are closed against them; as regards the Aliens Act, you can drive a carriage and pair through it and aliens are coming here on three months' and six months' leave to get naturalization.

Under this kind of pressure the Government could hardly afford to relax the rules for alien refugees. Complaint after complaint issued from the Labour benches that immigration officers were sending Jews back to Germany. Wedgwood alleged that the first question the alien was asked by the immigration officer was 'Are you a Jew?' and that in defence Jews were lying, declaring that they only intended to stay for three months and would not take any work. Sir Samuel Harper, the Home Secretary in March 1938, under constant left-wing pressure, refused any change in the law 'in spite of the huge demand for asylum by Austrian refugees'. The alien rules, he said, had been 'slightly relaxed'.

By this time the anti-alien lobby in the House had been taken over by a Captain A. H. Ramsay, Tory M.P. for Peebles, who believed that all political processions of protest were led, organized and inspired by foreigners – usually Jews. On 28 June 1938 Captain Ramsay asked leave to introduce an Aliens Restriction Blasphemy Act 'to prevent the participation by aliens in propagating blasphemous or atheistic doctrines calculated to interfere with the established religious institutions of Great Britain'. Leave to introduce the Bill was carried by 165 to 134, with Sir Samuel Hoare voting in favour of the Bill. Another enthusiastic supporter of the Bill was Mr Roy Wise, the Member for Smethwick.

The Bill had to be withdrawn that year, because Ramsay had forgotten to table the backers of the Bill, but leave was given to reintroduce the Bill again in November. Nothing more was heard of this extraordinary measure, perhaps because its sponsor, Captain Ramsay, was interned at the outbreak of the Second World War for pro-Fascist activities.

One of the question marks which still hangs over the mass slaughter of Jews in Germany during the 1930s, is why so few of them fled the country. One answer is that they could not. The world-wide depression had shut the door of escape to every available country. Indeed, one of the more nauseating aspects of the British Conservative Government's approach to Hitler's Germany in the late 1930s was the manner in which it continued its harsh immigration policy to the extent of refusing entry to Jews (thus, inevitably, driving them back to the concentration camps). If anyone seriously believed in the right of political asylum in Britain before 1933, the Government's immigration policy after that date must surely have disabused them.

*

While the Conservative Party's attitude towards alien immigration thus slipped into racialism, the Labour Party went through a violent change of attitude. Josiah Wedgwood, aided by Captain Wedgwood Benn, had spoken out clearly against the Aliens Restriction Act of 1919 and spoken too for free right of entry by foreigners into Britain. They got support in February 1923 from a new Member representing a constituency in the East End of London, Mr Clement Attlee, who said: 'In my opinion these Aliens Restriction Acts are thoroughly bad Acts . . . they are inspired by a sort of crude nationalism.'

Yet the Labour Party was shortly confronted with that element which has so often dissipated so many of its principles – power. A flurry of opposition during the few months of Labour–Liberal Government in 1924 frightened the Government into operating the legislation against aliens even more firmly than their predecessors had done. That year, for instance, there were only 934 foreigners naturalized, while in the next year (under Joynson Hicks!) the figure rose to 1,034, and in the year after that, to 1,345.

In the 1924 'Red Letter' election, which flung Labour from office, the aliens issue was played on ruthlessly by many Tories eager for cheap votes. In spite of the fact that alien immigration had gone *down* since the war, the Tories still drove Labour into restating their position on control. This was a party manoeuvre unconnected with the problems of further immigration. In the opinion of Mr A. C. N. Dixey (Cumberland, Penrith):

One of the great reasons why the Labour Party did so badly at the General Election was that people generally in the country, not without foundation, think that the party opposite prefers to consider the interests of aliens to the interests of our own people.

Major Yerburgh (the Tory Member for South Dorset – a county with 672 foreigners living in it) rubbed salt in the Labour wounds by introducing a Private Member's Bill on 11 February 1925, 'That this House approves the possession by the House of full and sufficient authority to control alien immigration'. Cruelly, he underlined the Labour dilemma:

Provided that the Socialist Party takes its stand as a national party and not as an international party, they are given the chance by this motion of throwing off an encumbrance which I am sure from my experience in my own constituency has very sadly impeded their progress.

John Scurr, a member of the I.L.P. from East London, proposed a compromise amendment, recognizing the need for immigration control, but complaining that the present rules were too stringent, and declaring that the present administration could be more sympathetic and humane. Scurr was an internationalist of the old socialist school who personally rejected the basic case for control. The amendment had been forced on the party by the right wing and constituted the first official acceptance by the Labour Party of the case for immigration control.

Yet Scurr, goaded by Tory interruptions, could not restrain his basic principles.

'We are áll internationalists,' he shouted.

HON. MEMBERS: All of you?

G. LANSBURY: Yes, and why not?

SCURR: We are not afraid to say that we are internationalists – all of us (Laughter). The boundaries between nations are artificial.

The Labour leaders writhed on their benches.

They understood what the more naïve Scurr did not: that immigration control is imposed in the interests of the people of one nation – not of all nations. Macdonald, Thomas, Clynes and the rest had already rejected internationalism in their struggle for Parliamentary power.

This they demonstrated when power came their way again – in 1929. Almost the first act of the Labour Home Secretary John Clynes was to refuse political asylum to the most hunted of all political refugees in this century – Leon Trotsky. His reasons for this read strangely:

Persons of mischievous intention would unquestionably seek to exploit his presence for their own ends, and if in consequence he became a source of grave embarrassment, the Government could have no certainty of being able to secure his departure.

The 'right of asylum', if it ever existed, had been buried by a Labour Government. It is ironical that Karl Marx, Frederick Engels and Lenin had all lived in Britain under Tory and Liberal governments. Yet the fourth of that revolutionary quartet was banned by a Labour government.

On 26 November 1929 Clynes was again faced with trouble over aliens from his own back benches. Scurr put forward an amendment to the Aliens Restriction Act along the lines of his amendment four years earlier. Clynes could not accept it:

War conditions have altered things very much and have kept before us economic and industrial questions which come close up to this question of the incoming of aliens into this country.

Clynes continued with restrictionist policies which must have overjoyed Joynson Hicks. On 28 July 1931 he told a Tory frontbencher:

The restrictions relating to aliens and the general conditions under which they have been permitted to enter this country have not been in any way loosened.

In reply to criticism that the £10 naturalization fee put naturalization out of the hands of many working-class people he declared that 'British nationality is a possession which ought to be highly prized by anyone receiving it, and therefore is so good a thing as to be worth paying for'. Finally, triumphantly, he announced that a Labour Home Secretary had naturalized fewer Russians than his Tory predecessor. John Clynes was the first in the line of that curious political phenomenon: the Labour Home Secretary. He laid down two basic principles for his successors, who, for the most part, have followed them scrupulously. First, behave in office in direct contrast to your promises and principles when in opposition; second, strive mightily to be less humane than the Tories.

Thus the attitude towards foreigners of both Labour and Conservative Parties throughout the inter-war years remained thoroughly restrictionist. The Liberal Party, though it clung to its Free Trade doctrines, seldom raised the aliens issue, and indeed Sir Herbert Samuel, Liberal Home Secretary in the National Government of 1931, went out of his way to refuse temporary entry to several distinguished foreigners on the grounds that they were connected with Communist organizations.

The treatment of aliens during the 1939–45 war followed the same pattern as during the 1914–18 war with one crucial difference. The political element in the Second World War – the strong feeling among a large section of the population that the fighting was not for national grandeur but against Fascism – meant that the Liberal Left could rely on considerable support over issues like the aliens question. The Home Secretary was not forced to collapse in the face of the chauvinist Right as he had done during the First World War. Further, many of the so-called 'enemy aliens' were refugees from the régime which Britain was fighting, and could not be regarded as potential spies. Thus Sir John Anderson, Chamberlain's Home Secretary, announced at the outbreak of war that in the treatment of aliens the Government would show 'no unnecessary interference' with the individual liberties of the refugees. Liberals like Lord Birkett were put in charge of the Aliens Advisory Committees, and by the end of 1939 only a few hundred of the 35,000 refugees had been interned. Yet, as Holland, Belgium and France were invaded, so chauvinist pressure began to influence the Home Secretary. On 23 July 1941 Anderson announced that the Government was pursuing a general policy of internment – a statement which evoked the fury of the ageing 'Josh' Wedgwood. Not only were all enemy aliens interned – including thousands of Jews who were eager to fight against the Nazis – but 13,000 *friendly* aliens were restricted in their movements. Further, some 4,400 enemy aliens were shipped across to Canada, and another 2,200 to Australia – almost all of them Jews. On one of the ships taking Jews to Australia – the *Dunera* – the sailors, influenced by current Fascist propaganda, grossly ill-treated the deportees, locking them up for days on end in the hold, robbing them and insulting their women. The plight of these Jews, arriving, robbed, raped, unwanted and suspected, thousands of miles from the countries and cultures they knew – all because they had fled from Nazi terror to Britain – is one of the saddest stories in the whole miserable saga of the British treatment of foreigners.

Yet the wave of chauvinism soon passed, and the new Home Secretary, Herbert Morrison, was forced to listen to complaints against the treatment of German and Austrian Jews and socialists in internment camps. By the middle of 1942 only some 8,000 aliens remained interned.

In August 1945 a Labour Government was elected with an enormous majority on a policy of full employment. Peace-time full employment had been an unknown phenomenon since the industrial revolution, and the leaders of the Labour Party at the outset, like most other people, never really believed that it could be produced. The haunting fear of recession and mass unemployment dictated the Government's policy for the first two years of its life – particularly in its attitude to the serious shortage of labour (which quickly became obvious) and the recruitment of foreign workers. In 1945 and 1946 it agreed to the recruitment of a mere 1,000 Central European widows to help in the hospitals, sanitoria and mental asylums which had become seriously short of labour. Mr Hugh Dalton, the new Chancellor, and Mr Stafford Cripps, President of the Board of Trade, came under fire for their restrictionist immigration policy not only from their own left wing, but also from certain sections of the Conservative Party. The two Tories most prominent in the campaign to recruit more foreign labour were Mr Peter Thorneycroft and Mr Martin Lindsay, two gentlemen who were to become leading opponents of further Commonwealth immigration in similar conditions of labour shortage fifteen years later. On 21 November 1946 Thorneycroft declared:

What about other foreign workers ? The fact is that with a shortage of manpower in this country every kind of administrative and bureaucratic difficulty is put in the way of the volunteer who tries to get into this country to work. I find something a little contemptible about a party which preaches internationalism abroad and yet takes every step to prevent free men from coming here to work.

Cripps replied: 'The fear of unemployment still exists. The admission of large blocks of foreign labour is looked on with considerable caution.'

Thorneycroft and Lindsay were joined in their campaign, for a fleeting moment, by a Mr Cyril Osborne, M.P. for Louth. Osborne asked on 4 April 1947 whether the Minister of Labour 'will now widen the arrangements for ex-Italian prisoners of war who wish to return to this country to work on farms and to marry English girls'. Mr Osborne was to become celebrated in later years through his obsession with immigration, but no one will remember him for his commendable efforts to get more foreigners into Britain shortly after the war.

The pressure on the Government was led from within its own ranks – by a young ex-union official, James Callaghan. Callaghan put down a special adjournment motion on 19 June 1946 calling for a reversal of current immigration policy.

In a few years, [Callaghan predicted, rightly] we will be faced with a shortage of labour – not with a shortage of jobs. We ought now to become a country where immigrants are welcomed. We should break away from this artificial segregation of nation from nation . . . who is going to pay for the old-age pensions and social services unless we have an addition to our population, which only immigration can provide in the years to come ?

Although Callaghan was supported by a small number of Labour M.P.s and one Tory (Lord Hinchingbrooke), the Under-Secretary of the Home Office, Mr George Oliver, found that he 'could not agree'.

Yet the Government was very soon forced to agree. The fuel crisis of 1947 was due largely to shortage of labour in the pits, and despite Attlee's personal radio appeal to the nation, many of the 750,000 women conscripted to work during the war had left employment to look after their families.

The first 'large block of foreign labour' to be recruited was forced on the Government rather than recruited by it. During the war there had collected in Britain some 50,000 Poles, who had fought in France. There were also another 70,000 members of the Polish 2nd Corps, better known as General Anders's Army, languishing in refugee camps in Italy. General Anders had in his early days fought for the Russians, by whom he had been awarded the Order of St George for bravery, yet he strongly resisted the Russians after what he regarded, together with many of his countrymen, as a terrible betrayal – the German–Soviet pact of 1939. With war declared, he led the Polish 2nd Corps through the Middle East and Africa where he was cruelly starved of supplies and rations by the Russians. Yet eventually the Poles came through from the Middle East to Italy with a series of legendary victories at Monte Cassino, Piedmonte, Ancona and Bologna. After the war Anders himself and his officers were subjected to a Stalinist tirade for supporting undercover movements in Poland against the new Stalinist regime.

The Poles in Britain and in Italy presented a serious problem for the Labour Government. There had been some resentment against them, particularly in Scotland, where they were regarded as non-fighting spongers, many of them on the German side. Immediately after the war the Poles in Britain received a letter from the Prime Minister personally urging them to return to their country. By October 1945, a third of the Poles in the country had volunteered to return, but of the 207,000 Poles under British control in Europe, only 37,000 wanted to do so.

By the middle of 1946, therefore, the Government formulated the only possible policy in the circumstances – allowing those who had volunteered to go home to do so, but absorbing those who didn't into British society. It was helped in this decision, not so much by its own humanitarianism, as by the growing shortage of labour. On 12 February 1947 the Home Secretary introduced the Second Reading of the Polish Resettlement Bill, aimed at setting up a Resettlement Corps, in which the Poles would be trained to take jobs in the British labour market. As Ernest Bevin had put it a year earlier:

We cannot launch all these people, not even knowing our language, onto the labour market and leave the whole thing in chaos.

The Resettlement Bill was opposed by the Communist Party and a section of the Labour left wing. The main speakers against the Bill in Parliament were Mr Phil Piratin, Member for Mile End, and Mr William Gallacher, Communist M.P. for West Fife. The Communists had treated the problem of the Poles with accustomed shabbiness and chauvinism. Labour and Liberal candidates particularly in Scotland were besieged by questions from Communist sympathizers about 'sending the Poles home'. On every occasion when the matter was raised in Parliament, Gallacher would produce such interruptions as 'the Poles should get coal in their own country', or 'Why can't the Poles go home?' The Communists, upset that anyone should not volunteer to enjoy the rigours of Stalinism in the Russian satellites of East Europe, attacked the Poles in terms of the most squalid nationalism. Thus far had the great international ideal which had inspired men like Gallacher in their early years been twisted by their obsession with Russia.

Yet the 120,000 Poles who in two short years got jobs in Britain were not enough to fill the labour gap, and by May 1947 the Government was announcing its 'Westward Ho' scheme for the recruitment of displaced workers in Europe. In two years some 90,000 workers had come to Britain under this scheme (and a smaller one dealing with Ukrainian prisoners of war), with the bulk of those recruited Ukrainians (30,000); Poles (14,000); Latvians (12,000) and Yugoslavs (10,000). There was very little opposition, either in the country or in Parliament to these schemes, although Mr Cyril Osborne started his long campaign against foreign immigration (having apparently changed his mind from a few months earlier) by asking the Minister of Labour in June 1948 if he would suspend the schemes 'now that we have thousands of our people unemployed'.

There are three interesting aspects of the European Voluntary Worker schemes which throw some light on the general problem of immigration and race in British politics. The first is that the immigrants were all brought in *outside* the Aliens Restriction Act of 1919, for that law did not allow the Government enough scope to recruit large numbers of workers. It says much about the cynicism of British politicians that, while insisting to some of their own supporters that the Aliens Act must continue, they were prepared, if the economic necessity arose, to move outside the Act.

Secondly, the E.V.W. schemes laid harsh restrictions on the immigrants, mainly in the areas of work and dependants. The immigrants were expected to work in whatever job the Ministry of Labour deemed fit.

In the scheme for Ukrainian prisoners of war, the foreign workers were liable to deportation if their health made them unfit. One boy who had lost his sight through falling off a farm lorry was deported to Germany. Ernest Bevin, with characteristic sensitivity, replied to a questioner in the House of Commons on this case that 'they (the Ukrainian P.O.W.s) had only been brought here to save them from forcible deportation to the Soviet Union and that they had no claim as prisoners of war to remain here'.

Some impression can be gained of the harshness of the labour restrictions on E.V.W.s in Britain by the accusation against the U.K. delegate at the Fourth Session of the United Nations that displaced persons in Britain were 'the victims of an official policy of discrimination'.

For the first six months of the E.V.W. scheme dependants were allowed into the country, although in many instances families were split up, with the wife working in one part of the country and the husband often hundreds of miles away. After January 1948, however, recruitment was confined to single persons only and prospective workers had to sign a statement declaring that they were 'single, unattached and had no dependent relatives'. Later, under the Distressed Relatives Scheme, the worker could bring over his dependants provided that he could guarantee work and accommodation. But this was so difficult a business that only 4,018 dependants had been admitted under the scheme by 1952.

Such examples demonstrate the inhumanity and economic cynicism behind the methods of recruitment. The rigid control exercised over the types of workers coming in and the conditions laid down for them inevitably caused much misery and distress among the Europeans when they arrived. Yet there were other, more congenial aspects of the scheme underlined by Bevin's comment that 'we cannot simply throw them onto the labour market'. Considerable trouble was taken with teaching the workers English (only ten per cent of them had any knowledge of the language on arrival), and those workers hired for the mines had to go through a compulsory ten-week language course for safety reasons, with voluntary courses available for most other E.V.W.s.

Although the housing shortage was a crucial problem, trouble was taken by Government and local authorities to see that the refugees enjoyed minimal hygiene and sanitation. The Central Office of Information published a book in eight languages about life in contemporary Britain which was distributed free to all the E.V.W.s. In 1948 the Central Co-ordinating Committee of Refugee Welfare Organizations was formed, aided by the Government, as was the British Council for Aid to Refugees, formed in 1950. All this activity arose because the Government understood that bringing tens of thousands of foreigners into a country whose culture and language were unfamiliar to them would create serious social problems – problems which it was Government responsibility to solve. In that respect at least the Labour Government's treatment of E.V.W.s differed from its Conservative successors' treatment of Commonwealth citizens in Britain throughout the fifties.

Such policies allowed the E.V.W.s to settle down and integrate themselves in factory and town with the minimum of fuss. There were isolated outbursts of resentment. One newspaper wrote that the new immigrants were the 'skim' of the milk of available European labour. M.P.s occasionally asked questions voicing constituents' worries that E.V.W.s were getting priority treatment with meat rations. But generally speaking there was little trouble. Many of the E.V.W.s soon left the type of work that they were recruited to do – particularly those recruited for agricultural labourers. But most of them stayed where they started – in the mines, in the wool mills of the West Riding and the cotton mills of Lancashire. Only a small percentage became naturalized British citizens. By 1951 there were 429,000 aliens in Britain compared with only 239,000 (80,000 of them refugees) in 1939. It was the official European Voluntary Workers and Poles who accounted for almost all the increase.

Then, from 1951 to 1964 a steady stream of aliens came into Britain – at an average rate of some 16,000 a year. The numbers each year differed sharply, and roughly corresponded to the employment situation in Britain. But in any event the figure of 16,000 a year was small when compared with the influx of permanent workers into countries like Germany, France and Switzerland.

From the end of the E.V.W. schemes, the only serious interest shown by Labour politicians in the aliens was to criticize the Aliens Act of 1919 as being too restrictive. Regularly over the last fourteen years, backbench Labour M.P.s have raised the issue under the Expiring Laws Continuance Bill, which, each year, seeks to continue the Aliens Act. The attack has been led by Mr Reginald Paget and Mr Sydney Silverman, helped occasionally by Mr Leslie Hale. The following people who became Ministers in Mr Harold Wilson's administration of October 1964 have spoken out for more humane aliens legislation: Mr James Callaghan (Chancellor); Sir Elwyn Jones (Attorney General); Sir Dingle Foot (Solicitor General); Sir Eric Fletcher (Minister without Portfolio); Mr Anthony Wedgwood Benn (Postmaster General); Mr Richard Crossman (Minister of Housing); Miss Jennie Lee (Parliamentary Under-Secretary of State for Education and Science). It goes almost without saying that the two gentlemen who tried most anxiously to keep the law intact during the tenure of the post-war Labour Government, Mr Chuter Ede and Mr Kenneth Younger, became sudden converts to the principle of changing the law almost as soon as Labour lost office. The arguments on the Expiring Laws Continuance Bill are almost always the same, so it is only necessary to quote one extract – from the speech of Mr Paget on 17 November 1964:

We, in this House, are for the fiftieth time to deny aliens the most elementary of human rights – the right to live under the rule of law . . . we are renewing emergency wartime provisions given to the Government on 4th August 1914 and renewed again without discussion in 1919 and renewed annually since then. These emergency powers give complete control to the Executive over the liberties of the people who come here. They are now more or less consolidated in the Statutory Rules and Orders, 1953, which provide the most Draconian powers to the Government. Entry to the country is subject to the say-so of immigration officers and from their decision there is not really even an appeal to the Executive. The immigration officer can say 'Back you go'. . . .

Why should we put ourselves in this false position and have to hang our heads at the United Nations and say we cannot ratify the Declaration of Human Rights?

I would urge the Government to get away from the excuse that we have heard year after year, 'Yes, but it is not time now', and now that fifty years of this prevarication have gone by say, 'Let the House of Commons solve this' . . .

Paget received some support on that occasion from Sir Edward Boyle, then Opposition spokesman on Home Affairs, another new devotee of the idea of a change in the Aliens Law. But the Government prevaricated as it had done for fifty years.

Under the law which provokes such continuous criticism some 100 people every year are deported from Britain for reasons which do not have to be given and without any right of an appeal. About four times a year a case takes place which shocks enough people for the matter to be raised in Parliament. The more famous cases in recent years have been those of Dr Soblen, deported to America, who committed suicide on the plane; Chief Enahoro, refused leave to stay in Britain and later imprisoned in Nigeria; and General Delgado, refused leave to land in Britain and later found murdered in Spain (the decision to refuse Delgado leave to land was taken by a Labour Home Secretary). These cases and many others like them have reduced the right of political asylum to sporadic farce.

The treatment of foreigners by British politicians in this century has involved a nasty mixture of chauvinism and cynicism. The chauvinism has come mainly from the Conservative Party which has not hesitated to use the issue against the 'radicals' in order to win votes for itself (as in 1906 and 1925). The cynicism has come from all parties, in continuing the emergency legislation of 1914, and, if for economic reasons labour has been needed in large numbers, in quietly shelving the Act while the labour has been imported. And of this cynicism the Labour Party has been especially guilty, in its violent shifts of policy when in power for fear of being trailed around the hustings as too friendly to the foreigner.

Before 1945, Britain was never faced with an influx of foreigners big enough at any one time to cause her lasting race problems. Although there have been substantial flows of immigrants from different countries throughout the centuries, she has, with the single exception of the Irish, never been faced with a minority as large as the Negroes in the United States of America or the Jews in pre-war Germany. Thus in this sense the bitter fruit of her anti-alien policies has never been tested. Certainly too, something would have snapped, had the post-war shortage of labour for the new, slumpless British capitalism persisted. If Britain had been forced to seek labour from Europe after 1951 then she would have had to drop the Aliens Acts, and allow much freer right of entry, and offer adequate inducements to attract aliens away from the high wages of expanding Germany, France, Switzerland and Belgium.

In the event, she managed to evade all such contingencies. As the labour supply from displaced persons in Europe appeared to be drying up, as the rigid controls of a timid, post-war Labour Government were relaxed, on 8 June 1948 the *Empire Windrush* set sail from Kingston, Jamaica, with 400 people on board seeking work in their so-called Mother Country. A new era in the story of immigration to Britain had begun – and one which was to test her unwitting politicians far more than any previous one.

7. Commonwealth Immigration and the Conservative Party, 1948 – 65

'There is enough experience in the Commonwealth to prove that harmony between the races on a basis of partnership is a practical policy. We believe the mingling of culture leads to a richer and better society.'

Conservative Political Centre Report, *Wind of Change*, 1960, signed (among others) by Mr Patrick Wall, M.P. for Haltemprice.

'We must for the moment reject the multi-racial state not because we are superior to our Commonwealth partners but because we want to maintain the kind of Britain we know and love.'

                                Mr Patrick Wall, M.P. for Haltemprice,
5 March 1965   Conservative Central Council

*

By the time the British Conservative Party started its longest uninterrupted period of political rule, shortage of labour had become the greatest problem facing an expanding British industry. New competitors, recently enemies in war, were rapidly constructing powerful, streamlined economies, and mopping up the pool of available labour, in millions, from Eastern Europe and Southern Italy. Such countries were not burdened, as was Britain, by restrictionist immigrant legislation, and could therefore import labour without undue strain on the authorities. Thus the first King's Speech written by a Conservative Government since the war declared:

My Government views with concern the serious shortage of labour, particularly of skilled labour, which has handicapped production in a number of industries.

The apparently insoluble problem of finding workers to man these industries without repealing the Aliens Act was solved for the Government by an accident, an accident stemming from the 'benevolence' of British imperialism, which had awarded automatic citizenship to the inhabitants of all the dominions in the British Empire. The Romans, when carving their Empire out of

Europe and Africa, adopted a harsher attitude than the British Empire builders towards the people they conquered. The Romans – like the British – soaked their conquered subjects economically for decades, living proudly off the produce of their industries. They gave citizenship only to those who most abjectly accepted the new masters. Citizenship was, in the Roman Empire, a prize for the most subservient and most able of the conquered. The British were more magnanimous. As all imperialists must, they robbed Indians, Africans and all other people lucky enough to be conquered by marauders sailing under the British flag; they robbed them of their indigenous industries and cruelly exploited their agricultural production to supply cheap food and materials for the insatiable 'Mother Country'. But, in the fine spirit of British generosity, they gave citizenship free to all their new subjects. The wogs, ran the theory, could hardly complain so long as they could call themselves British citizens. The concession had the added advantage of costing nothing.

This British citizenship was not granted by fiat or by law. In the words of a junior Conservative Minister:

It [the granting of citizenship] was not due to a deliberate act of policy formally announced and embodied in our law. It is not even a policy which gradually grew up and became established by custom, so far as I have been able to discover. It is simply a fact which we have taken for granted from the earliest days in which our forebears ventured forth across the seas.

	Mr David Renton,
5 December 1958	House of Commons

No one bothered with a formal announcement that all British subjects in the Empire were automatically British citizens because it did not make the slightest difference. No one, apparently, foresaw the one crucial privilege which citizenship entailed – the obvious right of a British citizen was to come freely and live in Britain.

This single, substantial privilege was not significantly exercised in the pre-war years of vicious slump–boom capitalism. Yet from 1948 onwards West Indians, followed by Indians and Pakistanis in greater and greater numbers, began arriving in the 'Mother Country' to man her labour-short industries. The figures for 'net' immigration (those who arrived from the countries minus those who left to go to them) from the West Indies, India and Pakistan for every year since 1953, when the Home Office first started making estimates, are given below.

	West Indies	India	Pakistan	Total 'Coloured' Commonwealth
1953	2,000	—	—	2,000
1954	11,000	—	—	11,000
1955	27,000	6,000	1,800	42,700
1956	30,000	5,500	2,000	46,850
1957	23,000	6,600	5,200	42,400
1958	15,000	6,200	4,700	27,450
1959	16,000	3,000	860	21,550
1960	50,000	6,000	2,500	58,300
1961	66,000	24,000	25,000	125,400

For the new Tory Government, and the labour-hungry employers, this must have seemed a heaven-sent gift. The Commonwealth citizens came in freely – unhindered by the legislation on aliens. They cost the Government nothing. In sharp contrast to the European Volunteer Workers schemes of a few years earlier, the Government could not automatically be held responsible for the accommodation and integration of the new workers. After all, the Government had not recruited them, and furthermore, special grants for accommodation and other forms of assistance could, if demanded, easily be refused on the grounds that such assistance would amount to racial prejudice! The Government could sit back, happily relieved of the desperate shortage of labour, while a handful of harassed local authorities grappled with the problems of absorbing tens of thousands of immigrants into their areas.

Most of the Commonwealth immigrants were coloured. There had been coloured people in Britain before, but never in substantial numbers. Some 15,000 emancipated slaves brought over in the eighteenth century had been absorbed totally into British society. A few thousand coloured beggars, landed in Britain after the war with the American colonies, had been swiftly established in Sierra Leone. At the end of the First World War a certain number of coloured seamen had taken root in Liverpool and Cardiff, and their presence in a time of intense unemployment had provoked serious riots and demands for repatriation. Schemes had been promoted for lending money to facilitate repatriation, and many coloured immigrants had made use of them. The Government, in the racist fever of the time, had even insisted that some Commonwealth citizens should be subjected to the restrictions of the Aliens Acts by passing the Special Restrictions (Coloured Alien Seamen) Order, 1925. The numbers involved, however, had been extremely small. A special survey published in 1940 on coloured people in Liverpool had found only 206 male coloured adults, and seventy-four per cent of these were unemployed, compared with thirty-four per cent unemployed among the indigenous population.

During the Second World War – a time of acute labour shortage – a number of West Indians had come to Britain to work both in war factories and the R.A.F. Many of them had returned after the war, but, finding home conditions intolerable, had decided to return to the 'affluence' of post-war Britain. These were the men who, with their friends, set sail on the *Empire Windrush* in June 1948. The tens of thousands who were shortly to make the same journey came to a country almost without experience of coloured people.

The reaction of the British to this new phenomenon was, at the outset, both suspicious and interested. There were many examples of strikes and other forms of industrial action against the employment or promotion of coloured workers. Such action was particularly prominent among busmen and railwaymen who saw the coming of the coloured man amongst them as the symbol of their own demotion from the aristocracy of British labour. As soon as both groups of workers found, however, that the coloured workers joined the union immediately, eagerly supporting all moves for higher wages and better conditions, they dropped their opposition. In the main, throughout the numerous engineering factories and mills into which the immigrants were absorbed, the degree of hostility and bitterness at work was remarkably small.

Opposition built up *outside the factory*. The immigrants' main problem had been accommodation. They were packed into once-fashionable 'multi-occupied' houses on the inner rim of large towns and cities where conditions were insanitary and foul. As their families joined them, so children speaking no English enrolled in the schools. Living habits and social standards, jealously guarded by the British working class, were – through ignorance – openly flouted. Surveys on the degree of prejudice and resentment against coloured immigrants differed sharply in their findings. In 1956 Mr John Darragh conducted a survey of 1,000 people in Birmingham, many of them living in 'immigrant areas'. To the question, Would you have a coloured person in your house as a lodger? 985 answered No, and fifteen Yes. Sixty-four per cent of those interviewed thought that coloured people were intrinsically less intelligent than white people, and only seventeen per cent thought intrinsic intelligence was the same in black and white. In the same year Dr Michael Banton found that half the people interviewed in a nation-wide survey considered it wrong for a landlady to reject a tenant because he or she was coloured. Such discrepancies can be put down largely to different areas of interview. But from all such surveys a common pattern emerges. There is a small group of people 'severely' prejudiced, and a somewhat larger group who can be described as 'tolerant'. In the centre is a large number of people who are 'mildly' prejudiced, but who are ashamed and embarrassed by outright racialism and discrimination. These are the people who will eventually decide whether or not Britain will have to face racial problems on the scale existing in the United States of America.

Tory councillors and local politicians reacted, in the main, benevolently to the influx. Except in the West Midlands, extremists were frowned upon. Nowhere outside the West Midlands did a Tory local council group tolerate a Councillor Collett of Birmingham or a Councillor Finney of Smethwick. For example, when Councillor Robert Churchill of Nottingham publicly condemned the appointment of a West Indian as a magistrate in 1962, the local Tory chairman hastened to dissociate his party from this 'personal view'.

The same cannot be said of all Conservatives in Parliament. Right from their first year of office, the various Ministers dealing with immigration were persistently nagged on the issue by a group of their own backbenchers. This opposition revolved around the bespectacled, somewhat comic figure of Sir Cyril Osborne (knighted June 1961). As early as 1950 Osborne was demanding figures of immigration from the Labour Government, with 'separate figures for coloured immigration', and in 1952 he started his long, finally successful campaign against his own front bench for legislative control of Commonwealth Immigration.

His main arguments were that Britain should not import the criminals, the sick and the lazy of the underdeveloped countries; that the Welfare State was a 'honey pot' to people of poorer lands; that Britain should not import 'a race problem'. Despite all protests to the contrary, Osborne could never disguise his bias against coloured people. For example:

This is a white man's country, and I want it to remain so.
7 February 1961   *Daily Mail*

It is time someone spoke out for the white man in this country, and I propose so to do.
29 October 1958   House of Commons

I refer to the urgent need for restriction upon immigration into this country, particularly of coloured immigrants.
29 October 1958   House of Commons

If the rate of increase continues the time will come when there will be more coloured than white people in England.
11 October 1961   *Daily Telegraph*

Those who so vehemently denounce the slogan 'Keep Britain White' should answer the question, do they want to turn it black? If unlimited immigration were allowed, we should ultimately become a chocolate-coloured, Afro-Asian mixed society. That I do not want.
4 December 1964   *Spectator*

I do not like to regard the Irish as immigrants. I regard the Irish as British as I am. When I fought in the First World War, I was glad to have a good Irishman by my side.
23 March 1965   House of Commons

In view of this sort of comment, it is difficult to accept Sir Cyril's assertions that colour never enters into his considerations. He would like to have it both ways. He would like to keep the blacks out, regardless of race, colour or creed.

For many years, Osborne was alone in his campaign, shunned by the modernizing Tory 'radicals' on his own side of the House, and snubbed by his own Front Bench. Only Churchill afforded him a fair hearing. Eden and Macmillan treated his queries about unemployment and disease among immigrants with undisguised contempt. He got similar treatment from the two Ministers of the Colonial Office who received the brunt of his complaints – Mr Henry Hopkinson (later Lord Colyton) and Mr Alan Lennox Boyd (later Lord Boyd). On 24 January 1957, for instance, shortly after taking office as Prime Minister, Mr Harold Macmillan answered a supplementary question from Osborne with the crushing rebuke: 'I would deprecate any reflection that may be cast on the standard of health and conduct of these immigrants.'

But Osborne is an indefatigable campaigner, and he set to work to forge a powerful anti-immigrant lobby. He received support after 1955 from Mr Norman Pannell, M.P. for Liverpool Kirkdale until 1964, who was tireless in his search for knowledge about leprosy, crime and prostitution among immigrants. Two other Tory M.P.s from the fashionable suburbs around Birmingham rallied to Osborne's cause. They were Mr Harold Gurden, M.P. for Selly Oak, and Mr Martin Lindsay (knighted in 1962), M.P. for Solihull. Gurden took the view that the housing problem in Birmingham was largely the fault of immigration, while Lindsay used language which is the very stuff of racialism:

We all know perfectly well that the core of the problem is coloured immigration. We must ask ourselves to what extent we want Great Britain to become a multi-racial community. . . . A question which affects the future of our own race and breed is not one we should merely leave to chance.

5 December 1958   House of Commons

In those early years, there was little to comfort Osborne in Parliament, and even in the constituencies, where he could normally expect considerable support, his views were known as being 'out of favour' with the Cabinet. Yet as early as 1955, the Central Council of the Conservative and Unionist Associations (the real policy-making body of the party) approved, albeit by a narrow majority, a motion calling for the application of the laws against aliens to Commonwealth immigrants. The first sign of support in the Government for Osborne's views came in October 1958, when Lord Home (later Sir Alec Douglas Home),

Minister of State for Commonwealth Relations, speaking in Vancouver, said that 'curbs will have to be put on the unrestricted flow of immigrants to Britain from the West Indies'.

Fired by this success, and by the passing of an immigration control motion at the Conservative Party Conference later that month (the Home Secretary, R. A. Butler, spoke against the resolution but did announce the likelihood that the 'Government will seek a power of deportation'), Osborne speeded up his campaign. Speaking on the Queen's Speech in 1958, he raised the immigration issue in strong language, alienating not only his own front bench but many fellow backbenchers as well. On 5 December he moved a Private Member's motion demanding control in line with other Commonwealth countries. He eventually withdrew his motion after a long debate in which both sides of the House agreed that control was unnecessary. The Government spokesman, Miss Pat Hornsby Smith, who outside Parliament called attention to the dangers of unrestricted immigration, refuted all Osborne's charges. The immigrants were, she announced, no more sick, no more criminal, no more lazy than the British. Early in 1959 the Government, in effect, rejected the case for deportation of immigrant criminals. Pannell moved an amendment to the Street Offences Bill calling for the deportation of all foreigners convicted of living off immoral earnings. The Government replied that immigrants came into this country 'without prejudice' – that Commonwealth immigrant criminals must be treated like British criminals. This is the only time, indeed, that the Conservative Party officially aired this reply to a demand for the deportation of criminals. It may to some extent have been influenced by the violent riots in Notting Hill and Nottingham through the summer and autumn of 1958.

During all the years of immigration from 1954 to 1964, Conservative Ministers were faced with a different type of question than the wholly negative demands for control from their own backbenchers. This was the 'integrationist' question, over what Government machinery was being set up, what methods were being employed to ensure that the immigrants settled down in Britain with the minimum strain and exploitation.

To a question on 19 October 1954 on why the entire immigration problem was being left to local authorities, Mr Harold Watkinson gave no answer. Mr Henry Hopkinson, Minister of State for the Colonies, said on 5 November 1954: ' In the long run this problem can only be solved by building more houses, and I can assure Honourable Members that the Ministry of Housing is very much alive to the question.' He announced a committee of inquiry into such matters. On 15 December he declared that the report had not yet been completed. 'The Government', he declared, 'are doing their best to deal with this matter as rapidly as possible.'

Two years later there was still no report. But by now the Government had abrogated all responsibility for such problems.

On 19 April 1956, Major Lloyd George, answering a set of questions on what the Government was doing to help immigrants settle down, said:

We look after them, as we look after every other citizen, to the best of our ability. I have no information that there is any particular problem as far as these people are concerned. . . . There are certain areas which have even more difficulty than others.

This devastating analysis was confirmed some months later by the Colonial Secretary himself: ' I am satisfied', he said, 'that adequate arrangements have been made by the British Caribbean Welfare Service, in cooperation with the London County Council and other voluntary welfare agencies.'

Finally, on 22 November 1957 Mr Reginald Bevins, Parliamentary Secretary to the Ministry of Housing, spoke on immigrant housing conditions:

There is a problem, [he admitted] and we certainly intend to scrutinize it most carefully again in the light of what has been said and in the light of information available to the Minister. When we have done that we will consider the wisdom of initiating discussions with the interested local authorities and perhaps other Ministries to see if we can make a real contribution to what, I admit, is a real human problem.

Mr Bevins may have scrutinized for some years, but his Government never produced a policy on these matters. In that crucial decade of Commonwealth immigration, the Conservative Government had no programme for the immigrants who came. There was no policy about meeting them at the port of arrival; no policy about accommodation; no policy about schooling their children.

Not until 27 November 1963 did Sir Edward Boyle inform the House that his Government was opposed to separate schools for immigrants, and by then, as he himself admitted, one school in Southall was already 'doomed' as an immigrant school. The local authority had not tackled the problem forcefully enough. The Government had not bothered with it at all.

During the decade from 1954 to 1964 the Government both found that there was no problem, and admitted that there was. It set up committees which never reported, and instigated inquiries which reached no published conclusion. No one knew whether the immigrant problem was a matter for the Colonial Office, the Home Office, the Housing Ministry, the Education Ministry, the Ministry of Pensions, the Ministry of Health, or, for that matter, the Arts Council. No one took the responsibility. The matter was left entirely to the 'British Caribbean Welfare Service, in co-operation with the London County Council and other voluntary welfare agencies'.

While these organizations tackled, unaided, problems with which they were not equipped to deal, the Conservative Party prepared to reap political gain from the resentment and squalor which their own neglect had created.

Immigration was not an issue in the 1959 election. Only in Brixton was the Conservative candidate accused of raising the matter in order to get votes – and that accusation was dubious. The Conservative Party in 1959 – the heyday of its post-war political progress – needed no 'shady' issue. The votes of 'affluence' poured in from all over the country, and the Conservatives emerged triumphant. Yet the large number of new Conservative M.P.s who reached Parliament that October tipped the scales in favour of the Osborne campaign on immigration. Many of them were men drawn from the lower-class echelons of the Tory Party – men who listened with sympathy to the Pannell and Osborne views on immigration. For example, three new men were returned for Birmingham constituencies – Leonard Seymour from Yardley, Leslie Cleaver from Sparkbrook, and John Hollingworth from All Saints – and all three were to take a keen interest in the campaign for immigration control which rapidly gained momentum.

Through 1960 the questions about immigration doubled and

redoubled in number and in force. They were all negative, un-helpful, clamouring for control. In July 1960 with Osborne and Pannell keeping up a barrage against the 'appalling flood' of immigrants, Butler still felt confident enough to declare that 'It is very unlikely that this country will turn away from her tra-ditional policy of free entry'. But that was the last time he was to speak so surely about a policy which he himself would abandon fifteen months later. Nowhere in any of his replies to questions on the subject did it occur to Butler or his junior Ministers to point out the real reason for the higher level of immigration – the econo-mic 'boom' which Tory economics and election planning had created, the most expansive boom in post-war industrial history.

In December, and again in January 1961, Harold Gurden or-ganized a series of meetings of backbench M.P.s from immigrant areas – almost all in the Midlands – to talk about different forms of control. The M.P.s suggested to Butler that immigrants should be admitted only if they had a job to come to, a house to live in, funds to support them, a clean bill of health and a record of no criminal offences. At future such meetings, the M.P.s would draft a letter to Butler asking what could be done about control. Further-more, this sort of Parliamentary activity must be seen against the background of the nationwide propaganda (again loudest and strongest in the Midlands) of organizations like the Birmingham Immigration Control Association (see Chapter 9).

In late January the Home Office (by special request of the Home Secretary) produced a report on the different possible methods of controlling immigration, and Butler, according to a story in the *Birmingham Evening Mail* of 9 February, told senior Ministers at a Cabinet meeting that Commonwealth immigration would be con-trolled. There was powerful opposition from Mr Iain Macleod, Mr Duncan Sandys and Sir Edward Boyle, Ministers respectively for the Colonies, Commonwealth Relations and Education.

The Cabinet meeting had been called because, by some un-happy accident, Sir Cyril Osborne had once again been successful in the ballot for Private Members' Bills, and he intended bringing forward yet further demands for Commonwealth immigration control in the following week. Osborne's motion was opposed by the Government in no uncertain terms. Winding up the debate, Mr David Renton, Under-Secretary at the Home Office, told

Osborne that the Government refused 'to contemplate legislation which might restrict the historic right of every British subject, regardless of race or colour, freely to enter and stay in the United Kingdom'.

By April 1961, the Cabinet was still set against control. Sir Edward Boyle could tell the officers of the Birmingham Immigration Control Association that 'it is impossible that the Government will introduce immigration control' (*Birmingham Evening Dispatch*, 6 April 1961). And in May, the Cabinet circularized each M.P. with the definite news that there would be no control legislation for at least a year. The *Sunday Express* surmised that the real reason for the circular was the fear among Cabinet Ministers that there might be a big rush of immigrants to 'beat' legislation which might never be passed.

The fears were well grounded. Throughout the spring, summer and autumn of 1961 the case of the anti-immigrant lobby, itself inspired to further activity by the Cabinet's circular, was considerably assisted by the large flow of immigration from the 'coloured' Commonwealth. The figures for the first nine months of 1961 were more than double those for the peak year of 1960, and Osborne could point to these figures with the assertion that 'the nation is alarmed' at the mounting 'flood'. In fact, the reasons for the increase could largely have been laid at the door of Sir Cyril himself. For the ordinary flow of immigration had been grossly distorted by the constant suggestions of control, coupled with the Government's refusal to declare that it would not bring in control legislation. Furthermore, it has been shown that immigration movements correspond to the employment situation with a slight time lag at either end. Therefore, just as the immigration figures for 1959 had been too low properly to meet the labour requirements of that year's boom, so now in 1961, as the boom petered out, the immigration figures were still geared to the situation some months previously, and were, therefore, too high. It was a combination of these two aspects which drove immigration to such comparatively huge proportions in 1961.

Pannell and Osborne were not, of course, interested in this sort of scientific analysis. They were concerned solely to raise the cry, 'Keep Them Out!' and this they did to some considerable effect, helped by the newspaper correspondence columns, particularly of *The Times* and *Daily Telegraph*. They used their influence, too, in the Conservative Party. Ably assisted by Harold Gurden they lobbied the constituency associations, and by 13 September Osborne could tell the *Daily Mail*:

I can guarantee that it [control] will be one of the first proposals announced in the Queen's speech at the start of the session in November.

Osborne's confidence was reflected in the Tory Party conference agenda for October: forty of the 576 submitted resolutions featured immigration, thirty-nine of them, in varying degrees of militancy, calling for control. (There were only twenty resolutions on education and forty on the Common Market.) The powerful Birmingham Conservative Association submitted a resolution giving the Government a blank cheque to introduce whatever measures of immigration control it thought fit.

Two further factors united to assist the anti-immigrant campaign during that summer. The increased activity of extreme right-wing groups dragged the more disreputable anti-immigrant propaganda into the centre of the political stage. Moreover, the Conservative Party, for the third time in ten years, had instigated a recession to pay for its election-year boom. Mr Selwyn Lloyd's pay pause and seven per cent Bank Rate of July 1961 heralded a period of deflation and depression throughout Britain, for which the Tories had to pay in votes. Political bankruptcy, as in 1904, made the leadership more amenable to the demands of their extremists.

The tendency to emphasize more disreputable issues in the search for popularity and votes was followed by prospective candidates in the constituencies. In March 1961, a by-election was fought at Small Heath, Birmingham. The Labour candidate was Mr Dennis Howell, former M.P. for Birmingham All Saints. The Conservative was Mr Bernard Owens, a founder member of the 'radical' Bow Group, who immediately decided that 'immigration is *the* issue in the campaign' (*Birmingham Mail*, 21 March 1961).

As his campaign wore on and as it became clearer that the voters of Small Heath found little to inspire them in the official Conservative policy, Owens placed more and more emphasis on the issue. Eleven clergymen in the area who asked him to leave immigration alone, met with a flat refusal. In spite of his efforts – and the deep, apparently irrevocable split in the Labour Party – Mr Howell won with an increased share of the poll. Mr Owens could only scrape together some 5,500 votes. But his lead was followed nonetheless. Mr Dudley Smith, Conservative candidate for the marginal Brentford and Chiswick constituency, declared publicly that more and more people in his area were getting worried about immigration, and Mr Toby Jessel, Tory candidate in Peckham, organized a straw poll which found only one in ten of his constituents opposed to immigration control. Later in the year, the Tory candidate at the Moss Side by-election in Manchester declared that immigration would not be an issue 'unless someone stirs it up' – an obvious reference to his Union Movement opponent – but later admitted that immigration control was one of the main points in his programme.

Delegates assembled for the Conservative conference in Brighton on 11 October, depressed both by their own party's failures and by the sudden unity of their opponents. As they filed into the first session of the conference they were handed printed copies of a letter, published that morning in the *Daily Telegraph*, and signed by Sir Cyril Osborne.

It was the lead-letter on the centre page, and was headed in large type:

IMMIGRATION LUNACY
Even Nearer an Afro-Asian Britain

The letter contained the usual arguments about scarce housing, and, for Osborne, the usual arguments about colour. Some 5,000 copies of this letter were printed, and distributed on the steps of the conference hall, by Osborne and his colleagues. In a letter to me about this incident, Osborne states, no doubt correctly, 'I believe this was the final action that clinched the issue and made the Conservative Party leaders most reluctantly bring in the Bill'.

The first debate that afternoon centred around a composite motion, moved by Councillor David Clarke of Hayes and Harlington, which expressed 'concern at the very serious problems being created by the uncontrolled number of immigrants flowing into the United Kingdom', and asked the Government for urgent action.

The motion was supported by Miss Barbara Maddin (Southall), Mr Toby Jessel (Peckham), Mr Frank Taylor (Moss Side) and Mr Pannell. All the speeches were mild and reasoned, save possibly that of Pannell. Three delegates spoke powerfully against the motion – Mr Nigel Fisher (M.P. for Surbiton and co-chairman of the British Caribbean Association), Mr Christopher Barr (Yorkshire Provincial Area) and Mr Michael Buck from London University – the only branch organization to submit a resolution favouring unrestricted entry. Mr Buck spoke of a 'most carefully thought-out campaign promoted by Mr Pannell, Sir Cyril Osborne, Mr David Clarke and others'.

The Home Secretary's speech was very much more conciliatory than it had been in 1958. Indeed, Butler seemed entirely to agree with the mover's arguments. What worried him was that 'if the immigration outruns at some stage the economic capacity to absorb, we might be faced with real concentrated difficulties in certain areas, both from the social angle and from the employment angle'. Yet although it must have been clear to delegates as they voted overwhelmingly in favour of the motion that Butler would introduce legislation sometime soon, no one could have assumed from his speech that he would be moving the Second Reading of a control Bill only four weeks later. The last paragraph of his speech read:

This is obviously a matter in which we have to have the fullest consultations with the Commonwealth and the overseas Governments. This must be carried through. Also, the Conference will know that the final decision must be that of Her Majesty's Government and must be taken at the time of year when decisions are taken about the forward legislative programme. That is the constitutional position and we cannot go behind it.

These were, clearly, not the words of a man in a hurry. And indeed when the time of year for taking decisions about forward legislation did come (in the following week) the Conservative Party must have decided to bring forward the Immigration Bill. For on 31 October, just twenty days after Butler's conference declaration, the Queen's Speech indicated that 'legislation will be introduced to control the immigration to the United Kingdom of British subjects from other parts of the Commonwealth and to give powers for the expulsion of immigrants convicted of criminal offences'.

The Bill, which was published on the following day, empowered the immigration officers to refuse entry to anyone who could not support himself without working or who did not hold a labour voucher from the Ministry of Labour. It allowed in students and visitors almost without restriction. It enabled the courts to recommend deportation of Commonwealth immigrants and insisted on a period of five years (previously the period had been one year) before a Commonwealth citizen living in Britain could be registered as a British citizen. Ministry of Labour vouchers were classified into three groups; those with a specific job promised by a specific employer (A vouchers); those proclaiming a definite skill or craft (B vouchers); and those for unskilled workers without a definite job promised them (C vouchers). Any grant of these last, said the Bill, would vary 'subject to any limit which the Government from time to time consider necessary'.

Although this Bill commended itself to the rank and file in the constituency parties, it caused grave misgivings among the Conservatives in Parliament. There is little doubt, however, that it would have got almost unanimous support were it not for the strange bungling of the Irish question.

Citizens from the Irish Republic were allowed into Britain free of restrictions even after the Free State seceded from the Commonwealth. The reasons for this departure from the normal aliens rules were that the Irish were useful workers who spoke the language, and that no one wanted to antagonize the strong pro-Irish element in Britain. Further, the cost of policing the Irish border was not worth the dubious advantage to Britain of keeping immigrants out; and no one would dare suggest restrictions on the Northern Irish.

When on 1 November Mr Gaitskell asked the Prime Minister, Mr Macmillan, whether the Irish were to be included in the Bill, Macmillan replied: 'Yes, certainly.' But by 17 November – the day set aside for the Bill's Second Reading – the Irish had disappeared from its provisions ostensibly, according to Butler, because the policing of the border was unworkable. The Opposition leaders were quick to drive home this unexpected advantage in the argument. The Irish, they said, were the 'fig-leaf'

– now ripped away – of the Tory colour-bar policy. If Germany or America could police their vast frontiers, why could not the British police the Irish boundary?

So powerful was this argument that, during the Second Reading Debate, a group of Conservative backbenchers told Iain Macleod, the Leader of the House, that they would vote against the Bill on its Third Reading unless the Irish were included in the control provisions. On the following day Sir Douglas Glover, Chairman of the Central Union of Conservative and Unionist Associations, cracked any outward impression of Tory unity by declaring in a Bradford speech that 'We have got to incorporate the Irish into this Bill'. The Government promised to take note of the matter, and eventually came up with a compromise. The Irish would be allowed in free, but Irish criminals would be subject to deportation procedure. In other words, Irish criminals could be deported, but nothing could stop them coming back on the next boat.

Such anomalies played havoc with conscientious Tories, and many spoke against the Bill in its various stages. These included: Humphrey Berkeley, Lord Balniel, John Biggs-Davidson, Sir Thomas Moore, Robin Turton, Nigel Fisher and Lord Colyton (in the Lords).

Even more remarkable than the omission of the Irish, was the method of control laid down by the Bill. Employment was the main criterion of control, even though no one had suggested that unemployment was a reason for control. On the contrary. Some ninety-five per cent of the immigrants got jobs within a few weeks of arrival, and their contribution to the economy was undisputed. The question which presented itself immediately to politicians reading the Bill was: *Why keep people out on an employment basis when there are less than enough here for employment purposes at the moment?* The main argument against the rate of Commonwealth immigration was that the social services could not cope with the influx; but when it came to *controlling* immigration, the only method that the Government found possible was control through employment vouchers.

Moreover the control provisions promised to produce absolute confusion. It was impossible from the type of control envisaged in the Bill to say how many people would arrive from abroad at any particular period. First, dependants and students were subjected to no restriction. Secondly, the mere issuing of labour vouchers to workers did not mean that they would in fact be used. 1,000 labour vouchers might be issued of which as few as 200, or as many as 800, could be presented in the six months before the voucher lapsed. Thus the Immigration Act did not 'control' immigration at all. It set up a substantial bureaucracy which would not solve any problems of the immigrants already in Britain, nor of immigrants coming there, but would make it more difficult for workers desperately needed by the economy to get into the country at all.

Because of this, it was clear from the outset that no one had the slightest idea what sort of effect the Immigration Act would have on the rate of immigration into Britain.

The Bill was opposed fiercely by both opposition parties, and the Government was forced to introduce the guillotine. The Third Reading in the Commons took place on 27 February, and became law on 1 June 1962. Sir Cyril Osborne and Mr Norman Pannell, like Sir Howard Vincent and Major Evans Gordon fifty-seven years previously, had successfully stampeded their party into introducing laws to keep the foreigner out. Like Evans Gordon before him, Osborne was knighted in the year the control legislation was introduced.

During the Christmas recess of 1961–2, and in the middle of intense national discussion about the Act, a smallpox epidemic had broken out. One of the victims had been a Pakistani, and Sir Cyril had lost no time in announcing his diagnosis of the tragedy. He told the *Daily Express* on 16 January 1962:

This week-end's smallpox deaths should lie heavily on the Labour Party's conscience. But for their bitter, fanatical opposition, my proposal that all immigrants must have a clean bill of health would have become law and these poor folk need not have died.

The Bill contained no provision that immigrants should have a clean 'bill of health'.

During the six months after the Act was passed, immigration from the Commonwealth dropped to almost nothing. The striking difference between the figures for net immigration in the first six months of 1962 (before the Act) – 86,700 – and the second six months (after the Act) – 8,290 – showed not so much that the Act was working, but that a large number of prospective immigrants, including a number who never intended to move at all, came to Britain before the Act rather than run the risk of being prohibited by one of its provisions.

Despite this sharp fall in the figures, and despite some evidence that the issue had lost its bite in the country at large, the Conservative extremists, having tasted blood, were thirsty for more. Osborne and Pannell continued their accustomed questions on immigration, exploring loopholes in the Act. As early as 5 March 1963 Mr Norman Pannell submitted a motion to tighten up the Act's deportation provisions. He was worried that not enough people were being sent 'home'. Drug-pedlars and those living on immoral earnings were getting away with heavy jail sentences. Pannell's motion was defeated – but only by forty-one votes. The Government stayed away from the lobbies, as did the senior members of the shadow Cabinet. Eighty-seven Tory back-benchers voted for the amendment, but a small handful, including Sir Godfrey Nicholson and Mr Richard Hornby, voted against it.

Outside Parliament, two by-election candidates followed the lead of Pannell and Osborne – Alderman Hawkins at West Bromwich and Mr John Brimmacombe at Deptford. Both used immigration centrally in their campaign, and Mr Brimmacombe issued an eve-of-poll leaflet on the issue. Both men were soundly beaten. The Labour majority in West Bromwich soared, and in Deptford a Liberal candidate, running for the first time in decades, beat Mr Brimmacombe into third place.

The formation of the Southall Residents Association in September 1963, however, showed that resentment against immigration was boiling over, despite the Act. In October 1963, Sir Edward Boyle addressed a meeting of some 400 Southall parents where he made it clear that Government policy was set against the formation of separate 'immigrant' schools. The rise and fall in resentment and indignation against immigrants no longer bore any relation to the number of immigrants entering the country.

As another General Election approached, so the question whether or not to revive the issue became crucial for Tory strategists. In June, the British Caribbean Association, fearful that what was going on in Smethwick might spread as election fever rose, sent out a circular to all prospective candidates asking for an assurance that immigration would not become a party issue in the elections. The B.C.A., rather stupidly, did not publish a list of assurances received, but did announce that about half the prospective candidates, including a substantial number of Tories, had signed the assurance. Perhaps disturbed by this move, and by his own party's tacit approval of those who had signed, Mr Geoffrey Lloyd, the Member for Sutton Coldfield, an ex-Minister of Education and undisputed leader of the Birmingham Conservatives, called a special meeting in his London house on 23 July to discuss the role of immigration as an issue in the election. The meeting was attended by Dame Edith Pitt (Edgbaston), Mr Leslie Seymour (Sparkbrook), Mr Leonard Cleaver (Yardley), Mr John Hollingworth (All Saints) and Mr Harold Gurden (Selly Oak). It was markedly *not* attended by Sir Edward Boyle (Handsworth) and Mr Aubrey Jones (Hall Green), both of whom held known liberal views on immigration. Indeed shortly before the meeting, Mr Jones had told his constituents that too great a restriction on immigrants would be disastrous for the British economy. Sir Edward has since denied that his failure to attend was due to political disagreement.

The meeting released a written statement, which received wide publicity in the Birmingham Press. After warning the electorate to remember the race riots in Harlem, this read:

The size of the problem avoided by the timely passing of the Immigration Act in 1962 is shown by the fact that at June 26th there were 315,000 outstanding applications for work vouchers by intending immigrants. The friction engendered by overcrowded housing, unequal opportunities and job discrimination must be sought and rooted out wherever they may be found. Better, they must be avoided by forethought.

The good relations which the inhabitants of Britain enjoy, whatever their country of origin, must not blind us to frictions to be avoided when different cultures live side by side, or excuse us if we are not alert to solve them before they harden into ingrained prejudice. Had it not been for the Act, this flood would have been channelled to a few great cities like Birmingham, which, though doing what they can to ease the absorption of welcome and necessary labour reinforcements, cannot but be aware of the inseparable frictions.

The effect of the statement, of course, whatever its careful wording, was to raise the immigration issue centrally for the

Conservatives in Birmingham. Yet despite this lead many Conservative candidates in the Birmingham area refused to accept such an association. Mr H. Banner Adkins (Northfield), Mr A. M. Beaumont Dark (Aston), Mr T. G. John (Ladywood), Mr Prescott (Small Heath) and Mr D. L. Knox (Stechford) all refrained from bringing the issue into the open, despite the temptations of marginal majorities and substantial immigrant settlements in their areas. Mr Beaumont Dark expressed himself in vigorous terms:

> I have an immigrant problem in Aston, but I have gone out of my way to speak to the coloured immigrant population, putting forward the set policy of my party that immigration must be controlled for the good of all concerned . . . I would not want a vote from anyone because I was against coloured immigrants. I would rather lose by 10,000, even 20,000 votes, than be accused of being against immigrants. I do not agree with Alderman Griffiths's approach.
>
> 25 September 1964   *Birmingham Post*

Indeed, in spite of attempts by both Gurden and Lloyd to set the pace on the immigrant issue in the early part of the campaign, and in spite of the finding of a special *Birmingham Evening Mail* poll that 'Immigration is *the* issue in Birmingham this election', even the signatories of the July statement played the issue down during the campaign. Cleaver, Seymour and Hollingworth – former militant advocates of control – made remarkably few public statements on the issue. The Sparkbrook Association refused permission to the Birmingham Immigration Control Association to campaign on its behalf.

The same was true of the large majority of candidates in the Black Country. In Wolverhampton North East, for instance, where Mrs Renée Short was defending a majority not much larger than Patrick Gordon Walker's at Smethwick, and where an anti-immigrant foundation had been laid by the British Immigration Control Association three years previously, the Tory candidate, a mild housewife called Mrs Miranda Greenaway, announced, 'My party does not regard the colour of a man's skin as an election issue', and scrupulously avoided raising the issue in any public statement (*Wolverhampton Express and Star*, 30 September 1964).

Indeed only in Smethwick, Perry Barr and Selly Oak was the

issue raised more than incidentally in the public utterances and election addresses of Conservative candidates.

The July meeting of Birmingham M.P.s was the only organized attempt by a group of election candidates to bring the issue to the fore. Elsewhere, the pattern of restraint was followed faithfully. In London, Nottingham, Bristol, Slough, Bradford and other immigrant areas there is little evidence that the Conservatives made electoral capital out of immigration.

Southall and Birmingham Perry Barr were conspicuous exceptions. In Southall the Tory candidate, Miss Barbara Maddin, trailed behind the British National Party in a drive to capture the anti-immigrant vote. She devised a special policy of her own – a complete ban on all immigrants for two years (excepting 'top-priority' ones). Her election address put immigration top of the list of issues, and she devoted a special leaflet to the subject. In an interview with me during the campaign she explained that 'the Labour council makes it so easy for the immigrants in Southall, so they all stay'. She refused to say whether or not, in her view, Southall rejected the idea of a multi-racial society.

At Perry Barr, Dr Wyndham Davies, inspired by the Birmingham Immigration Control Association, did not hesitate to raise the issue in the crudest terms. On the eve of poll a leaflet, bearing the imprint of his agent, was distributed throughout the constituency. It showed a huge thick arrow pointing to the heart of Perry Barr. Across the leaflet was written: '300,000 immigrants: This *could* happen if you Vote Labour.' (There are only a handful of immigrants in the Perry Barr constituency.) Such propaganda is morally and intellectually grotesque. Its social consequences are, without exception, negative and dangerous.

This account of the attitudes revealed by Conservative candidates during the campaign is based on the public evidence. No one can know in every detail what instructions were handed out to canvassers on this issue; no one can know how this issue was raised on the doorsteps. One Conservative canvasser in the Midlands explained it to me this way:

The candidate may well decide not to raise the issue, and instruct that the matter should not be brought up by canvassers. But often the voters themselves bring it up. In the general hurly-burly of canvassing, it is almost impossible to resist the temptation of saying: 'We stopped floods of these people coming in uncontrolled. Labour opposed us.'

But the fact is that not all that many people do raise it. Very few people ever raise any issue when being canvassed. If the candidate does make a public fuss of it – I've no experience of it myself – it must make an impact on the electorate.

Why, then, did so few candidates raise the matter in the 1964 election? Why, with so very few exceptions, did Tory candidates, many of them not averse to mentioning the issue in the past, fail to follow the lead so patently set by Mr Geoffrey Lloyd?

The first answer is that a great many Tory 'radicals', like, for instance, Mr Beaumont Dark, will not – on principle – be associated with any form of anti-immigrant propaganda. But the second is probably more relevant: political self-preservation. The Tory organizers in London made their views quite plain to candidates everywhere. There were to be no more Smethwicks. The party leadership was already too embarrassed by Smethwick to face up to similar situations elsewhere. The organizers made it plain that they would frown on any candidate who used the issue unnecessarily.

What were the implications of such a warning on a man like John Hollingworth, the Member for All Saints? He had a majority of twenty. Almost inevitably he would be swept away by the Labour tide. He had been a good local M.P., and had made some impression in the House. Above all, he loved being a Member of Parliament. In an interview with the *Birmingham Evening Mail* on 10 December 1964 Hollingworth said, about his defeat: 'Having tasted smoked salmon, you don't enjoy going back to bangers and chips. I'm intent on returning as soon as possible.'

Suppose then that Hollingworth had exploited the immigration issue, as Griffiths had done, and lost his seat. As prevailing opinion stood at that time he would probably never again be considered by Central Office a likely candidate for a safe seat. To fall out of favour with Central Office for the mere possibility of a few extra votes would be political lunacy. Thus eligible young Conservatives, defending marginal seats, or attacking safe seats, were best advised to keep quiet on immigration. What matters in the end is the view of Central Office. Obviously if Central Office gives the slightest indication of approval for anti-immigrant propaganda at election time, the issue may well play a leading part in official campaigns. Certainly, the change in the Conservative mood since October 1964 would indicate that bashfulness on immigration among Conservative candidates will be a great deal less common in future elections.

Thirdly, the immigrant vote must have worried men like Hollingworth. In All Saints there are an estimated 15,000 immigrants – about a fifth of the entire population, and five times more than in Smethwick. A direct anti-immigrant line could lose votes.

Fourthly, there was no indication before the General Election that an anti-immigrant campaign could deliver the votes. The evidence from by-elections – notably Deptford and West Bromwich – was very much to the contrary. Peter Griffiths had embarrassed Central Office and the leader of the party. And there was no concrete proof at the time that his campaign was succeeding. At any rate, Griffiths had been 'at it' for three years and more. There was no time to 'do a Griffiths', and a short spurt of anti-immigrant propaganda was unlikely to influence the electorate.

As well as alienating the party leaders, jeopardizing any chances of future 'safe seats' and losing the immigrant vote, there was no guarantee of electoral advantage to the Conservative candidate in immigrant marginals by making an issue of immigration. Small wonder then that Geoffrey Lloyd's July manifesto flopped in 1964. Manoeuvres of that kind are unlikely to flop again.

Clearly, the party leaders were initially inclined to let the matter rest. The Conservative election manifesto included only the briefest reference to the issue:

A Conservative Government will continue to control immigration from overseas, according to the numbers which our crowded country and its industrial regions can absorb. We shall insure that the working of the Commonwealth Immigrants Act, which we passed in 1962 against bitter Labour opposition, is fair and effective.

Yet as the campaign wore on, and as Labour made more and more of the running, so the election machine gave way to pressure for more immigration talk. The campaign pamphlet entitled *Advance on the Home Front* carried a large section on immigration, castigating the Labour Party's attitude as 'blind, weak, muddled, and hypocritical'.

On 6 October Sir Alec Douglas Home threw his hat into the ring. In a major speech in Bradford, one of Britain's main immigrant centres, he perpetrated the old saw that 300,000 immigrants would have come in had there been no control. He went on:

What had been a trickle of immigrants from the Commonwealth was developing into a flood. We saw that if it was not brought under control it would create very serious social and economic problems – problems of employment, housing and education, for instance. So we brought in legislation. The Socialists – aided by the Liberals – opposed it all along the line. Any immigrant who enters Britain is treated just like every other British citizen. But the immigrants themselves will realize how much it is in their own interests to avoid the social and economic problems which have created so much trouble elsewhere. Most people will agree that it is necessary to keep the conditions and the number of permits under the strictest review, and to strengthen the safeguards against evasion.

Sir Alec repeated his speech almost word for word in the Birmingham Rag Market on 8 October, and extracts on immigration were prominently reproduced in the Birmingham newspapers. Following Home to Birmingham, and to Oldbury and Halesowen, came the most glamorous of all Tory electioneers, Mr Quintin Hogg, who also put it about that 300,000 immigrants would have flooded the country under Labour.

Yet the effort was half-hearted, ill-organized, and spasmodic. It was a fight for which few of the Tory strategists had any stomach. They fought on this front, indeed, only when out-manoeuvred on every other.

Defeat at the polls in October 1964 was, for the Conservative Party, as if God had personally revoked the Divine Right of Kings. The inevitability of the result, in keeping with all the forecasts, did nothing to subtract from the overall gloom and disarray into which the party was plunged. In the grim aftermath of the result, one fact stood out clearly from the figures. Smethwick was a notable and unique exception. Only twenty-six constituency results showed a swing towards the Conservatives, and of these swings fourteen were under one per cent. All others showed swings of 3·5 per cent or less, yet the swing in Smethwick was 7·2 per cent.

However 'fishy' the campaign that Griffiths had conducted, two factors almost immediately commended him to the Tory

Party throughout the land. First, he had won – polling far better than any other Conservative in the country. Secondly, whatever his faults *he had got away with them*. We have already seen how, with the single exception of the 'leper' comment, Griffiths was treated with uneasy respect by his colleagues in Parliament, by the Press and even by the Labour Opposition. Indeed, after those first cautious moments, as people waited to see how far the attack on Griffiths would escalate, Griffiths himself escalated to respectability in the Tory Party. No speaker was more sought after during the first six months of the Labour Government than Peter Griffiths. He spoke at universities, constituencies, Young Conservative rallies. The Conservative Party joyfully distributed Press advances of his speeches. Speaking at a meeting of the London Young Conservatives in December, Griffiths voiced the feelings of thousands of party members by saying that 'there are at least twenty seats we could win at the next election if we take a firm line on immigration'.

A firm line on immigration! What more could the bruised and battered leadership require? Had not Labour, on assuming office, ruthlessly exposed Conservative mismanagement of the economy over the last year? Was not Labour, while making the running on every other political issue of the day, obviously frightened and bashful on immigration? Were not the constituency parties crying out for blood and thunder from their unsuccessful leaders? Were not all the forces neatly stacked to drive the Conservative Party off the main road into the political gutter?

For a time the 'radicals' in the Conservative Central Office managed to hold their own. They were assisted considerably by Mr Aubrey Jones, a former Cabinet Minister, and Mr Norman St John Stevas, the new member for Chelmsford, both of whom made powerful pro-immigrant speeches in the Commons debate on 17 November. Even as late as 28 January 1965 Mr David Howell, the director of the Conservative Political Centre, wrote a document on immigration which emphasized the necessity for 'integrative' measures. Control was relegated well to the bottom of the list. The party's parliamentary spokesman on immigration was Sir Edward Boyle, who held progressive views, and in the November debate on continuing the Act, Boyle made a startlingly constructive contribution.

But by February the pressure within the party, both nationally and in parliament, had risen to fever pitch. On 4 February Sir Alec Douglas Home went to Hampstead to speak for Mr Henry Brooke, the local M.P., and there made four new demands on immigration which received widespread publicity. First, he said, all immigrants who entered illegally should be repatriated. Secondly, there should be Government assistance for those who wanted to go back to their countries. Thirdly, dependants should be included in a limit set on the overall immigrant numbers. Fourthly, there should be a further reduction in the numbers allowed entry. These were demands hitherto unexpressed by Conservative leaders. The provision on dependants meant inevitably that not all wives or children under sixteen would be able to join their husbands or fathers in Britain. 'Further reduction' would involve decreasing to almost none the number of labour vouchers issued – a mere 14,000 in 1964, most of them for highly skilled workers.

Sir Frank Soskice, the next day, announced tighter restrictions on immigration; Home was understandably delighted. He congratulated Sir Frank warmly, and asked him to take a closer look at the overall figures with a view to reducing them. The fact that Soskice's obviously prepared statement came the day after Home's Hampstead speech, seemed, to the Tories, rather too good to be coincidental. Nevertheless Home's speech did cause some disarray within the ranks of the Tory radicals, and on television that night Home announced, disarmingly, that he did not want immigration to become an issue between the parties.

Home's desire to keep the matter out of party politics was shortly put to the test. On 6 February Sir Cyril Osborne sought leave to introduce a Bill under the ten-minute rule which would prohibit all immigrants from the Commonwealth, except for those whose parents or grandparents had been born in the United Kingdom. The immediate reaction of the Conservative leaders was to oppose his motion as they had opposed his much milder motions in 1958 and 1961. But by now extremist flames were rising high in the parliamentary party, assiduously fanned by Osborne and Gurden with questions about repatriation and health checks. Gurden asked that British nationality should be withdrawn from Commonwealth citizens and that fingerprints be included on immigrants' passports. On 11 February immigration was, according to the *Daily Telegraph*, 'raised surprisingly' at a backbench meeting of Tory M.P.s, and Mr Selwyn Lloyd was appointed to look into the matter. On 16 February, in a Shadow Cabinet reshuffle caused by Mr R. A. Butler's retirement to the Lords, Mr Peter Thorneycroft, known for his 'toughness' on immigration, took over from the 'liberal' Sir Edward Boyle as front-bench spokesman on Home Affairs. Mr Angus Maude, one of the more 'intellectual' figures in the Tory Party and normally associated with its liberal wing, summed up his party's feelings in a speech on 21 February: 'It is not unreasonable', he said, 'for a white people in a white country to want to stay a white country.' (Regardless, no doubt, of race, colour or creed.)

Although Sir Alec Douglas Home, in his frequent statements on the matter, constantly referred to the need to treat immigrants 'as equals', as British citizens, by March all the emphasis in the Tory Party was on control. Thus, Sir Cyril Osborne's motion, instead of being rejected out of hand by his own party as in the past, was considered carefully by Thorneycroft and the other leaders, and Sir Cyril was persuaded to water it down. Ensured of support from influential members of the Conservative front bench, Sir Cyril enthusiastically obliged, and his motion – debated on 2 March – called not for an outright ban but for 'periodic and precise limits on immigration', together with further powers to deport criminals. In his speech, Sir Cyril could afford to be moderate and magnanimous. Anyone who stirred up racial hatred, should, he said, be 'punished to the uttermost of the law' (a statement which clashed strangely with Sir Cyril's later opposition to the Government's Racial Discrimination Bill), but he called for more restriction on behalf of the 'majority of the British people not because they hate other races but because they love their own country and want to leave their heritage to their children as they found it'.

The Bill was defeated by a large majority of ninety-nine. But several members of the Shadow Cabinet voted in favour of it – including Sir Alec Douglas Home, Mr Thorneycroft, Sir Martin Redmayne, Mr Enoch Powell (who is opposed to all controls except those on immigration), Mr Michael Noble, Mr Selwyn Lloyd, Mr Edward Heath, Mr Joseph Godber, Mr William

Deedes, Mr Anthony Barber and Mr Julian Amery. Sir Alec Douglas Home's vote was, of course, crucial. The day before the debate a group of Tory and Labour M.P.s had issued a special statement asking that immigration be taken out of party politics, and requiring opposition to Sir Cyril's Bill on the grounds that it was wholly negative. In spite of Sir Alec's own expressed view that immigration should be taken out of party politics, he marched into the lobbies against his own supporters who were trying to do just that.

Seven Tories voted against the Bill, and many more, including Mr Iain Macleod and Sir Edward Boyle did not vote. Yet three days later, at a meeting of the Central Council of Conservative and Unionist Associations, Mr Thorneycroft called in the strongest terms yet used by Conservative spokesmen for further legislation to control immigration. Deliberately raising the bid from Soskice's moves to tighten control, he remarked scornfully that 'the issue of circulars to immigration officers is not likely to suffice'. The motion which Thorneycroft supported was moved by Mr Patrick Wall, the Member for Haltemprice, who said that 'Britain must for the moment reject the multi-racial State'.

When Mr Peter Griffiths a year earlier had said the same thing about Smethwick in a relatively obscure local newspaper, he had brought on himself a vigorous rebuke from politicians of all parties. Even his own leader had admitted that 'we should not say things like that'. Now an experienced and well-known M.P. could say the same thing publicly at a Conservative conference without a squeak of criticism from the Press or from the Labour Party, much less than from his own party. Mr Wall's speech, indeed, was enthusiastically received.

At a meeting of the Conservative Parliamentary Party's Home Affairs Committee on 15 March, a flood of resentment was unleashed against St John Stevas, who had consistently opposed the anti-immigrant extremism. Backbencher after backbencher rose to complain that people like St John Stevas were 'letting Wilson off the hook'. What was required was a militant policy, including assisted passages for the repatriation of immigrants already in Britain.

Now, however, the radicals staged a counter-attack. At another meeting of the Home Affairs Committee, on 21 March, the Tories decided to emphasize integrationist measures, while calling vaguely for 'drastic cuts'. An adjournment debate the next day was a model of parliamentary 'responsibility'. All the speakers except Sir Cyril Osborne, were moderates. Not an angry word was spoken, and both parties cheered and complimented each other. Mr Peter Griffiths and Mr Harold Gurden, who sat together throughout the debate, rose on every occasion, but were not called to speak – a fact about which Griffiths complained bitterly to the *Daily Telegraph* three days later.

It looked as though the radicals had stopped the rot. Yet not much later, on 19 April, 1965, a front page article in the *Daily Express* reported that the Tories had now finally decided to go all out on the subject of immigration, pressing for a complete ban on any new immigrants until the problems of integration were solved by the local authorities. Though we must leave the story arbitrarily, at the start of the 1965 summer, the pattern seems well-established. The current political bankruptcy of the Conservative Party, coupled with pleas from the constituencies for militant opposition, will result in a tough line on immigration, with no holds barred.

*

The British Conservative Party can be conveniently divided into three theoretical groups. No one suggests that every member of the party can be classified accordingly, but such a general division will help the student of Conservative politics to appreciate the party's reactions on the immigration issue.

First, there is the 'Tory Radical'. He is fundamentally opposed to any form of racial discrimination, and is normally in favour of some form of organized activity to 'help the immigrant'. In 1962 the Conservative Political Council – West Midlands Area – produced a pamphlet called *Helping the Immigrant*, which proposed several serious, sensible ideas for Government activity to assist the immigrant – none of which was taken up in a decade of Conservative Government. The chairman of the group which wrote the pamphlet was Mr Reginald Eyre, later to be M.P. for Birmingham, Hall Green. Yet this group is distinguished not so much for its general bias towards philanthropy, nor for its radical drive, but for its understanding of modern economics.

Above all, these people understand that the economic 'miracle' of post-war Germany and Japan* is largely due to the enormous supply of immigrant labour from which the countries have profited. They have realized, in consequence, that any attempt to shut off Britain's only ready supply of labour would have disastrous economic consequences.

The most able and coherent of this group was Mr Aubrey Jones, M.P. for Hall Green, and a former Minister of Supply, who, in April 1965 left Parliament to become Chairman of the Prices and Incomes Board set up by the Labour Government. Even before the Immigration Act, which he did not support, Jones was describing strict immigration control as 'a tragedy'. In a speech to the Commons on 17 November 1964 Jones expounded clearly the views of the 'radical' group. He gave figures to contrast the immigration of workers into Britain with that into Germany, Switzerland, France and Belgium, and went on to say that 'the population of this country is increasing while the working force is practically stationary. It is difficult to see how one can service a community of this kind of composition without some element of immigration.' Jones also spoke about the immigrants already here:

What has worried me of recent weeks is the suggestion that if we reduce the numbers of immigrants, then automatically the immigrant population already here will be assimilated and everything will come right. I believe that this is the wrong way to look at the problem. We should look at it precisely the other way round. In other words, we have to deal with the problem of the immigrant already here.

Jones was joined in the debate by Norman St John Stevas and other prominent Tories in and out of Parliament on his side were Mr Humphrey Berkeley, Mr Richard Hornby, Mr Peter Kirk, Lord Balniel and Mr Nigel Fisher. Mr Arthur Tiley, a Bradford M.P., and Mr Tom Iremonger have in the past supported legislation to make racial discrimination and incitement illegal. All, at different times, have made very similar noises, and between them they constitute a powerful and intelligent pressure group.

The second main group is the Traditional Right. These are the

* Koreans from outside, and, within the country, movement from the rural to the industrial areas.

Conservatives emotionally and intellectually dedicated to the greatness and majesty of the British Empire. They believe firmly in the 'civilizing mission' of Britain in the countries of the Empire. For them, the word 'disloyal' means putting the interests of one's own country before those of Great Britain. These men and women are drawn largely from the aristocracy and many of them have personal experience of governing in the colonies, an experience which has produced an overpowering desire to speak up for the people they have governed.

Such a man, for instance, was Mr Henry Hopkinson, later Lord Colyton, who, as Minister of State for the Colonies, spoke in the first Commons debate on Commonwealth immigration. 'In a world', he said proudly, 'in which restrictions on personal movement and immigration have increased, we still take pride in the fact that a man can say *Civis Britannicus Sum* whatever his colour may be, and we take pride in the fact that he wants and can come to the Mother Country.'

Similarly, a later Colonial Secretary, Mr Alan Lennox Boyd, ruthless in opposition to growing nationalist movements in Central Africa and Cyprus, could say repeatedly and sincerely that the ending of the right of free entry to Britain for Commonwealth citizens would be a tragedy. Even Sir Thomas Moore, perhaps the most extreme reactionary in the Conservative Parliamentary Party of the fifties, abstained on the immigration debate because he regarded it as discriminating against the Commonwealth. Lady Molly Huggins, ex-wife of a former Governor of Jamaica, and ex-chairman of the Conservative Party's West Indian group, voiced the sincere feelings of this group in a speech on 25 April 1959:

The increase in West Indian immigration in recent years has created domestic difficulties in this country. But what is the Commonwealth worth? Is domestic difficulty here an adequate reason for abandoning the whole concept of the Commonwealth? If we are not prepared to pay that price we shall imperil our whole colonial policy and our whole Commonwealth ideal.

To the Traditional Right, most of whom vehemently opposed their party's moves to join the European Common Market, the Empire was, precisely, an 'ideal'. Any measure calculated to end the old relationship between imperial governor and governed was, for them, anathema.

The Conservative Party managed to resist demands for immigration control during some eight years of mass Commonwealth immigration, largely because of a strange alliance between the Radicals and the Traditional Right. The authors of the 1960 Conservative Party document on racial discrimination and the Commonwealth, entitled *Wind of Change*, bear out this point. They include, on the one hand, the young radical Bow Group enthusiast, Mr James Lemkin, and on the other, Lord Colyton and Lady Tweedsmuir.

The Radicals draw their strength from the universities and technical colleges, and command considerable support among the organization men in Central Office, while the Traditional Right have a large representation on the Government Front Bench. Many of the influential Traditional Rightists went to school with the Prime Minister. The understanding by the Radicals of the economic demand for immigrant labour combined with the Traditional Right's sentimental attachment to the colonial peoples to outvote demands for control. Both groups were, however, at the same time, singularly silent about the need for integration initiatives by Government. Aubrey Jones only emerges as the champion of 'integrative' measures *after* the Immigration Act, and with the single, notable exception of a Bow Group pamphlet, it is difficult to find a single contribution from a Conservative 'radical' during the years 1951–61 in which intelligent demands were made for Government action to help assimilate the immigrant into the social structure.

The third relevant grouping in the Conservative Party can be known, for want of a better name, as the Goldwater Right – so-called because it draws its support not from the big industrial combines, nor from the public schools, but from the ranks of small business, the professions and the lower echelons of retired colonial and civil servants. The attitude towards immigration of those belonging to this group is one of shocked horror. Their over-riding characteristic, which acts as a defence barrier against their waning role in a centralized, bureaucratic society, is ultra-chauvinism. The 'invasion' of immigrants appears to them as a disastrous process of 'mongrelization'. Their 'Britishness' to them is crucial. And now, no doubt in their view, due to some monstrous Communist conspiracy, even that is to be taken away. The 'Communist conspiracy' theme is constant. Thus, for instance, Mr Harold Gurden told the Commons on 16 November 1961:

> I quote a newspaper report of a Birmingham case. When arrested the man said: 'I am an agent for Russia.'
> MR MACCOLL: Why quote such rubbish?
> MR GURDEN: Because I was talking about crime.

The Goldwater Right concentrates on three aspects of immigration; the number of immigrants, their health and their criminal record. Norman Pannell, for instance, has shown an extraordinary interest in the health and crime records of immigrants, delving into cases of leprosy and immigrants living off immoral earnings in London. It horrified him that the criminal and sick should be coming to Britain from abroad.

The Goldwater Right has little power in parliament and through most of the fifties its members were treated with some contempt both by the Radicals who despised their ideas and by the Traditional Right who didn't really like 'that type of chap' in the Tory Party anyway. Few of the Goldwater Right went to 'proper' public schools. Yet they received much additional support after the 1959 election and were joined by Mr Peter Griffiths and Dr Wyndham Davies after October 1964.

Their main strength comes from the constituencies, from the shopkeepers, lawyers and accountants who run the local party organizations. Such men attracted to the Traditional Right by snob instincts, find their political interests closer to those of men like Osborne and Pannell. Attacks on the immigrant invasion of foreigners warmed the heart of many a constituency chairman and secretary. And it was in the constituencies, where members of both other sections of the Party were no more than respected outsiders, that the battle for immigration control was won.

One further factor which greatly assisted the Goldwater Right was the political bankruptcy of the Tory Party throughout the 1960s. The pay pause of 1961, bringing with it the highest post-war rate of unemployment, proved beyond all doubt that the Conservatives were fixed rigidly in a 'stop-go' economic cycle.

From the summer of 1961 the Conservative Party floundered – with nothing left to do and no role to perform. For the opening session of Parliament in the autumn of 1961, the Conservative Government introduced only two major Bills – the Immigration Bill and the Army Reserve Bill. Both were irrelevant to the main political issues of the day; both wasted a large amount of Parliamentary time; neither solved nor sought to solve any of the problems which confronted the British people. And this measure of political bankruptcy was to be underlined by the final breakdown of the Common Market talks.

The result was a break in the alliance between the Traditional Right and the Radicals, leaving the way open for the Goldwater Right. Many of the Traditionalists who opposed the Immigration Bill were swept along and later became champions of tighter control. Mr Robin Turton, for instance, who with Mr John Biggs-Davidson opposed the Bill with a 'wrecking amendment' early in 1962, two years later became a keen supporter of more drastic restrictions,

A large number of Conservative Members of Parliament fall into none of these groups. These are the 'realists', the 'empiricists'. Such a man was Mr R. A. Butler. As early as 1954, Butler was making noises about control, but he never ceased to put the other point of view. The state of policy struggles which take place within the Conservative Party can be measured most accurately by the decisions and reactions of the 'realists'. When things are going well for the Tories, as in the fifties, or when a deep reappraisal of classical class theory is required – as in 1947–50 – the realists side with the Radicals. In times of electoral defeat, theoretical and political bankruptcy, they become reactionaries. Upon such criteria are race relations in Britain largely dependent.

*

What, in summary, has the approach of Conservatives been to the problems caused by Commonwealth immigration? They were in power during the first thirteen years of this process. These were crucial years, if any foundations for integration and the peaceful absorption of the immigrants were to be laid. But between the years 1951 to 1961 the Conservative Party did nothing whatever about the problem. There were no Government arrangements for meeting the immigrants and dispersing them to their destinations in Britain. There were no arrangements made for health inspection on arrival or on departure. As the wives and children of immigrants came over in the late fifties, no Government arrangements were made for the teaching of English. No Government encouragement was given to voluntary organizations struggling to solve the numerous social problems caused inevitably by a large influx of men and women of different cultures and histories. Worst of all, no provision was made by the Central Government for accommodation. The exploiters' paradise which immigration created – for airport 'taxi' racketeers, for unscrupulous landlords, for a rat-pack of ravenous employers – was watched over benignly, even encouraged, by the Conservative Government. The 1957 Rent Act – surely the most pernicious post-war social legislation enacted – with its provisions for 'creeping decontrol' laid the immigrants open to still more exploitation, squalor and resentment. There was no Government propaganda, much less legislation, against racial discrimination or incitement, and not until 1962 was any Government organization formed to help cope with immigrant problems. Even then, the Immigrants Advisory Council was inadequately conceived for the task.

All these problems were left to the local authorities. How the local councils, their resources strained far beyond their requirements, were expected, out of rating revenue, to deal properly with this new, awkward problem, no Conservative bothered to explain.

When the ten years of neglect reaped their inevitable resentment, bitterness and racialism, the Conservative Party, in Mr Hugh Gaitskell's words, 'yielded to the crudest clamour – Keep Them Out'. Far from trying to counter the difficulties of housing, education and assimilative work, they simply decided to 'turn off the tap'. In doing so, they gave full credence to the slander of their extremists, who blamed the immigrant himself for the social problems resulting from Government neglect. As could have been predicted from historical experience, 'turning off the tap' did nothing to appease the bitterness and resentment against the immigrant. And the Conservative Party, having once given in to their extremists, could not hold them back. The party itself has moved further and further to the Right against the counsel of its own intelligent economists, and out of all proportion to the actual figures of immigration. It has, in keeping with its most prejudiced supporters, limited its complaints almost entirely to coloured immigration, although white immigration has recently been as large.

The story of the Conservative Party's reaction to Commonwealth immigration is a story of undiluted cynicism, chauvinism and human neglect.

8. Commonwealth Immigration and the Labour Party, 1948 – 65

'We on this side are clear in our attitude towards restricted immigration. I think I speak for my Right Honourable and honourable friends by saying that we are categorically against it.'

Rt Hon. A. G. Bottomley,
5 December 1958 — Labour Front Bench

'There should be no doubt about the Government's view. The Government are firmly convinced that an effective control is indispensable. That we accept and have always accepted . . .'

Rt Hon. Sir Frank Soskice,
17 November 1964 — Labour Front Bench

*

Post-war Commonwealth immigration started under a Labour Government. As the *Empire Windrush* set sail from Jamaica in June 1948 Mr Tom Driberg, M.P., asked a series of questions of the Minister of Labour, Mr George Isaacs, about their arrival. Isaacs replied:

It is very unlikely that a similar event will occur again in the West Indies. . . . Accommodation has not been arranged. . . . They will be met and told how to register. The arrival of these substantial numbers of men under no organizational arrangement is bound to result in considerable difficulty. I hope no encouragement is given to others to follow their example.
8 June 1948

Despite this somewhat churlish approach from a Minister of Labour who desperately needed every man he could get, Isaacs did arrange for the West Indians to be met and assisted to their destinations. Those who had no addresses – about 200 out of 440 altogether – were housed in an underground air-raid shelter at Clapham. And similar makeshift arrangements were made for the few hundred other Commonwealth immigrants who arrived under the Labour Government. Although Labour, presumably, expected to be returned to power in 1950, no long-term plan was devised to deal with the problems arising from any further immigration from the Commonwealth; indeed, no one thought of looking to the Commonwealth for a solution to Britain's labour shortage problems. When in 1951 the Labour Government was finally dispatched into long years of limbo, it had contributed nothing to the problem of Commonwealth immigration.

During the fifties, the bulk of immigration problems fell on the shoulders of Labour local authorities, problems which were well beyond their limited resources. The local councils had no estimate from the central Government of the numbers coming to their area, no guidance from Health or Education Ministries on the possibilities of different health and sanitation standards or on the difficulties of teaching children who could not speak English. Commonwealth immigration sneaked up on the local councils, without warning. Had every local councillor been a humanist of soaring imagination, pledged unequivocally to assist his brothers from abroad, the problems would still have been insurmountable without some assistance or guidance from the centre.

The local treatment of the problems varied enormously. The most common attitude among Labour councils was to 'play safe'; not to be suspected either of attacking the immigrants or of favouring them. There was little possibility in the fifties at any rate of 'council house trouble' since most councils enforced a residential 'qualifying period' of at least five years, before anyone could get a council house. The male immigrants who started the influx kept to themselves, without impinging overmuch on the local authority. Very few of the local authorities provided hostels or other accommodation for the immigrants, and it was not until the late fifties that councils began special schemes for teaching English, for training nurses in foreign languages and health habits, for tightening up on the regulations against overcrowding (which legislation did not allow them to do properly until the Housing Act of 1961). A problem which particularly worried the councils was that of slum clearance. By law, anyone living in a house cleared by the council had to be offered alternative accommodation in council property, and where immigrants were living in slums due for clearance, the council responsible was faced with the problem of offering them a house ahead of many indigenous people on the waiting list. Many councils, including

Smethwick, faced this responsibility bravely by housing immigrants in decent council homes. Others got round the problem by offering alternative accommodation in tumbledown 'stop-gap' sites, picked up by the council in the course of redevelopment, or even in some cases by not clearing the houses in which immigrants lived.

To the general rule – 'muddling through' without fuss and without success – there were among Labour councils some honourable and dishonourable exceptions. Among the former were a number of mayors throughout the 1950s who went out of their way to welcome the immigrants in whatever meagre way they could, even if it was only by attending their functions, opening bazaars and even temples, and holding special receptions. The more constructive local authorities were those whose housing shortage was least marked. In Halifax, for example, where there was no real shortage of housing despite a considerable immigrant community, the local authority was able to get on with ordinary integrative action without fear of losing votes. Bradford and Nottingham corporations both employed coloured immigrants in important posts. At the other extreme there were unhappy examples of Labour councillors who were not ashamed to voice anti-immigrant propaganda. In 1961, for instance, two Labour councillors in Deptford, Mr Carroll and Mr Agambar, organized a petition calling on the Government to control immigration from the Commonwealth and from Ireland. They were not disciplined by the local Labour group, despite its opposition to the policy of control, but they became more militant in their opposition to the group itself, and were not selected to stand when they had outrun their terms of office in 1964. In the General Election both councillors gave considerable assistance to a Mr Atkins, an ex-colonial servant, who burst into Deptford only a few weeks before polling day to stand as an Independent candidate. His election address dealt solely with immigration and ended with the stirring words: 'Repatriate all coloureds already here. This can be done without hardship. Remember this is our country, not theirs. . . .' Mr Atkins was no doubt delighted to get help from such well-known ex-Labour councillors.

Since 1956, Mr Tommy Steele, a Labour councillor in Southall, has taken a strong line against immigration, on the thesis that immigrants were ruining his native Southall. Steele is a popular councillor, and many Southall voters no doubt associated the general Labour line on the issue with Steele's comments – particularly as none of his colleagues intervened to correct that impression.

When in July 1962 a Jamaican girl called Carmen Bryan was threatened with deportation for shoplifting, Mr Eric Fletcher, Labour M.P. for East Islington, fought a long and eventually successful campaign to annul the deportation. On the Wednesday after the deportation was cancelled, a meeting of the East Islington General Management Committee took place. Mr Pat Haynes, a delegate from Mildmay Ward, moved a resolution congratulating Mr Fletcher on his successful fight. The other delegates, promptly and unanimously, moved 'next business', and passed on from such undesirable activity.

Most Labour groups contained one or two members anxious to adopt an anti-immigrant posture, but they were led and instructed by people with some theoretical training in the Labour movement who were quick to expose and oppose any blatant racialism within their ranks. The exceptions were the councils without racist tendencies amongst them and those dominated by anti-immigrant elements. Southall is probably the nearest example of the latter.

The attitude of the Labour local authorities was throughout the period of Commonwealth immigration well to the right of the local Labour constituencies, and even trade-union branches. The 'mind' of the Labour rank and file in the constituencies is always difficult to assess. People rarely take polls of Labour Party members. It is a customary myth that Labour members and trade unionists are just as prejudiced against the immigrants as are their Conservative counterparts, if not more so. One of the more revolting aspects of Conservative anti-immigration propaganda from Joseph Chamberlain to Cyril Osborne has been the claim of such men to speak for the working class.

A fair estimate of the differing views held by the rank and file of the two parties is shown by the 1961 party conference agendas. There were two resolutions from local Labour constituencies demanding immigration control, while there were thirty-nine such resolutions from Conservative constituencies.

Similarly, the hysterical anti-immigrant propaganda common among Conservatives is rare among trade unionists – particularly those who work with immigrants. Of course there are exceptions – as there are in the Labour constituencies. The exceptions are usually those people who have moved furthest away from intellectual or class commitment to the Labour movement. Labour Party General Management Committees and trade-union branches, many of them controlled by people with some intellectual or class commitment to the Labour movement, succeed almost without exception in staving off exaggerated racialist sentiments. Yet the people they represent are more delicately balanced. The story of the engineering workers in Smethwick who drink with their Indian mates after work, and then go home and abuse them in front of the neighbours accurately sums up the situation. The workers are balanced on a knife edge. If the field of propaganda is left clear for the Tories, then they will eventually stop drinking with immigrants after work. If the Labour Party responds more forcefully and logically, appealing all the time to traditional solidarity, then they will stop abusing immigrants at home.

In the parliamentary party, during those early years, the pace was set by Labour's right wing. The first Commons debate ever held on the immigration issue was instigated by a Labour Member, Mr John Hynd, a former Minister and Member for Sheffield (Attercliffe). In the spirit of his distinguished Sheffield predecessor, Sir Howard Vincent, Mr Hynd complained bitterly that '11,000 to 12,000 [immigrants] are pouring in every year'. He went on to talk about the dangerous possibilities of a recession, and mused approvingly about the 'technical question as to whether there should not be some kind of control or regulation over the rate of influx of these people'. Hynd even went as far as to excuse the local dance hall proprietors in Sheffield who had imposed a colour bar. (House of Commons, 5 November 1954.)

Between 1954 and 1958 the only statements on immigration from the Parliamentary Labour Party took the form of questions. There were two distinctive types of these – the 'integrative' and the 'control'. The former sought to establish some machinery for the better integration of the immigrant once he had arrived. The latter implied that the solution was to slow down the rate of influx.

For instance, early in 1954, Mr Kenneth Robinson asked the then Minister of Health, Mr Iain Macleod, what measures he was taking about immigrants who arrived suffering from tuberculosis. The innuendo was that they should be inspected, and, if suffering from the illness, hospitalized. Macleod replied, after some deliberation, that any action on the matter would be too expensive to make it worth while. In April 1956 Mr Frank Allaun asked if the Home Secretary would 'consider helping West Indians by giving advice on arrival concerning jobs, industrial retraining and housing problems rather than leaving it to charitable organizations as at present?'

The most persistent 'integrative' questioner was Mr Marcus Lipton, M.P. for Brixton, the area which had received the bulk of the first batches of immigrants. In 1954 Lipton led a deputation from the Lambeth Borough Council to the Home Office, suggesting various helpful transitory social measures which could be taken to help the immigrant on arrival, such as transit camps where they would be instructed in basic facts about life in Britain. He then followed the deputation with a series of questions throughout the fifties making anxious appeals of a similar nature to the Government. He raised the issue in 1957 and again in 1958 in reply to the Queen's Speech. His theme was persistent, consistent:

It [the immigrant problem] cannot be left to the local authorities who are already overburdened. . . . We cannot leave it to uncoordinated and sporadic private enterprise to solve the problem as best they can.
5 November 1954

Though Brixton at that time had more West Indians than any other constituency in Britain, Lipton never once deviated from his line of helpful, constructive suggestions. He never once suggested during this period that immigration control was the answer.

That was more than could be said for some of his colleagues. The most persistent 'control' questioners at that time were Mr Albert Evans (South West Islington), Mr George Rogers (North Kensington) and the two gentlemen called Hynd – John (Sheffield, Attercliffe) and Harry (Accrington). Harry Hynd, who led the Labour 'control' lobby in the Commons for some years, is – as he never tires of pointing out – a magistrate. Typical of his attitude to the immigration problem was the information which he gave to the Commons that:

Only yesterday in one of Her Majesty's Courts I had to deal with a Jamaican who had been arrested but was found unfit to plead and was therefore sent to an institution where he probably will be kept for the rest of his life at the expense of British taxpayers. Must this go on ?

Likewise did Evans and Rogers ask questions specifically directed against the immigrant community, demanding, either explicitly or implicitly, control of immigration as a remedy.

Outside parliament, the Labour Party was not wholly idle over the issue. On 1 March 1955 the Commonwealth Sub-Committee of the Labour National Executive issued a short report on colour prejudice. The sub-committee had no doubt that 'the [immigration] problem is based on colour'. After describing the reaction to immigration in various parts of the country, it suggested four alternative courses of action:

(1) to call upon all affiliated bodies to oppose racial discrimination;

(2) to seek Commonwealth discussions on immigration;

(3) to request that the T.U.C. establish a special committee to study problems of employment and union membership among immigrants;

(4) to call a conference of local authorities and coloured representatives to discuss the problem.

In September 1955 a joint sub-committee of the London Labour Party executive and the L.C.C. Labour Group reported on immigration in London. The committee included Mr George Rogers, Mr Arthur Skeffington and, strangely for a London committee, Mr Patrick Gordon Walker. It dealt in general terms with housing and welfare problems and ended by opposing 'any unilateral action by the Government to restrict immigration from the Commonwealth'. It called urgently for 'Government action to assist the integration of immigrants into the community'.

Despite these pointers to a coherent policy, the Labour Party did not formulate its views on the matter for three years after the report. A strongly-worded composite resolution against racial discrimination was passed at the Labour Party conference in

1956, but in 1957 a resolution on immigration was not discussed. There has, indeed, never been a discussion specifically on Commonwealth immigration at a Labour Party conference.

By early 1958, the political pace on immigration was still being set by the right wing. On 3 April Mr Harry Hynd followed his namesake by promoting a special motion on immigration in parliament. He made it clear that he was 'concerned only with immigration from the Commonwealth', thus absolving the Irish. 'The immigrants', he declared, 'are undoubtedly adding difficulties to our health authorities. When these people arrive in our country, they immediately become eligible for National Assistance. We know the financial difficulties which the Government have had in that connexion and it is something which cannot be ignored.'

Hynd then went on to make certain 'suggestions' for legislative action. They were:

(1) no restriction on visitors and students;

(2) admission, without limit, to those with jobs and homes guaranteed;

(3) the refusal of admission to those without visible means of support, and

(4) the refusal of admission to those who were obvious invalids, who might 'become a burden on the National Health Service', people with criminal records, absconding husbands 'and the like'.

Many of these provisions, particularly that relating to 'visible means of support', were far stronger than those encompassed by the Conservative Immigration Act three years later. Like that Act, they referred only to Commonwealth citizens – not to the Irish. They were proposed by a leading Labour backbencher, and were effectively demolished by the Conservative Government, in the shape, on that occasion, of Miss Hornsby Smith. Hynd's motion was supported by two other Labour Members – Mr Albert Evans (Islington, S.W.) and Mr Frank Tomney (North Hammersmith). In May two other Labour M.P.s, Mr Charles Hobson (Keighley) and Mr Charles Howell (Birmingham, Perry Barr) combined with a Conservative to put down a much stronger motion calling for immigration control. That motion – perhaps fortunately for the Labour Party – was never debated.

It looked as though the Labour leadership would be guided by such men as Hynd and Tomney. Shortly after the Notting Hill riots of that summer, the Labour M.P. for the area, Mr George Rogers, told the *Daily Sketch*:

The Government must introduce legislation quickly to end the tremendous influx of coloured people from the Commonwealth. . . . Overcrowding has fostered vice, drugs, prostitution and the use of knives. For years the white people have been tolerant. Now their tempers are up.

2 September 1958 *Daily Sketch*

Three days later Mr Maurice Edelman, the Member for Coventry North, wrote a leading feature article in the *Daily Mail*, insisting in strong terms on immigration control.

By now the left wing and the leadership were shaking themselves into action. On 29 September the Labour Party issued an unequivocal statement on racial discrimination, and this dealt categorically with the issue of immigration control in terms which must have shaken Hynd, Rogers and Edelman.

We are firmly convinced that any form of British legislation limiting Commonwealth immigration into this country would be disastrous to our status in the Commonwealth and to the confidence of Commonwealth peoples.

Front-bench spokesmen in parliament nailed the policy to the Labour mast. On 29 October Mr Cyril Osborne was interrupted by Dr Edith Summerskill. Surely, she said, he did not really mean that he would deny people access on grounds of ill health. Certainly he would, replied Osborne, and went on:

What would happen if a shipload of lepers came here from West Africa? Would there be any power to refuse them admission?

DR SUMMERSKILL: I hope not. The Hon. Member appeals to us on humane grounds. Is he seriously suggesting that if a sick person were diagnosed as a leper he should be sent away? Does not he know that in this country we have isolationist hospitals for lepers? Surely he would not ask the House to accept that inhuman proposition?

The Shadow Cabinet did not have the chance to express views from the dispatch box until Osborne instigated a full-scale debate on 5 December. On that occasion Mr Arthur Bottomley replied to the debate from the Opposition Front Bench. No one doubted that his speech summed up Labour's policy on the matter.

We on this side are clear on our attitude towards restricted immigration. . . . We are categorically against it. We are the most industrialized country in the world and we have a direct responsibility for our colonial subjects when they are poor, badly housed or unemployed.

[MR OSBORNE: And criminals?]

MR BOTTOMLEY: If, by an unfortunate error, one of them gets into this country, it is our duty to deal with him, whatever his race, colour or creed, according to the judicial requirements of the land. The central principle on which our status in the Commonwealth is largely dependent is the 'open door' to all Commonwealth citizens. If we believe in the importance of our great Commonwealth, we should do nothing *in the slightest degree** to undermine that principle.   [*Author's italics.]

The position was utterly clear. The Labour Party was opposed not only to general control, but also to controls based on health or criminal record. Moreover, it was opposed to such controls *on principle*.

Such statements and policies can be contrasted with the statement made on Independent Television News on 5 February 1965 by Sir Frank Soskice, the Labour Home Secretary, that *'we have always been in favour of control'*.

Through the 1959 election the Labour Party kept scrupulously quiet over the immigration issue, and, after the election, occupied itself with the arguments over defence and public ownership which brought it near to splitting point. It was not until Osborne's motion in February 1961 that Labour rethought its position, and came to the same conclusions as in 1958. No front-bench spokesman entered that debate, but on 23 May Cyril Osborne wrote to Mr Gaitskell for a statement on the attitude of the Parliamentary Labour Party to the issue of immigration control. He received a reply dated 2 June, and signed by the secretary to the Parliamentary Labour Party. The letter ran:

Mr Gaitskell has asked me to thank you for your letter of the 23rd May. The Labour Party is opposed to the restriction of immigration as every Commonwealth citizen has the right as a British subject to enter this country at will. This has been the right of subjects of the Crown for many centuries and the Labour Party has always maintained it should be unconditional.

Unconditional! No health restrictions, no refusal of men with a criminal record. For that matter, no right to deport criminals. That was the principled line of the Labour Party as late as mid-1961.

The agenda for the Labour Party conference of 1961 carried only two resolutions – from Peckham and Bermondsey – which suggested the control of Commonwealth immigration. Neither was debated. But Labour's policy and principles were still clear. As the Queen's Speech announced new measures to control immigration, it seemed obvious that Labour would oppose them outright. At the two-and-a-half hour meeting of the Parliamentary Labour Party on 15 November called to discuss the Bill, a small band on the right wing made a determined effort to push the party into accepting control. When the votes were counted, only twelve were prepared to stand out for control against the Leader they had so vigorously defended in the recent defence debates. Among them was Mr Christopher Mayhew, perhaps Gaitskell's most dedicated supporter on defence.

According to the *Birmingham Post*, Mayhew was supported by Mr Albert Evans and Mr Marcus Lipton, who by now was a strong supporter of control. From the statements already quoted, the names of the other nine will be evident.

Opposition from this small caucus left its mark on the Labour amendment for, although declining Second Reading to the Bill because it introduced control, and because 'it was widely held to introduce a colour bar into our legislation', the amendment gave qualified support to the imposition of 'health checks' and the 'deportation of criminals'. There is no record of any explanation for this departure from the wholesale opposition to all forms of restriction on Commonwealth citizens which the party had adopted in 1958.

Nevertheless, Labour's opposition to the Bill was powerful enough, both at Second Reading and through the early part of the Committee stage, which was held on the floor of the House. Throughout the period before the Christmas recess, both Gaitskell and Gordon Walker made devastating speeches against the Bill, greatly assisted by the Tory muddle over the Irish question. They were supported in that early period particularly by Mr Elwyn Jones, who described the Bill as 'inhuman and totally illiberal', Mr Sidney Silverman and Mr Michael Foot (both at that time deprived of the Labour Whip), Miss Jennie Lee, Mrs Barbara Castle, Lady Megan Lloyd George and Mr Donald Chapman, the Member for Birmingham, Northfield. Mr Chapman admitted that his stand against control was not popular, particularly in Birmingham, but added proudly that 'on matters of principle I do not give way to expediency'. During this period only three amendments were discussed, all of them in effect 'wrecking amendments' designed to obstruct the Tory Party to the utmost.

This opposition brought the Labour Party its rewards, both in votes and spirit through the length and breadth of the movement. A Gallup Poll published a few weeks after the Second Reading debate showed a sharp slide from seventy-six to sixty-two per cent in the number of people who favoured the Act. Though the majority still favoured controls, it was clear that Labour's opposition was making strong headway in the country at large. Constituency parties throughout the country rallied to oppose the Act. The Young Socialists found a Labour policy which they could support without equivocation.

Even in Transport House itself there was a faint stirring of idealism. The party issued a 'Guide to Action' leaflet entitled *The Integration of Immigrants*. 'The National Executive Committee of the Labour Party believes that Labour Party organizations should now reinforce the party's opposition to the Government's legislation by themselves taking practical action to deal with the problems of integration', ran the preamble. The pamphlet went on to outline several useful guides to action on integration. Nowhere did the pamphlet equivocate. It was a straightforward call to action based on the 'basic principles of the Labour Party'. In almost every area it was well received.

After Christmas, the Labour Party in parliament continued its opposition, infuriated by Osborne's crude remarks about smallpox during the recess. It violently opposed the imposition of the guillotine on 25 January.

Yet already Labour enthusiasm was waning. The constant warnings from Mayhew and his band began to have some effect, particularly on Mr Patrick Gordon Walker who was finding troubles of his own in Smethwick. Gordon Walker dropped out of the fight altogether, voting only for the more reactionary amendments.

The three allotted days of the Committee stage and the Report stage were dominated on the Labour side by Mr Eric Fletcher, the whipless M.P.s and Mr Donald Chapman, who proposed a stream of amendments.

So inevitable was the passing of the Bill that all Mr Fletcher and his friends could do was to make it slightly more tolerable to the immigrant. They set about this task with considerable skill and by the Third Reading the Bill had changed in several crucial details.

First, instead of operating for five years before parliament could examine it again, the Act would now only run until November 1963 – a mere eighteen months. Second, the instructions to immigration officers were published, as were the working arrangements for the voucher system. Third, the Home Secretary had included in the Bill a special reference to students. All along the Labour Party had insisted that there should be no check or bar on part-time students. Mr James MacColl (Widnes) had said: 'I am scared of something which will simply allow a smooth passage for the person who is officially accredited but which will not give the opportunity to what I might call the unofficial student to come here.'

There were also many concessions dealing with wives and children. 'Common law' wives from the West Indies were allowed in as a direct result of Labour pressure. The Home Secretary bent over backwards to meet Labour's demands. He also accepted several detailed amendments on the right to search and the right to keep documents, all of which favoured the immigrants. Mr Fletcher did not exaggerate when he declared that the Bill had been 'substantially improved since Second Reading' and that 'nearly all, if not all of the improvements were either inspired by or strongly supported by Hon. Members on these benches'.

As the Committee stage ended, Mr Denis Healey, Labour's front-bench spokesman on colonial affairs, addressed a mass meeting of all the Commonwealth organizations in Britain. He gave a solemn pledge that a Labour Government would repeal the Immigration Act. The pledge was short-lived. In the Third Reading debate on 27 February 1962 Mr Denis Healey summed up for the Opposition against the Bill. Towards the end of his speech he spoke in terms very different from those of his friend and colleague Hugh Gaitskell, three months earlier. He reaffirmed that the Labour Party could not see the necessity for the Bill at that time. In words which looked forward to future debates and future Labour attitudes, he went on:

If the information collected by a serious survey of the whole problem revealed that immigration control was necessary, we should regard it as essential to consult the other Commonwealth Governments. (Hon. Members: Oh!) We would consult other Governments to see how this could be achieved with the minimum damage to their interests and to their confidence of our loyalty and good will.

Despite constant interruptions, Healey refused to say whether or not Labour would repeal the Act. After only three months the party had abandoned its principled opposition to control. It was now in favour of control 'if the information collected revealed that it was necessary'. As with the revocation of its policy on health and crime checks, there was no analysis, no explanation of why this switch had taken place. In view of Healey's contribution, it was perhaps small wonder that the Government's majority on the Third Reading was higher than at any time during the course of the Bill. With official Labour and the Liberals in apparently unqualified opposition, and with several Conservatives abstaining, the Government majority was 107. Among the Labour names that did not appear in the division lists that evening were those of Mr Frank Tomney, Mr Marcus Lipton, Mr Maurice Edelman, Mr Patrick Gordon Walker and Sir Frank Soskice. That week the weekly paper *Tribune* promised to print the names of Labour abstainers but the Chief Whip, Mr Herbert Bowden, refused to give information on which Labour M.P.s had been 'paired'.

In January 1963, six months after the Act became law, Mr Hugh Gaitskell died. His own passionate opposition to the Immigration Bill had played a leading part in the Labour Party's principled stand. The deep split in the party over defence had rallied many right-wing M.P.s to his side over the Immigration Act, though in their hearts they had felt that he was wrong. Three features in Gaitskell's political make-up had combined to drive him into opposition to the Act. The first had been an understanding of and devotion to modern capitalism. He had recognized the economic demands of that capitalism, and had understood much better than his colleagues the general principles behind international migration of labour. Secondly, he had had a violent loathing of anything that smelt of racial prejudice. Thirdly, leading from the second point rather than the first, he had 'believed in' the British Commonwealth, partly through a desire to see a world-wide multi-racial community work. This combination of principle and economic understanding had led to what had probably been Gaitskell's finest hour throughout his long and tortuous leadership – his Second Reading speech on the Commonwealth Immigrants Bill. Although Gaitskell must have agreed to the party's ambiguous line during the Third Reading debate (he had been away from the House on that occasion), there is little doubt that the Labour Party's subsequent about-turn would have been a more difficult operation had Gaitskell been leading the party.

Unfortunately for it, the Labour Party, through its own vigorous opposition to the Bill, had procured the right and the duty to re-examine the Act every year. Yet when the Expiring Laws Continuance Bill loomed on the parliamentary agenda in 1963, with the inevitable Conservative demand to continue the Commonwealth Immigrants Act for another year, the Labour Party must have wished that it had accepted the period of review as the five years originally proposed by the Conservatives. The last thing that it wanted now was to make up its mind on the immigration issue and reveal its decision in debate.

In July the Shadow Cabinet instigated a straw poll of Labour M.P.s on immigration, and this confirmed the feeling that opinion had shifted sharply. In early September a group of M.P.s led by Mr Gerry Reynolds, Member for Islington North, lobbied Shadow Cabinet members and their colleagues on the back benches to permit a continuance of the Act without any opposition. This view was sharply opposed, however, by the two men who a few months earlier had fought each other for the leadership of the party, Mr Harold Wilson, the new leader, and Mr George Brown. Brown particularly was adamant that the Gaitskell line should be followed. He maintained, quite rightly, that nothing had changed to justify a switch in the Labour attitude. Wilson and Brown were met by firm opposition in the Shadow Cabinet, led by Patrick Gordon Walker and Sir Frank Soskice. Only Mr Michael Stewart, Mr Herbert Bowden and Mrs Barbara Castle could be relied upon to support the leadership. Then a counter-attack was launched by an alliance of ex-Gaitskell supporters and the left-wing. Finally a compromise was drafted which committed Labour to supporting control in principle, but to opposing the Act again, unless the Tories promised immediate Commonwealth discussions to formulate new methods of control. Brown and Mrs Castle opposed any reference to control at all.

At the Parliamentary Party meeting on the Tuesday before the debate, the compromise was carried by eighty-five votes to eight. The eight, including Reynolds, wanted unconditional support of the Act.

On 27 November, Wilson rose to move his compromise. Although his motion opposed the continuance of the Act, his speech differed sharply in emphasis from that of his predecessor almost two years previously.

We do not contest the need for control of immigration into this country, [he said, and went on to emphasize the shift in policy].

I must point out that there are loopholes in the Act and we would favour a strengthening of the legal powers. . . . We believe that health checks should become more effective. . . . We would be prepared to support a change in the law relating to deportation. At present the Act provides this limit of five years' residence in this country. If an indivi-dual found guilty of certain crimes has been in this country for more than five years, he is excluded from the operation of parts of the Act.

Twenty months earlier, on 7 February 1962, Mr Eric Fletcher had moved an amendment to the Immigration Bill aimed at re-ducing the period of residential immunity to deportation from five years to two. He had justified his amendment in these words:

We think that if a person has established himself here as a resident for a couple of years, even though he committed an offence for which he could be punished by imprisonment or fine like any other subject should have the same protection against deportation as a natural-born British subject or anyone else who has made this country his home. We do not want these novel, and, as we think, undesirable provisions for deportation to be any more extensive than is really necessary to meet the case in point.

When Fletcher had said 'we', he had meant the whole Labour Party, for 164 Labour Party members in Parliament had followed their Leader, their Whips and Sir Frank Soskice in voting for Fletcher's amendment to whittle down the 'undesirable provisions' of deportation.

Wilson's arguments in 1963 were the exact opposite of Fletcher's. Far from wanting to whittle down the provisions for deportation, he wanted to extend them. He wanted to close the 'loophole' which his party had fought to widen less than two years before. Wilson went on from such unexplained contradictions to explain his party's new approach to the Act as a whole. His party would not repeal the Act on achieving power, but would instigate discussions with Commonwealth countries to get control from that end, and until such time as that form of control was agreed, his party would keep the Act. He would keep the Act to prevent immigrants from 'jumping the gun' while his emissaries were talking to Commonwealth leaders.

He therefore made a generous offer to the Home Secretary that if the Conservative Government would instigate Commonwealth discussions, the Labour Party would not vote against the Act. Brooke replied scathingly that the offer was ridiculous. India and Pakistan had already tried methods of control at source and failed. The West Indian Governments had categorically refused to control emigration. Such a policy would, for any Jamaican Government in particular, be electorally catastrophic.

The degeneration of the Labour Party on the issue was underlined in the debate by a speech from Mr Frank McLeavy, the Member for Bradford East. McLeavy had remained silent throughout the entire dispute on the immigration issue in 1961 and 1962, but now, sensing the change of mood in his party, he chanced his arm. Speaking strongly in favour of immigration control, he made a clarion call to those, like him, who had worked in the Labour movement for many years. 'We cannot', he said, 'afford to be the welfare state for the whole of the Commonwealth. We have a responsibility to our people from a trade-union point of view. . . .' It was small wonder that Mr J. J. Mendelson, the Member for Penistone, was forced to plead with McLeavy to 'keep the Labour Movement out of this'.

Not only the official line, but the whole bias of the Labour

Party was changed. Its speakers in November 1963 spoke defensively, reluctantly.

Interruptions were guarded, conciliatory. The old campaigners – Silverman, Fletcher, Chapman – did not intervene in this debate. Only Mr John Diamond spoke in the Gaitskell tradition. The way was left open for Mr Frank McLeavy. Only 131 Labour Members followed their leader into the lobbies against the Bill that evening – not including Mr Patrick Gordon Walker, Mr Charles Howell, Mr George Pargiter, Mr Frank McLeavy, Mr Maurice Edelman, and Mr Frank Tomney. Sir Frank Soskice, however, voted loyally against the continuance of an Act which, less than a year later, he was ruthlessly to continue. During the entire debate, in the statements of the Labour Party's executive, in policy leaflets and periodicals, not a single explanation was given for this remarkable transformation. Was it the figures for applications from intending immigrants which changed the Labour Party's mind? Was it the declining importance of the Commonwealth in world affairs? Or was it simply that Labour, cock-a-hoop after a glorious conference, smelt victory and decided that no power on earth, much less political principle, could take it away from them?

Soon after the 1963 decision to oppose the Act, officials at Transport House began to notice the steady trickle of letters on immigration, most of which came from Labour supporters, and advised that Labour would probably lose the election on the immigrant issue; that the party's policy on immigration was inconsistent and unclear; and that it had better think out another one quickly. Most of the letters said that it was easy to sit in London and be idealistic about the matter, but that living with the problem was a more serious business.

After some weeks of these letters, Transport House devised a policy for answering them. A duplicated letter – two sides, foolscap – was sent to every correspondent. The text of the letter was not sent to the Press or made public in any other way. In general, it summed up Wilson's November speech, pointing out that the Labour Party now favoured controls, and that though it preferred voluntary controls after discussion with the Commonwealth, it would keep the Act while the discussions were in progress. Many further letters from correspondents then asked whether *after* the

Commonwealth consultations, Labour control would be more or less strict than Tory control. This question was not answered.

Throughout 1964, as the letters continued to trickle in, and the duplicated answers surreptitiously to trickle out, the attitude of the Transport House chieftains became increasingly clear. *On no account* was any policy on immigration to be made public. Party workers and spokesmen were expected to remain as quiet as possible.

This instruction filtered through to the Parliamentary Party, and when, on 29 July 1964, Norman Pannell moved one of his familiar motions calling for tighter control, no Labour M.P. rose to answer him. He was followed by three supporting Tories, before the motion's time expired. For this, Labour received a sharp rebuke from an unexpected source – the Fabian Society. Their Commonwealth Journal, *Venture*, called on the party leadership to sort out its ambiguities over Commonwealth consultations and present the electorate with a clear, principled line.

Considering the general atmosphere of secrecy, it is little wonder that the issue provoked some argument when it came to writing the Labour manifesto. Most other issues were comparatively easy to deal with, but not immigration.

The final draft read:

We believe that the Commonwealth has a vital part to play in grappling with the terrible inequalities which separate the developed and underdeveloped nations and the white and coloured races. That is why a Labour Government will legislate against racial discrimination and incitement in public places and give special help to local authorities in areas where immigrants have settled. Labour accepts that the number of immigrants entering the United Kingdom must be limited. Until a satisfactory agreement covering this can be negotiated with the Commonwealth, a Labour Government will retain immigration control.

Mr Harold Wilson in his whistle-stop tours found that hecklers were raising the issue everywhere, and he dealt with the matter a great deal more firmly than he had done in parliament the year before. He placed almost all emphasis on Labour's plans for integration and drew cheers from his predominantly sympathetic crowds by stressing the contribution that immigrants made, particularly in hospitals. In the Birmingham Rag Market on 6 October he brilliantly handled chaotic heckling on the issue.

Speaking without a Transport House script he emphasized the need for special help to the 'immigrant areas', and strongly attacked, as he had not done in 1963, the Tory 'alibi'.

There is a very real problem of overcrowding which the Government has neglected. But let's keep this in perspective. We are not having the immigration question used as an alibi for the total Tory failure to handle the problems of housing, slums, schools and education in this country.

In response to consistent pressure from the constituencies, Transport House published extracts from Wilson's Birmingham speech and distributed it, hurriedly and fitfully, through the relevant areas. It was the only guidance that candidates had as to how to deal with the problem. Queries to Transport House by harassed candidates and agents produced advice that they should stick to the 'traditional working-class issues' and underplay immigration. When the issue was raised by the Conservatives or by prospective voters, the less courageous candidates and canvassers followed the pattern set by Patrick Gordon Walker.

Thus Mr George Pargiter, in Southall, harassed by the Tories, the British National Party and the local Residents Association, was quoted in the *Middlesex County Times* of 5 October 1964, as saying:

Labour has not been in power for thirteen years to control the flow of immigrants, and before that Southall had not been in difficulties.

Considering that Pargiter was one of the leading speakers against the Commonwealth Immigrants Bill in November, 1961, and that he had voted against the Bill's Third Reading, such a statement does not bear serious consideration.

Pargiter's campaign in Southall deserves more attention. He relied to a very large extent in his marginal seat on the support of the Indian community which could gather some 2,500 voters. The Indian Workers' Association, which has a very strong pull over its members, loyally supported Pargiter, despite quarrels with him in the past. The leaders even called a Press conference to declare their support for Labour in view of the Tory candidate's utter disregard for their problems. The president, Mr S. S. Gill, and secretary, Mr P. S. Khabra, two of the most cheerful characters in British politics, worked day and night in the Labour cause.

A mass round-up and canvass of Southall Sikhs resulted in one of the highest immigrant polls in the country.

Considering that Pargiter won with a reduced majority of only 1,800, he had every cause to thank the Indian community. Yet when, some days after the poll, he held his celebration party neither Khabra nor Gill nor any other Indian was invited.

Many other candidates showed no reluctance to tackle the issue in the same way. Mr David Kerr, the prospective candidate for the marginal seat of Wandsworth Central, issued a leaflet throughout his area entitled: '*Things About Immigration the Tories Want You To Forget.*'

The first two points stated were:

Large scale immigration has occurred only under this Tory Government.

The Tory Immigration Act has failed to control it – immigrants of all colours and races continue to arrive here.

What possible construction was the elector to draw from those words? Surely that 'large-scale' immigration was both undesirable and the responsibility of the Tories, who had never tried seriously to stop it. So incompetent were they, in fact, that immigrants '*of all colours and races* continue to arrive here'. It is difficult to see what Mr Kerr meant by that last remark, unless he was implying that it would have been much better if those of only one race and one colour had arrived.

Some fourteen per cent of Labour candidates (to only eight per cent of Tory candidates) mentioned immigration in their election addresses – and almost all the Labour candidates who did made it clear how keen their party was to continue controlling immigration. A substantial number made no mention of the need to integrate the immigrants already here. Considering the theoretical void into which the Labour Party had slipped over this issue, it could count itself lucky that the Conservatives showed as much scruple as they did in raising the matter at meetings and on the doorstep. The Labour Party will never be so lucky again, and in future elections it will have to think out a more convincing, more forceful approach than the one it half-adopted in October 1964.

On taking office, Sir Frank Soskice, the new Labour Home Secretary, applied his legal mind to the problem of immigration.

One feature occurred to him immediately, and was rammed home by his chief officials in the Home Office. The Act was not working. It could, as drafted, never have worked. The first main flaw was that no one could tell how many immigrants were going to come into the country simply by the number of labour vouchers issued. No one could say what percentage of the vouchers would be used. Secondly, there were two types of immigrant over whom there was no control – dependants and students. These could come in at will, and this free entry seriously damaged any possibility of foreseeing the rate of influx. Many immigrants were arriving as students and getting jobs soon afterwards, and it was difficult with the machinery of the Act to stop them. Several thousand immigrants, moreover, were coming in by forging passports and vouchers – thus 'evading' the Act. The civil servants were worried about all this, and so was Sir Frank. Yet it is worth pointing out again that all these 'loopholes' were the direct result of the Labour battles against the Bill in 1961 and 1962. Sir Frank himself must surely have remembered those forty-six divisions against the Bill – on issues like students, dependants and vouchers – in which he helped so earnestly to loosen the provisions.

Now what mattered to him was to tighten them up. Reporting the number of 'evasions' to the House in the debate on the Expiring Laws Continuance Bill on 17 November, he agreed:

That there should be more long-term and elaborate legislation. We must watch the problem as it develops and so shape our legislation as to deal with it in its various phases. For the present, we are merely asking for control to continue for a year. I end with this remark so that there should be no doubt about the Government's view. The Government are firmly convinced that an effective control is indispensable. That we accept, and have always accepted, although we couple it with the feeling that the Commonwealth must be brought in. We must have an effective control whatever else we have.

The wheel had turned full circle. From outright opposition to all forms of control the Labour Party had moved to support health checks and the deportation of criminals, and from these on to conditional support for control if the Commonwealth were consulted, and then further to unconditional support for effective control, *whatever else we have*.

Winding up the debate, Mr Ray Gunter, Minister of Labour, underlined the trend by announcing an almost complete ban on C vouchers for unskilled immigrants.

On 5 February 1964, the day after Home's Hampstead speech, Soskice announced, in a special statement, that he would seek powers to repatriate all immigrants entering illegally and would tighten up the regulations in every way he could. He mentioned 'further steps' that might be taken if these did not work. A month later, on 9 March, the Prime Minister himself bewailed the 'fatal erosion' of the Act which he had himself opposed three years earlier. 'Since the Act is not working as was intended,' he said, 'a fresh examination of the whole problem of control is necessary.' He therefore proposed a high-level mission, to be led by Lord Mountbatten, to 'examine what can be done to stamp out evasion at source, and to discuss whether new methods are needed to regulate the flow of immigrants into the United Kingdom'.

This was patently *not* the form of Commonwealth consultation which Wilson had insisted on in 1963, and without which he could not at that time accept the Act. This Commonwealth consultation was instituted '*because the Act is not working as intended*'. If the Act was working as intended, presumably, the Labour Party would not have bothered with the mission. Evasion was the reason for the mission, not the political principle of Commonwealth consultation before exercising immigration control.

While the attitude towards control tightened in Parliament, so the spokesmen for the Government made similar, generally coarser statements outside. Most notable of these was the speech of Mr Richard Crossman, the Minister of Housing, to a West Midlands Labour Party rally at Hanley. Crossman's speech must have been vetted by Transport House. A statement on immigration in the West Midlands by a senior Minister is no off-the-cuff affair. *The Times* reported him as saying:

Two years ago the Conservatives instituted completely ineffective controls and now they blame us because the flood of illegal immigrants is threatening to undermine the efforts which local authorities are making to integrate these new citizens.

In a debate on 23 March, Soskice dropped further hints of stricter legislation to come. After saying that 'we are not in controversy' about the Commonwealth Immigrants Act, he went on: 'To go further would be to do something which we would be most reluctant to contemplate. If it must be done, in due course, we shall have to consider it.'

An interesting episode on 28 March gave some indication of the state of the Labour mind on immigration. Mr George Brown, a consistent, coherent advocate of large-scale immigration, addressed a meeting in Sheffield. 'It is mad', he said bluntly, 'to talk of restricting immigration.' He pointed to the shortage of labour in the nation at large and the absurdity of the anti-immigrant argument. He declared that there was resentment against all immigrants because of the shortage of houses, schools and the like.

His statement provoked uproar. The entire machinery of Transport House was set in motion to 'correct' Brown's statement, and Brown himself was forced to explain that he had not really meant what he had said. Mr Maurice Edelman contributed an article in reply, to the centre pages of the *Daily Express*. '*Full Stop! We Cannot Accept A Two-Nation System*', ran the headline. Labour spoke with one cantankerous voice. In the view of the party, Brown was 'mad' to want more immigrants.

The incident demonstrates, not only the xenophobic bog into which the Labour Party had sunk, but also the alliance between the Gaitskell 'radicals' in the Labour Party and the 'radicals' among the Conservatives. For shortly before his speech, Brown had hired Sir Aubrey Jones, Tory M.P. for Hall Green, to take charge of his Prices and Incomes policy. On the immigration issue, as indeed on many others, the views of Brown and Jones were almost indistinguishable.

Some weeks later the *Daily Mail*, in a leading front-page article entitled '*Axe on Immigrants*' (20 April 1965), reported rumours that the Cabinet was set on introducing tighter immigration controls – even to the extent of ruling out B vouchers altogether and only allowing entry to those with specified jobs assured them. Further checks were expected on dependants and students.

There seems little doubt that Labour will shortly introduce

new restrictions of a most stringent nature, possibly even by bringing forward new legislation such as the Tories would never have dared to contemplate.

Throughout this twisting and turning over the control issue, two aspects of the Labour attitude to immigration and race offer some encouragement. The first is the party's constant insistence on coordinated Government measures for assisting immigrants in this country, and for special Government funds to further that purpose. This theme was underlined by several anxious demands from young Labour M.P.s representing immigrant areas and elected for the first time in 1964 – in particular Mr Roy Hattersley (Birmingham, Sparkbrook) and Mr Ivor Richard (Barons Court). Accordingly, on 9 March, Mr Maurice Foley, a junior Minister and M.P. for West Bromwich, was appointed head of a special Government inquiry into integration measures. Almost immediately, Foley left for Holland to find out how the Dutch have integrated some 300,000 non-whites with the minimum of fuss.

It is in its support for 'integrative' measures that the Labour Government differs most sharply from its Conservative predecessor. It has demonstrated that however abrupt its switch to control, it does intend to coordinate Government action on integration and welcomes new ideas on the subject. Although both parties *talk* in the same clichés on this matter, only the Labour Party is prepared to act. Foley's powers, however, are negligible. Neither he nor any of the Co-ordinating Committees throughout Britain possess the powers which, for example, are possessed by the Human Rights Commissions in many large American cities. In terms of practical political power, Foley's appointment and what few other measures the Labour Government had taken by April 1965 hold out small hopes for any substantial success. This is not to detract from the importance of the effort. What it does demonstrate is that enthusiasm for integrative measures is in many respects closely tied to the attitude of control. There is an inherent contradiction in saying: 'We want to keep these people out: we do not want many more of them here. But when they are here we want them to be like us in every way.' The first position involves hostile, the second friendly, propaganda. It is hardly surprising that as the Labour Party lost its militant opposition to control so enthusiasm waned within the party for strong measures to promote integration.

The second aspect concerns racial discrimination and racial incitement. From 1953 Mr (later Lord) Fenner Brockway strove to get through Parliament a Bill making racial discrimination and racial incitement criminal offences. His Bill, which he put forward seven times, and which was regularly supported by a loyal band of a few Labour M.P.s including Miss Jennie Lee and Mr Maurice Orbach, varied in militancy with the years – but it always failed. After the racial disturbances in Notting Hill and Nottingham in 1958, however, the Labour Party incorporated Brockway's demands in its official policy, and consistently promised to bring in a Bill against racial discrimination and incitement. Then, in April 1965 the promise became a reality and a Racial Discrimination Bill was published. It dealt in the main with incitement and with discrimination in places of 'public resort'. Contrary to the expectations of those who had been eagerly pressing for such legislation, it did not deal with housing or employment – the two areas which affect the immigrants most. Yet in establishing a clear Government line on the matter, the Bill, which was also supported by the Liberal Party, is a positive measure of which the Conservatives never showed themselves capable.

Remarkable as the Labour Party's change of attitude over immigration has been since 1958, it falls very clearly into an established historical pattern. In 1905, in 1919 and in 1961–2, the Labour Party in opposition bitterly opposed immigration controls which it described as a 'fraudulent remedy' for the social evils of the day. Yet possessed of power in 1924, 1929, 1948 and 1964–5, it manipulated these controls much more ruthlessly than had its political opponents. Side by side with this reversal has been a reasonably consistent attitude towards integrating the foreigners and helping them on arrival, as for instance with the European Volunteer Workers in 1948 and the Commonwealth immigrants in 1965.

There has been no official, real explanation from the Labour Party for its sharp change in line over controls. The most extraordinary aspect of the affair, indeed (a sad comment on the present state of theory in the Labour movement), is total official silence on the matter. It has been possible for Labour to turn a complete theoretical somersault without ever finding it necessary to tell its opponents or supporters why. It is as though each time the problem is discussed the record is swept clean; as though past statements, theories, principles never existed.

Why did the Labour mind change? Were there any arguments – used so forcefully in 1958, 1961 and 1962 – which were overtaken by events in 1964 and 1965?

One of the most powerful arguments had been the economic one, and Hugh Gaitskell had put it superbly in the 1961 Second Reading debate:

> The rate of immigrants is closely related, and in my view will always be closely related, to the rate of economic absorption. There has been over the years an almost precise correlation between the movement in the numbers of unfilled vacancies, that is to say employers wanting labour, and the immigration figures. As the number of unfilled vacancies goes down, the immigration figures go down, and as the number of unfilled vacancies rises, the immigration figures go up. It is in my opinion an utter and complete myth that there is the slightest danger or prospect of millions and millions of brown and black people coming into this country. Anyone who is trying to put that across is only trying to frighten people into believing it.

Has that situation changed? Has the 'economic regulator' ceased to work? Is there any evidence that the Labour Party changed its mind on control because it lost faith in this 'economic regulator'?

If we are to believe Conservative Party propaganda there has been a dramatic change in this respect. Sir Alec Douglas Home and Mr Quintin Hogg made great play during the 1964 election campaign out of the applications for unskilled-labour vouchers – totalling some 300,000 by the end of 1964. It was easy for Home and Hogg to point to these figures and say: 'Were it not for control, 300,000 would have come in – far more than the labour market could absorb.' This suggestion, however, has been contradicted by no less a person than Mr Henry Brooke, who said in the House of Commons when Home Secretary, in November 1963:

> There are over a quarter of a million applications for vouchers which have not yet been granted. Neither I nor anyone else would seek to

argue that if control were lifted a quarter of a million people would immediately arrive in this country.

Mr Brooke's statement, which seriously underestimated the capacity of his colleagues for false logic, was based on the wide differential between the number of applications for vouchers granted, and the number actually used. In the first eighteen months of the Act's operation, for instance, 66,000 vouchers were granted, and only 35,000 used. Further, many of those used were A and B vouchers – for skilled workers and immigrants with jobs already assured in this country.

The vast bulk of applications, however, come from unskilled workers, and most of these in turn come from India and Pakistan. In the first year of the Act's operation only twenty-one per cent of the vouchers granted to Indians and Pakistanis were used. Only fifty-five per cent of all Asians issued with work vouchers since 1962 have come to Britain. The percentage of unskilled Indians and Pakistanis who would have come to this country if all the applications had in fact been granted would probably have been even less.

The main reason for this differential is the racket in application forms directly created by the Immigration Acts. Many of the Indian and Pakistani villages which have supplied immigrant labour to Britain over the past fifteen years are manipulated by touts and moneylenders. And after the Act, these men paraded through the villages, flouting application forms as 'passports to paradise' and even selling them at substantial prices, though they were freely available from the proper authorities. It was only after obtaining the forms that the villagers realized a fare to Britain and the disruption of their families were necessary conditions for their arrival in Britain. Many other prospective immigrants filled in forms as a safeguard without seriously intending to move; they wanted to wait and see if a job could be found for them in Britain and in the meantime took the precaution of applying for a voucher.

In short, the whole process was distorted by the ludicrous methods of control promoted by the Tory Government. If control had not existed, at the very most a quarter of those who applied for vouchers would have come to Britain, entailing an extra 40,000-odd immigrants a year. Given the probable synchronization of Irish and alien immigration with such figures, these additional arrivals would have done no more than meet the needs of a labour-hungry British economy.

No one can argue from the figures available that Gaitskell's thesis has been proved wrong. Even less persuasive is the suggestion that the British economy during 1964 and 1965 did not need more workers. For example, on the same day as the *Daily Mail* announced that the Government was considering a still further cut in Commonwealth immigration, the *Daily Telegraph* reported on its front page a serious shortage throughout the economy of both skilled and unskilled workers.

No Labour spokesman has dared to suggest that the economic case against the Act has in any way changed. Many have dealt instead with increased housing and hospital shortages. Yet these have not been created by increased Commonwealth immigration. Since the Act, Commonwealth immigration figures have kept very close to the norm in the late 1950s. The Milner Holland Report on London housing tore to shreds the argument that immigrants are responsible for bad housing conditions.

The Labour thesis that Commonwealth immigration is irrelevant to the housing shortage remains as valid today as it was in 1961, while the argument of 1961 that Conservative emphasis on immigration was a 'decoy' from the real political issues remains true today.

Why then did the Labour mind change? Like the Conservatives, the Labour Party can be divided into three main groups – the 'Radicals', the 'Left' and the 'Right'. The Radicals are almost indistinguishable in their views on immigration from their Tory counterparts. They understand the economic case for increased immigration, and they hate the smell of racialism. Like the Left, they love the Commonwealth, and uphold, at any rate in theory, the brotherhood of man. The Left cherish old-world sentiments about the Commonwealth which bind them close to the Conservative Traditional Right. Thus one of the main pro-Commonwealth amendments to the Bill in 1962 was moved by Mr Robin Turton and Mr John Biggs-Davidson, from the traditional Tory Right, and Mr Sidney Silverman and Mr Michael Foot from the traditional Labour Left. Affection for the Commonwealth and hatred of racialism bound the Radicals and the Left together in dedicated, powerful opposition to the Immigration

Bill. The Labour Right, on the other hand, like Osborne and Pannell in the Conservative Party, saw large-scale immigration as a peril to the privileges of the British working class. Mr Frank Tomney, the Labour Right's most virulent spokesman, was not ashamed to employ openly racialist terminology:

The coloured races will exceed the white races in a few years' time by no less than five to one. This will be a formidable problem for the diminishing numbers of the white races throughout the world. Whether we like it or not, there is now a political, psychological pull towards the Eastern part of the world on the political outlook, aspirations and developments of nationalities. . . .

There is the constant dread of the people that the immigrants are seemingly better served than the indigenous population. These are facts which we can ignore only at our peril.

5 December 1958   House of Commons

Just as the Conservatives have their waverers, Labour has its 'rotten centre'. Fabians and 'left-wingers', whether their principles come from Tawney or from Marx, have always occupied common ground on the race issue. The 'rotten centre', however, the non-thinking, 'practical politicians' have always been ready to veer to the xenophobic Right. With Gaitskell dead, with the alliance between the Radicals and the Left beginning to crack, this 'rotten centre' led by Soskice, Crossman and Edelman 'yielded to the crudest clamour: Keep Them Out!'

There are four main reasons why, with so many of their arguments still intact, the Radicals and the Left permitted this collapse. The first was the inevitable decline of the 'Commonwealth ideal'. Gaitskell himself, the most principled of the Radicals, had spoken with some fervour on the subject:

We are responsible for them, and they think of themselves, as anybody who has been there knows, as British people. Oh yes they do. It is rather moving. I found when I was there that they look on us as the Mother Country in a very real sense . . . I simply say that we are the Mother Country and we ought not to forget it.

16 November 1961   House of Commons

Mr Arthur (later Lord) Royle had said: 'The second reason why they come is that they are loyal members of the Commonwealth and turn as of right to the Mother Country to obtain the things which the Mother Country alone can give them.'

And Mrs Barbara Castle had exclaimed, in a peroration of deep emotion:

I do not care whether or not fighting this Commonwealth Immigration Bill will lose me my seat, for I am sure that the Bill will lose this country the Commonwealth.

This obsession with the Commonwealth is a fetish of the modern British Labour Party. It stems from an inverted chauvinism. Labour members, many of whom were associated with the fight for political independence by colonial peoples, adopted an attitude towards them, once independence was won, which can only be described as maternal. Citizens of a country which has been conquered and exploited by Britain are, in the eyes of many well-meaning Labour parliamentarians, superior in some way to citizens of countries conquered by foreigners. On this basis, a man living in Ghana has a right to greater privileges than a man living in Algeria. The difference is that one country was ruled by the British, the other by the Frogs.

Although Labour arguments in favour of the Commonwealth are usually phrased in terms of 'a bridge between the rich and poor nations' and other such apparently admirable sentiments, it is impossible to avoid their basically chauvinist content. Their irrelevance to modern politics is one of the main reasons why the attack from the Left against the Immigration Act fell off and never recovered. Men like Royle had put all their force into the 'maternal' argument, and as its essential patronage and irrelevance to progressive politics became clearer, so the voices raised in its defence inexorably faded.

For more cynical Labour supporters, the Commonwealth had always provided convenient slogans which would raise a cheer at conferences. Besides, appeals to the 'Commonwealth ideal' had the great advantage of electoral irrelevance. Only after large-scale Commonwealth immigration started did the 'ideal' mean something in terms of votes. And then the mere possibility of losing votes because of the 'glorious Commonwealth ideal' was enough to make most former Commonwealth enthusiasts forget all about it.

Second to the Commonwealth in the hierarchy of Labour platitudes is 'planning'. 'We want planned growth of the economy', said Lord Sorensen at a Leyton by-election meeting in January, 1965, 'and planned control of immigration.' The left-wing weekly, *Tribune*, for more than six months after the election kept silent on the issue of control, then hinted that it was impossible to plan the British economy without controlling the numbers of immigrants settling in the country. This argument encounters two serious objections: first, that the 'economic regulator' itself would control the numbers coming in; secondly, that the 'planning' which is so fashionable nowadays is *national* planning, in the interests, at best, of the people of only one nation. It is reasonable certainly to deny such privileges as the free movement of labour, provided that the people so restricted benefit from the overall plan. The Pakistani or Jamaican refused leave to enter Britain, however, does not benefit from this 'planning' by the British authorities. A large number of Labour supporters have relaxed their opposition to control because of their mere love of planning for planning's sake. Yet such are precisely the Socialists who claim allegiance to international humanity.

There remains the small group of Labour M.P.s who still reject both the social and economic arguments for control but who have preferred not to attack the Immigration Act, because, in their view, the people of Britain need some reassurance before proper integration of those immigrants already here can be attempted.

This is the patronizing view that although we all know there will be no flood of immigrants unless there are jobs for them, the ordinary man in the street wants some comforting that the Government has the situation in hand.

Yet, despite doubts on the Commonwealth, on planning and on reassurance, that the main reason for Labour's switch on immigration lay elsewhere was explained by Mr Roy Hattersley, Member for Birmingham, Sparkbrook, in a Commons speech on 23 March. This speech, indeed, is the only public record of a Labour M.P.'s serious attempt to explain his change of view on immigration.

Hattersley admitted with a candour lacking in his colleagues that he thought his party should have supported the Act in 1961, although at the time he himself had bitterly opposed it. He agreed that the economic arguments all favoured increased immigration, but he went on:

I now believe that there are social as well as economic arguments and I believe that unrestricted immigration can only produce additional problems, additional suffering and additional hardship unless some kind of limitation is imposed and continued.

What were these additional problems? What was this additional suffering? Hattersley did not explain. He could not have meant housing or National Assistance problems. He would be the first to deny that immigration is significantly responsible for housing shortages, or that most immigrants live on National Assistance. So, too, he would agree that the rate of crime, disease or dirt among immigrants is not startlingly higher than similar rates among the British. He gave a clue to the 'social problems' which worried him later in his speech:

We must impose a test which tries to analyse which immigrants . . . are most likely to be assimilated in our national life.

Such a test, he went on, would fall most heavily on Pakistanis.

Hattersley came nearer than any other Labour spokesman to the real reasons for Labour's shift on the control issue. Labour was simply frightened of the 'social problems' caused by immigrants not easily 'assimilated into our national life'. What mattered to an increasing number of Labour supporters were the different habits, the different languages, dare we say it, the different colour of the immigrants, and the 'social problems' that arose from such. If this analysis is correct, what does it mean? It means precisely what the Labour Party itself feared in the original Commonwealth Immigration Bill. It means that the chauvinist, xenophobic element in the British people is assuming control over the politicians. It means that West Indians are to be preferred to Pakistanis and Irish preferred to both. A policy that welcomes all immigrants, whatever their race, colour or creed is a policy with which Labour is not prepared to face the electorate. The anti-immigrant resentment which long years of Conservative cynicism and neglect helped to create has taken its toll of the Labour Party. If Mr Hattersley is right, Labour, like Sir Cyril Osborne, would like to keep the strangest of the strangers out of

Britain. The more alien their culture or religion, the more striking their apparent differences, the more anxious is Labour to exclude them.

It is, in many ways, the most dangerous argument of all. It is the argument once used against the Irish, against the Jews, against the European Voluntary Workers, against the West Indians. 'We do not mind the ones we're used to', it runs, 'but we must stop these *new* people from coming in.' Although Irishmen, Jews, and West Indians are all 'assimilable' now, they were all 'unassimilable' in their day. Despite its apparently humane gloss, Hattersley's argument about control, representative as it is of his party, differs in no essential from the arguments of Sir Cyril Osborne and Mr Norman Pannell.

It is, as Hattersley himself admitted, 'a melancholy view'. It shows that the Labour Party has collapsed in face of what it believes to be 'public opinion': that it has changed its line on immigration not because economic circumstances have changed, not because of any new problems of housing or education, but, as its predecessors in 1925 acted, through fear of losing votes.

9. Anti-Immigrant Organizations

Political reactions to the process of immigration have been shaped to a significant extent by pressure groups formed with the main purpose of campaigning against immigration. Groups of this kind did not take shape until well after the process had established itself.

The most powerful of these by far is the Birmingham Immigration Control Association, which started with a small meeting in the Shard End housing estate in Birmingham on 13 October 1960, called by an engineer who described himself as a 'trade unionist' – Mr Albert Mucklow. Mr Mucklow's little meeting at Shard End, called to 'press at city council and Government level for restrictions on immigration to Birmingham' received generous publicity in the *Birmingham Mail*. Mucklow and his friends then organized a petition signed by some 1,200 people which they presented to the city council, and which called for tighter immigration checks.

One of the many letters that Mucklow received congratulating him on his move came from a Mr John Sanders who lives in the fashionable suburb of Sutton Coldfield. Sanders is a 'consultant in estate duty finance', a big, burly man with an accent half-American (he has lived in the United States for a large portion of his life) and half-Midland. On his return to England from California in 1952 he was 'filled with horror' by the immigration invasion.

Because he considered himself an intellectual, he quickly rationalized his prejudices. He was, he claimed, 'not racialist, not against any race – but simply opposed to a multi-racial Britain'.

Sanders has by now developed a long specious argument:

If by civilization we mean free men ruling themselves, then we are the only civilized nation in the world. Only twice has this self-rule been achieved in history – in Athens and in Britain. Since the end of feudalism this principle of self-rule has been practised only by nations around the North Sea (the American civilization stems from us, so that is no exception). We have the Magna Carta and the Bill of Rights and Habeas

Corpus – a very precious heritage which we are now throwing away. No country has ever solved its racial problems. The Afro-Asians are feckless peoples with cultures different from our own. By our standards they are barbarous.

No one really bothers about the Irish. They don't peddle dope and they don't kill chickens in the kitchen.

This civilization of the North Sea and of Kipling's five nations is in danger of destruction through this flood coming in. It must be stopped.

Although Sanders strongly rejects the view that he is colour-prejudiced, his only real objection is to coloured immigrants. He can tolerate immigration, provided the immigrants concerned are white.

Sanders has frequently vented his feelings in the Birmingham Press usually signing himself 'Sacred Briton' or 'True Briton'. For instance, in the *Birmingham Mail* of 20 October 1954, he wrote:

Am I to understand that when jobless I, a ratepaying Briton whose forbears have inhabited these islands since before there was an England [*sic*], am I to stand at the counter of the labour exchange office on a par with these new arrivals ? Or must I labour to keep the stranger on the dole – to pay for his food, housing and clothing ?

In similar vein Sanders wrote to Mucklow in October, 1960, conveying 'the gratitude which I feel is owing to you and your supporters'. In a simultaneous letter to the *Birmingham Mail*, Sanders wrote:

Are we resigned to seeing our homeland made into a racial cross-roads; converted into an impoverished society similar to those from which the immigrants are coming; to seeing our children disinherited ? If not is it not high time we followed the example of Mr Mucklow and his petitioners ?

Mr Sanders was busy on that day – 17 October. Not content with these rhetorical questions to the local Press and sending warm congratulations to Mr Mucklow, Sanders also wrote to a Conservative city councillor – Mr Charles Collett.

That he should have chosen Collett from among all the Birmingham councillors is not surprising. For ten years Collett has conducted a frantic campaign against immigration and the immigrant community. As early as 1956 he had shouted for committees in the council to investigate the colour problem. Three extracts from his letters to the Press are worth quoting, since the man remains a Conservative councillor with the full sanction of Conservative authority. They occur within a few weeks of each other, and they are not exceptional.

He [an Indian who had been sent to prison] had no fear of starvation, as we should have in his country. His friends would soon put him wise to the National Assistance Board. What a foolish race we are to tolerate the uncontrolled, unhealthy influx of coloured immigrants.

10 November 1959   *Birmingham Evening Dispatch*

Birmingham needs protection from coloured marauders. I would that there were 500 of us grouped together with one ideal: to stop the uncontrolled influx of coloured immigrants.

8 December 1959   *Birmingham Evening Dispatch*

Colour discrimination springs from . . . a genuine desire to protect our own people, which in no sense violates Christian teaching. Some of our Birmingham folk, and these merit most consideration, have nowhere to run; others have no desire to leave home because of foreign pressure. When will this city awake to the menace of coloured infiltration and a piebald population ?

7 January 1960   *Birmingham Evening Dispatch*

One story about Collett affords light relief in this melodrama of racial rancour, while underlining his own frenzied prejudices. In February 1956 he was called to the witness-box by the defence in a case involving the prosecution of a Pakistani for violence. The defence suggested that Collett by his anti-colour activity in the street where the Pakistani lived, had helped to provoke the man. Mr G. Brown, for the defence, asked Collett:

You have got the reputation of being a violent anti-coloured man, have you not ?

COLLETT: I don't know about that.

BROWN: I put it to you in this case that you are the nigger in the woodpile.

COLLETT: I am no nigger!

Thus it was that Sanders wrote to Collett on 17 October 1960:

You are not alone in your concern for what is being allowed to happen to our country, and in the hope that the knowledge will encourage you to drive some sense into the skulls of that shower of confused sparrow intellectuals and well-meaning but misguided doctrinaires in control of Birmingham City Council.

Small wonder that within a few days Sanders, Collett and Mucklow found themselves meeting together at Queens College Chambers, Paradise Street. There an embryo committee was formed and another, larger meeting arranged for all Mucklow's correspondents. At this meeting, held in the Imperial Hotel, Collett was elected chairman, Sanders treasurer and Harry Jones secretary. At that time the organization was still known as the Birmingham Immigration Control Committee. Sanders's business-like mind got to work, and on 4 February 1961 the Committee was formed into an Association under the Companies Act, 1948.

The new Association was soon tormented by factionalism, with the main argument centring around the political role of the organization. Was it to remain strictly outside party politics and campaign accordingly; or should it try not to offend the Conservatives? A dispute arose in April over tactics in the municipal elections. Harry Jones together with a new recruit, Tom Jones (no relation), were for putting up an independent B.I.C.A. candidate in the elections. Collett objected strongly after pressure was brought to bear on him by fellow Conservative members of the Birmingham council. The Joneses had singled out a solid Tory ward, Sandwell. Collett pointed out that standing for Sandwell would only take votes from the Tories – a prospect which did not deter Harry or Tom Jones. Tom, in fact, had for several years after 1945 been a member of the Labour Party.

In early April the executive committee, including the two Joneses, Collett and Sanders went to London on a deputation to see Birmingham Tory M.P.s on the issue of immigration. Harry Jones describes the incident:

All the way down on the train Collett tried to get me to stand down from the municipal elections. He said that the Tories would easily fix me up with a seat the next year if I stood down as independent candidate that time.

When we got to the House of Commons, I was sitting between Harold Gurden [M.P. for Selly Oak] and John Hollingworth [M.P. for All

Saints]. They pointed out to me that if I stood as an independent at Sandwell I could only get a small percentage of the vote, while if I stood as a Tory in 1962 I'd get onto the council.

These people were loyal first and foremost to the Tory Party – not to the cause. I told them I was interested in the issue of immigration, and would stand, not to get in, but to make an impact.

On 19 April Collett resigned from the chairmanship of the Association, while remaining on the executive committee. He pointed out that he could not be chairman of an organization sponsoring anti-Tory candidates. The executive committee had decided to back Jones's candidature. Sanders and Mr A. J. McIntyre, the vice-chairman, wavered on the issue. They brought their cars to help Jones on polling day, but did little else to assist him in the campaign. Tom Jones acted as agent. The result of the election in Sandwell ward surprised everyone:

Mrs A. F. Wood	(Tory)	4,886
Harry Jones	(B.I.C.A.)	1,839
W. A. Poulton	(Labour)	926

After the result, Sanders wrote to Jones congratulating him on the 'magnificent achievement'. Sanders agreed that he had been 'entirely wrong' on the matter of opposing the Conservatives. He hoped that there would be no ill feeling.

Yet the ill feeling steadily grew, and only a few weeks after the May elections trouble broke out again. Sanders explains that 'he was having trouble with a lot of B.N.P. members selling *Combat* at our meetings and shouting slogans'. His official explanation of the faction-fighting is that, with his election as chairman on 21 April, he was 'immediately confronted with the problem of enforcing the conduct of the Association's campaign in a manner and spirit consistent with the intentions of its founder members'.

Tom Jones says that the main difficulty remained the old one of the Tory Party; that he himself wanted a definite statement of non-party allegiance, and outright opposition to the Tories on all occasions, a statement which Sanders refused to make. Harry Jones says that 'there was pressure from some of the younger members for a more progressive, forceful organization . . . they were demanding a national organization with a national name'.

At one meeting of the executive a motion of no confidence in

Collett was proposed because he had resigned on the Tory Party issue. It was defeated, and a number of members, led by Tom Jones, refused to stand for re-election. At a meeting in the Red Lion Hotel, Handsworth (Handsworth was always the centre of the Association) Tom Jones was voted out of the room after a violent row with his namesake and with Sanders. He then formed his own group, the Vigilant Immigration Control Association, which was based in Handsworth and had strong links with Sutton Coldfield. One of the main proposals of this Association was that immigrants should not receive the benefits of the Welfare State until they had paid contributions to it for at least a year.

Meanwhile Harry Jones had also broken with Sanders, principally, it seems, over the desire for a national association, coupled with intense disappointment in Sanders himself. He was 'a long-winded stick-in-the-mud' says Harry Jones.

Harry Jones called his new Association the British Immigration Control Association, and he was joined before long by Donald Finney and his Smethwick branch who felt that Jones's forcefulness was nearer to their way of thinking than the pompous academics of Sanders.

Their difficulties thus resolved, the three organizations set about the task of spreading the gospel. Sanders's Association stuck to Birmingham, while Harry Jones and his friends moved out to Wolverhampton, West Bromwich and Smethwick. Strong branches of the British Association were formed in Wolverhampton and West Bromwich. Mr Norman Smith, then a leading member of the Association, who has, since its demise, joined the British National Party, explained the pull which the organization had over the public.

We went into Wolverhampton one Saturday in July. We had booked a room in the Wolverhampton Grammar School which could hold up to 300. There were only eight of us and we pushed out leaflets for a couple of hours during the afternoon. That was just about the only advertisement the meeting had. But it was packed. Packed to the doors. At least sixty people came forward at the meeting to form a branch, and later in July we got forty to a pub branch committee meeting.

At these meetings we pointed out that if things went on for much longer we would be having black M.P.s and black councillors. We said that there were hundreds of thousands more waiting to come where the other blacks came from.

The British Association also moved into West Bromwich, and in early September held a mass meeting in the West Bromwich town hall, where again a number of people formed a branch. The Mayor of West Bromwich refused to attend the meeting which he said was directed against the immigrants in the town. In a forthright statement he declared that 'these are now my townspeople entitled to the same rights and privileges as people who were born here'.

The Association printed several different leaflets, each of them calling on the ordinary man and woman to *Wake Up*. West Bromwich, Wolverhampton, Handsworth and Smethwick were all advised to wake up and face the fact that their houses and women were being stolen in the night by a silent invader. Typical of these leaflets was the one addressed to trade unionists:

WAKE UP, TRADE UNIONISTS!
You fought for better pay and conditions, why see your efforts go down the drain because of
UNCONTROLLED IMMIGRATION.
Stop this Cheap Labour Now.
Protest at your next branch meeting.
Why pay the Political Levy and not use the Political Machinery?
Make Your General Executive Committee come to heel.

The meetings, however, were muted compared with the barrage of protest which the three organizations unleashed against their Members of Parliament and councillors. The Birmingham Association had special postcards printed, addressed to the House of Commons, which declared that the senders, with their families, were 'suffering the consequences' of uncontrolled immigration, and called on the relevant M.P. to 'vote against the "come-who-may" policy' or lose the sender's vote.

The precise number of these postcards actually sent to M.P.s is impossible to establish, but it must have been in the region of 20,000. In August Mr John Hollingworth, M.P. for All Saints, complained that he had received 300 such postcards from constituents in one week.

A joint target of all three anti-immigrant organizations was Sir Edward Boyle, Conservative M.P. for Handsworth, the centre of most activity. Boyle showed a masochistic willingness to meet the organizations whenever they asked to see him, but he would not associate himself with their strident racialism. Sanders himself speaks today with as much venom of Sir Edward Boyle as he does of Patrick Gordon Walker, describing them as 'two of the worst M.P.s the Midlands have ever had'.

Sanders also made full use of the 'business' contacts he had established with Conservative Party supporters and officials.

He had another postcard printed, reading this time:

Like most of my neighbours I disagree most strongly with Sir Edward Boyle's unrealistic and evasive attitude towards uncontrolled immigration.

Until he *faces up* to the issue and agrees to represent the views and interests of his electors in Parliament I shall refuse to subscribe any more money to Conservative funds.

Again, no one knows how many such postcards reached Tory headquarters in Empire House, Edmund Street, Birmingham, but anyone with experience of local party offices and the electoral sensitivity of political agents will appreciate the commotion that such letters and postcards caused. The feud between Sanders and Boyle continued right up to and after the General Election of 1964.

Not content with postcards and meetings, the B.I.C.A. workers busied themselves in collecting signatures for Sir Cyril Osborne's nation-wide petition in favour of immigration control. Of the 12,000 signatures submitted to Parliament by Osborne, 5,000 were collected in Birmingham and the surrounding towns. In other petitions, the B.I.C.A. officers collected some 50,000 signatures.

Sanders more than the others kept close contact with the Conservative Party, and he claims many friends and contacts, some of whom hold powerful positions in the local party organizations.

Of the thirty-nine resolutions calling for immigration control submitted to the Conservative conference of 1961, five came from the Midlands; and one – from the Birmingham City Party – gave the Government a blank cheque to control immigration as it wished. For this Mr John Sanders and his cohorts could assume a great deal of responsibility.

In November 1961, after Butler had promised legislation at the

Conservative conference, and had published it, the Birmingham Association met to hear Sanders discuss the Bill. It decided that the Bill gave the Government sufficient powers to keep out the immigrants. After writing to the Home Secretary asking for further control based on accommodation they decided to 'suspend' campaigning activities and see whether the Government would use the new powers sufficiently.

Predictably, after such fame and fury, political limbo did not appeal to John Sanders, and in the summer of 1964 the Association decided to start up again. In September its committee pledged itself to 'break the conspiracy' among politicians to keep immigration out of party politics.

Sanders had previously been distressed by the attitude of the then Conservative Member for Sparkbrook Mr Leslie Seymour and his constituency association who specifically refused the Birmingham Control Association permission to work on their behalf in Sparkbrook. Seymour's personal attitude had then changed. In February 1961 he had proclaimed, for instance, that it was 'un-Christian to let in any more immigrants'. Sanders says that he had visited Seymour before his election campaign started, and that Seymour had shown 'more good sense' than most other M.P.s at the time, though 'smothered by the overall conspiracy to keep the issue out'. Similarly, Sanders has nothing but contempt for Mr John Hollingworth, former Tory M.P. for Birmingham All Saints. In 1961 Hollingworth had been at one moment violently in favour of control, at another 'against any hasty action' (this last after meeting a delegation from the British Caribbean Association). Hollingworth had appeared on the agenda as the mover of the Birmingham motion at the 1961 Tory conference giving a 'blank cheque' for immigration control, yet he had not spoken in the debate. Nor had he personally raised the matter officially during the election campaign.

Thus Sanders was driven, by the 'conspiracy' he so detested, into the Perry Barr constituency where he concentrated his forces. The Tory candidate at Perry Barr – Dr Wyndham Davies – was delighted to get the B.I.C.A.'s help, and soon found that the immigration issue, if skilfully exploited, could work wonders. On the day before the poll he issued a leaflet implying that 300,000 immigrants would invade Perry Barr if Labour was elected.

Sanders says that he did not design the leaflet, but his members were happy to distribute it.

On 1 October, Sanders published a leaflet that called for immigration, 'the leading political issue', to be brought into the General Election. The leaflet did not set down any clear policy except opposition to all future immigration from the Afro-Asian countries. On this, however, it was firm.

Clearly we cannot afford immigration. It is the sure road to ruin. And certainly there is no necessity for Britain to become a multi-racial society which, very clearly, our people *do not want*. But apparently these simple truths have not yet penetrated the minds of our legislators, many of whom appear to be living in a vacuum untouched by the atmosphere of reality.

The rest of the leaflet was based entirely on the economic argument – that Britain cannot afford immigration. Nowhere did Sanders point out that 'our' competitors are taking in three or four times more working immigrants a year than Britain, and that this is directly associated with their faster economic growth. To Sanders, 'we can effectively solve our problems . . . only by our own exertions'. 'We' and 'our' refer to British people. Irish are acceptable and so indeed are Europeans, provided that their skin is white and that they live within shouting distance of the North Sea.

Some 15,000 leaflets like this were distributed in the key constituencies of Birmingham during the few days which remained of the election campaign – a very large proportion of them in Perry Barr. Sanders also says that he sent several to Smethwick, where they were duly distributed, but he and his officers did not go and help Griffiths as they thought their presence might 'embarrass' him. The B.I.C.A. activities received considerable attention from the Press, and their impact on the election must have been considerable. Yet the Association mounted the hustings at a late date, with their organization rusty after three years of inactivity.

After the election the Association streamlined its organization, ready for a real campaign which would last, presumably, until immigration from Africa and Asia was completely banned. Sanders's office in Sutton Coldfield Broadway is almost a permanent office of B.I.C.A. His resources are considerable. Leaflets are well-produced, and a slick public relations service has been started. Sanders and his friends were, indeed, partly responsible for the threat in February 1965 to remove Mr Aubrey Jones from the Conservative candidature in Birmingham, Hall Green; the main opposition to Jones emanated from the Brandsworth Ward, where B.I.C.A. had some influence. But Sanders's pet hate remained Sir Edward Boyle, and at the height of the campaign against Jones, Sanders announced that many people in Handsworth were thinking of putting up Mr Norman Pannell – a veteran anti-immigrant campaigner – as an alternative candidate to Sir Edward in Handsworth. Boyle replied that there was no danger and that he had the complete support of his constituency association.

The British Association and the Vigilant Association did not re-form after the Immigration Act. Harry Jones had promised to close down the British Association after the Act, and promptly did so (he was furious with Finney for continuing with the Smethwick branch long after the parent organization had dissolved). Tom Jones tried to keep his Vigilant Association alive, criticizing the 'toothless bill' which the Tories had introduced. Yet his supporters had lost their enthusiasm, and V.I.C.A. faded.

The story of Harry Jones after he closed down his Association brings some relief to this otherwise gloomy chapter. He had been perhaps the most militant of all the anti-immigrant campaigners, save only for his namesake, Tom. He had, moreover, been a powerful speaker, effectively employing the distorted imagery of sex and disease. He had whipped up audiences of ordinary people into feelings of fear and horror about the immigrants in their midst. He had stomped the Black Country from Solihull to Wolverhampton, calling down fire and brimstone on uncontrolled immigration. It was Jones who had said that the Smethwick council was building two leper hospitals for immigrants, Jones who had talked about the spitting and sexual perversions of our 'coloured brothers' (irony had been his favourite weapon). When a B.I.C.A. branch had wanted a speaker from outside, they had almost always sent for Harry.

He had been, throughout all this, a general wholesaler. Shortly after he wound up his Association, business got worse, and he had to move out of his native Handsworth to live in East Birmingham, in Great Barr. Few of his original political friends or adversaries now know where he lives. They imagine that he left the anti-immigrant movement because he had two daughters who were constantly threatened and accosted by black men. This is not the explanation which Jones himself gives for losing contact with his old activities:

When my business folded, I took up a job as a receptionist and tele-phonist in a hospital in East Birmingham. Since then I've seen quite a lot of these people, these immigrants . . . West Indians mainly, but some Indians too. Before I'd never really met any in the course of my work, and the only ones I knew at all were those who used to come along to the meetings.

Since moving into the hospital and meeting these people, I have to a very great extent changed my views about them. I think there must be a better class of immigrant coming in now, or something. They are trying to live more as we live, and we can't expect them to change their habits overnight. You can't expect West Indians suddenly to like the idea of marriage after years without it.

I still blame the Government for letting them come in such big numbers. But I couldn't go back now and say the same sort of things as I was saying in 1961.

Once his life had settled down into a set pattern, once the in-security of small business was removed, once he associated at work with immigrants, Jones found himself revolted by the out-right racialism and hate which he himself had propagated.

Most of his followers either walked out of political life altogether, or, like Norman Smith, their appetite for such activity whetted, joined the British National Party. Others, when Sanders announced that he was opening up in business again, re-joined the original parent body – the Birmingham Immigration Control Association. A few helped Peter Griffiths in Smethwick.

After the 1964 election the old factions began to come together and get down to work. If, as seems likely, their 'work' prospers in a continuing political vacuum, if opposition to their activities is muffled by the fear of losing votes, the prospect for B.I.C.A. is one of almost unhindered advance.

That these organizations are crucial to Birmingham politics is obvious from the constant *political* content of their propaganda. The themes are always the same: the Government must do this, the Government must stop that. Votes must be withheld. Pressure groups must be formed in the local Conservative and Labour Constituency Parties. The declared aim of Sanders himself at the end of 1964 was to 'bring the politicians to heel at the next General Election'.

Yet the dispute which first split the movement in Birmingham survives today – whether to continue as a pressure group wherever pressure is likely to be most successful, or set up as an independent political organization sponsoring candidates in the local elections. The advantage for B.I.C.A. of the latter course is that propaganda becomes easier, there is no need to support people many of whose policies are objectionable, and the room for enthusiasm among the Association's workers is accordingly much larger.

On the other hand, there are serious disadvantages. The first is that the organization loses the official support of men like Councillor Collett and Councillor Finney. All the heavy spade work done in the local Tory Party is rendered useless by the call to the Tory rank and file to close ranks in the face of a declared enemy. Sanders himself has recognized more and more the possibility of influencing the Tory Party, particularly after what he calls 'Peter Griffiths's magnificent and courageous victory in Smethwick'.

There is, however, a more serious objection – the danger of being associated with extreme right-wing political parties. Such parties have never had great support in Birmingham, and are almost all centred on London, from which they draw most of their membership.

The most important of these are the Union Movement (formed in 1948 by Sir Oswald Mosley); the British National Party, formed in 1960; and the British National Socialist Movement. Of these, the Union Movement is the largest and the most moderate. It calls for a united Europe, and an Africa divided into white and black areas. Its 'European socialism' is not the National Socialism of Hitler but a strange mixture of Poujadism and syndicalism. No one will divulge the membership figures, but the Union Movement probably has about 1,000 members, and its potential support is much larger than its paid-up membership. The official party line is opposed to the cross-fertilization of races and cultures.

The British National Party is led by a Norfolk farmer, Andrew Fountaine, a Spanish War veteran (on Franco's side) and a Tory candidate in 1950 (he was eventually expelled from the Tory

Party), and by John Bean, a thirty-seven-year-old industrial chemist. Its monthly paper *Combat* pours out hatred and bitterness against coloured immigrants. The Party has some 500–700 members (again, accurate figures are almost impossible to get).

Bean has described himself as a 'British Goebbels', and admits that he regards coloured people as 'inferior to British people'. He also admits that coloured immigration is his one real recruiting issue, and that it is bringing in a constant flow of members. He leans towards the Fascism of the Nordic School, and is a super-patriot. He calls for the compulsory repatriation of all coloured immigrants, and, generously, he says that the 'Government should pay their fares if they can't'.

The National Socialist Movement is the most extreme of the three groups. Its leader, Colin Jordan, was a school-teacher in Coventry until the local authority dismissed him because of his activities. His main slogan is that Hitler was right. To Jordan, the Jews are even more dangerous than the blacks.

There are of course numerous other such groups, but they are all minute. Jordan himself has slender numerical support. Organizations like the Greater Britain Movement and the United Kingdom Defence League or the British Ku-Klux-Klan serve little more purpose than to pacify the Fuehrer complexes of their founders, and seldom have more than a handful of members. The present groups are also highly susceptible to factionalism and splitting.

Two vital features distinguish these organizations from the Immigration Control Associations in the Midlands. First, there is the Fascist connexion. It is difficult to convey the impression of 'super-patriotism' when your ideas are associated with those of the most hated enemy British people have known this century. Mosley's Union Movement can never get rid of this 'where-were-you-in-the-war?' tag, despite the constant disassociation of its younger members from Fascism. Similarly Bean and Jordan, strutting around calling themselves 'Goebbels' and 'Hitler', find it hard to convince the masses that their main aim is a Greater Britain.

The other crucial distinguishing feature is the political isolation of the neo-Fascist organizations – each doing its own bit to secure support, and each, if financially possible, putting up its own candidates in elections. The Union Movement has fought in several municipal elections, as well as in the famous Notting Hill (North Kensington) General Election of 1959. Similarly the British National Party regularly put up municipal candidates in London districts like Deptford, Islington, St Pancras and Ealing, and in 1964 John Bean stood for Southall in the General Election.

This political isolation brings with it all the problems of the fringe party. By and large the British electorate is stuck fast in its voting habits. The alternatives are clear: the Tories, the Labour Party and occasionally the Liberals. The enormous majority of people vote Tory or Labour out of class loyalty. Sometimes people will switch their vote, but usually between the three parties. A vote for a fringe party is a vote, inevitably, for an unsuccessful candidate and a party without a hope of forming a Government – a severe deterrent, as the Liberals with three million votes to their credit in 1964 still find.

The Immigration Control Associations in the Midlands over the years 1961–4 had no such disadvantage. Despite Harry Jones's two candidatures at municipal elections in 1961, no one associated the movement with electoral gain for its own purpose. Similarly, although there is little to distinguish the views of John Sanders on immigration from those of John Bean, no one calls Sanders a Fascist – and all of his committee members avoid the tag scrupulously. Thus the Associations command a very much higher degree of respect and attention than the official neo-Fascist parties, which at any rate are poorly represented in the Midland area.

The plain fact is that the Immigration Control Associations which arose in Birmingham and the surrounding area in 1960 and 1961, by means of their concentration on a single issue, their ability to move freely among members of established political parties and their disassociation from nominal Fascism, had a greater impact on British politics than any of the extremist right-wing parties could have done.

Why then did they remain *Birmingham* associations ? Why is it that an association called the British Immigration Control Association never established itself outside the West Midlands ?

The answer lies, partly, in time and resources. All these organizations were in active existence for only a few months during

1961, and the B.I.C.A. has only recently re-started propaganda. Harry Jones's British Association never contacted possible branch founders in Bradford, Bristol, Gloucester or Nottingham, and as yet Sanders, imbued with the isolationism of the West Midlands, is quite happy with his local organization.

The British Association did make an effort to start a branch in London. Harry Jones and some of his acolytes visited London during the summer of 1961, but they came away from their meetings in the metropolis sadly disappointed. 'They were all too much influenced by Colin Jordan,' says Jones.

The psychological misfits who gravitate towards modern Fascism inevitably congregate in London, even if, like Jordan himself, their home towns are elsewhere. The headquarters of all three main extremist groups are in London. Thus any approach from an outside anti-immigrant organization will inevitably be made to such groups, and will inevitably be met with the factional party-comes-first propaganda which dominates the British National Party and the Union Movement. In these new 'anti-blacks' such leaders see not the possibility of a growing movement, but more recruits for the party. Thus Jones's insistence that the British Association should remain free of official party or any Fascist tags was coolly met by his London counterparts.

Nevertheless, specifically anti-immigrant organizations have begun recently to take separate root in the London area.

In September 1963, a young couple advertised a house for sale in Palgrave Avenue, Southall, and the inhabitants of this hitherto highly 'respectable' road were shocked to notice eight Indians visiting the house to look it over. They immediately formed a Palgrave Avenue Residents' Association under a prominent local Conservative, Mrs Penn. Mrs Penn collected signatures from almost all the avenue's residents and petitioned the Labour-controlled council to buy the house so that it should not fall into the hands of coloured people. The council then placed a compulsory purchase order on the house and put one of their medical officers into it.

This development naturally received some publicity in the *Middlesex County Times* (Southall edition), and Mrs Penn was flooded with letters, one of them suggesting that the Palgrave Avenue Residents' Association should be turned into a Southall

Residents' Association. At a meeting in the Holy Trinity Church Hall in late September, this, indeed, was done, and a committee of thirty-two was elected. Mr Albert Cooney, a vehicle builder who had lived for some thirty years in Southall, became chairman.

The Association's work started enthusiastically. Its policy, as laid down in its initial charter, dealt with almost every social service problem which the town faced, and put immigration at the top of the list. It soon became clear, however, that immigration problems were to be the preoccupation of the Association. No other items ever reached the committee's agenda.

For the first few months the Association busied itself with attacks on the council. Mrs Penn claims that 'things which took the council years to act upon were cleared up in a few weeks'. Yet as the attack on the council spent itself, and as the committee searched around for new fields of activity a profound split developed within its ranks.

Mrs Penn, Mr David Baker, the treasurer, and two other committee members, Mr and Mrs Maughan, wanted to contact the local Indian Workers' Association and plan activities on a coordinated and friendly basis with them. But they, and Mrs Penn in particular, came under bitter and outspoken criticism from the other members, including Cooney. Mrs Penn had had several invitations from the Indian Workers' Association to attend their functions and discuss common problems. She argued strongly that she should go as a member of the committee, but permission was refused. Finally she went in her individual capacity and was, in her own words, 'extremely impressed both with the I.W.A. leaders and with all the other people who were doing their best to help these people integrate into our society'.

She and Baker reported back to the committee, where they were met with abuse and reproval, and at a meeting of the entire Association Mrs Penn was censured for her attitude of friendly cooperation with the immigrants. She and her friends hung on to their committee posts for a few more weeks, and then, in desperation, resigned. In all this time the committee had met the I.W.A. leaders officially only once – at what Mrs Penn described as a 'shameful and embarrassing meeting'. A great deal of hostility to the two Indian leaders – Mr P. S. Khabra and Mr S. S. Gill – was vented by the militant committee members.

After the resignation of Mrs Penn, Mr Baker and the Maughans, the Association degenerated into outright opposition to the immigrants and the whole process of immigration. A typical statement of its aims runs as follows:

To protect the interests and the rights of Southall people against the silent invasion of their homes by these immigrants . . .

The residents saw their whole way of life threatened and endangered by a flood of immigrants who were generally illiterate, dirty and completely unsuited and unused to our way of life. They overcrowd their properties to an alarming degree, create slums, endanger public health and subject their neighbours to a life of misery, annoyance, abuse and bitterness . . .

The responsibility rests directly on the politicians and can be solved quite easily . . .

STOP IMMIGRATION.

Cooney himself revels in this vicious propaganda, in stories about the Indians who come to work in Chrysler cars (or occasionally Vauxhall Vivas). He speaks with ill-disguised contempt of the Indian Workers' Association, or indeed of anyone who is trying to bring about a *rapprochement* between immigrants and indigenous Southall people.

Cooney's attitude towards his role and duty in the Association has much in common with that of the leader of a lynch mob. At a pre-election meeting of the Association, after the secretary alleged that she had been threatened by coloured men, Cooney shouted:

If ever such a threat is taken up, we shall not hesitate to take the law into our own hands. We shall not stand aside.

Yet my interview with Cooney was mild and considerate compared with a stifling hour I spent one evening at the home of the secretary of the Association, Miss Grace Woods. Miss Woods lives with two other women and a large cat towards which the conversation is continually diverted. Large, middle-aged, voluble, she bombarded me with the most gruesome tales about the immigrants in Southall.

The three, led by Miss Woods herself, were particularly anxious to explain the prostitution rackets which seemed to go on continually outside Miss Woods's front window. She personally had watched white girls picking up black men for five shillings. All three gave lurid details of these accostings. Their pet hatred, I gathered, was a West Indian called Harris, who was supplying white girls to the immigrants in the town. Harris, apparently, was accustomed to accosting old women of sixty-eight. (In three different immigrant areas – Birmingham, Bristol and Southall – I heard stories of an old woman of sixty-eight who had been accosted by a coloured man. One can only assume that there is a woman of sixty-eight who travels from town to town, a perennial aphrodisiac to Indians and West Indians alike.) Miss Woods assured me that she 'would kill him if he touches me'.

One exchange with this trio is worth repeating since it gives some idea of the vast gap between reason and prejudice. I interrupted a long tirade on the filthy housing conditions of the immigrants. 'Is it, then, a housing problem?' I asked. 'Oh yes, definitely,' said Miss Woods. 'Definitely a housing problem.'

'So all we have to do is to build more and better houses and there won't be a problem?'

This caused several moments' serious thought.

'Oh *no* . . . it's *them*, you see. It's the way *they* behave. You'll never cure that with houses.'

Miss Woods gleefully got out her files and showed me the letters she had received, many of them from well-wishers all over the country. A cheque for five pounds from someone on the other side of England is no rare enclosure in her large morning post.

She showed me letters from her M.P., letters from the council (desperate, short-tempered letters these – 'We have looked into the problem and we can do no more about it') and letters from building societies agreeing that the colour problem should be taken into account in the granting of mortgages. A letter from the general manager of the Goldhawk Mutual Building Society, for instance, dated 22 January 1965, said:

We have not lent for quite some time in most of the centre of Southall, as we were well aware that it was a difficult area on account of the colour problem, and I do not think that there will be any change in our attitude in this respect for some considerable time.

Miss Woods also showed me letters from prominent national

journalists with whom she was in touch about her problems. She had had letters from Robert Pitman of the *Daily Express*, Percy Howard of the *Sunday Express* (who, I explained, to her chagrin, is Robert Pitman in another guise) and Alfred Sherman of the *Daily Telegraph* – journalists renowned for their articles in favour of immigration control.

Robert Pitman for instance had written: 'I am most interested to read [your memorandum], and am most sympathetic concerning your problems.'

Yet of all her souvenirs, Miss Woods was most proud of her back numbers of the *Weekly Post* – Southall Edition. The *Post*'s attitude to the immigration problems of Southall makes the virulence of the *Smethwick Telephone* look like tolerance itself. In keeping with the traditions of the British yellow Press, its headlines and the main stories dealt almost exclusively with sex and violence, while its editorials adopted the highest moral tone towards such phenomena. Headlines on the *Post*'s front page taken from a small sample of issues in November and December, 1964, read as follows:

> *Pick Up! A White Prostitute Works!*
> *Vice – For Five Shillings.*
> *The Five Quid Sin Deal.*
> *Teenage Tarts in Ankle Socks.*

The stories told of the terrible 'vice rackets' in the town caused by the immigration problem.

Photographers were established at the home of Miss Woods in Townsend Road to take pictures of 'white girls picking up coloured men'. The pictures are as ludicrous as the stories.

When no vice story presented itself, the *Post* would satisfy its lust for news with features about the immigrants who 'terrorize innocent respectable white women and their families'.

The *Post* became a public relations sheet for the S.R.A. Miss Woods, who in normal circumstances would never have found her way to fame, was portrayed in a highly flattering picture on one front page with the caption: 'I'm not going to be ruled by prostitutes.'

'Scoops' of this kind were encouraged by the fact that the S.R.A. had announced a boycott of the more sober, more widely-read local paper, the *Middlesex County Times*. The *Times*, said Cooney, was 'not giving us a fair share of publicity' and was 'not printing most of our letters'.

One wonders what the *Post* editors would say to the suggestion (made by all responsible sources) that the best way to stamp out prostitution among immigrants is to encourage more of their families to come over here and provide decent home lives for them.

The political affiliations of the S.R.A. are confused by the sustained activity in Southall over several years of the British National Party. The B.N.P. had, in a ward election in Hambrough in 1963, pushed the Conservative into third place, and other local candidates had collected large shares of the vote. Standing in the 1964 General Election, Mr John Bean received 3,410 votes, or more than nine per cent of the poll – by far the highest percentage gained by any right-wing Independent anywhere, and a vote of which most Communist candidates would be proud.

In the 1963 local elections, two of the B.N.P. municipal candidates were nominated by Albert Cooney and Mrs Doris Hart, respectively chairman and treasurer of the Southall Residents' Association. Cooney was severely rapped over the knuckles by the majority of the committee for his action. Yet he is unrepentant: 'I agree with Bean and Co. on the immigration issue,' he says. 'Bean's a level-headed bloke – not the Colin Jordan type at all. I'm just not sure whether we should confuse this one issue with a lot of other political points.'

Before the 1964 election, the S.R.A. asked each of the three candidates (Conservative, Labour and B.N.P.) to address its members at a meeting. Miss Barbara Maddin and Mr George Pargiter (the Tory and Labour candidates) spoke at one meeting, while Bean addressed the Association separately. Both Miss Maddin and Mr Pargiter (particularly the second) were given a rough time, but Miss Maddin, by taking a 'tough line' on the issue, came through with flying colours. Pargiter could not get round the fact that he had voted (and spoken) against the Immigration Bill in November 1961.

Miss Maddin desperately tried to siphon the strong B.N.P. element within the Association into the Tory camp. She proposed a special policy – a total ban on 'non-priority' immigration for at least two years – and produced a strong leaflet dealing solely with immigration. Shortly before polling day she announced that 'there is no official affiliation between the Southall Residents' Association and the British National Party. Many prominent Association members are coming out to work for me.'

In this attempt she was remarkably successful. Both Cooney and Miss Woods, for instance, voted for her. At the count Bean remarked wryly, and probably correctly, that 'shortly before the election there was a big swing away from us to the Conservative'.

Since the election, indeed, the Association has moved further and further away from the B.N.P. Its spokesmen make every effort to establish the fact that they are not a party-political organization, although of course its main business is bringing pressure to bear on politicians of every party.

This disassociation was brought about in part by a further, more important development – what Cooney calls 'the attempt to turn this into a national organization'. Shortly after the election the secretary was instructed by the committee to write letters, sounding out the possibility of support, to everyone of significance in the London area who had shown the slightest interest either in the Association's work or, more generally, in the campaign against immigration.

Some twenty letters were sent. Many of them were to individuals like Mrs Rose Easter in Slough, who had stood in previous municipal elections on the issue of keeping out the immigrants and had polled a respectable number of votes. One, by way of 'keeping in touch', went to the Mayor of Smethwick, who answered it with exaggerated politeness.

Others went to Residents' Associations already formed, such as the Greenford Residents' Association and the Cardington Square (Hounslow) Association, whose sponsors were determined to expand their organization throughout Hounslow. Other areas to which letters went included Hornsey, Brixton, Heston and Isleworth, High Wycombe, Pinner, Wembley, Alperton and North Gifford. Hornsey quickly established an effective anti-immigrant Residents' Association.

The Cardington Square (Hounslow) Association was formed in August 1964 by an insurance branch manager, Mr Frederick

Perry. The reason was familiar – to stop the flood of immigrants into Cardington Square. Mr Perry says he is anxious to see a national organization composed of such associations but he is worried about 'political interference'. He is convinced that most of the people who have visited him asking to join his Association have been connected with extremist political parties. Mr Perry is, however, quite satisfied that the Southall Residents' Association is free from party politics.

Another organization in the London area which does not fit into the pattern either of the general control organization or the extremist neo-Fascist political party is the New Liberal Party, centred on the borough of Islington and the personality of Mr Alan Lomas. Lomas is a former E.T.U. shop steward and was a member of the Labour Party until not long after the war, when he left apparently because he disagreed with nationalization. He joined the Liberal Party after Suez (of which operation he strongly approved) and bustled around Islington recruiting members and building a powerful organization. He was for a short while prospective official candidate for the Liberal Party, but one of his main recruiting slogans was immigration control, and this led to racialist policies which were too much for the Liberal Party headquarters. Eventually Lomas and his group were expelled, and he then formed the New Liberal Party. The choice of name was shrewd, for it disassociated him immediately from any unfashionable extremist party. The word 'liberal', after all, conjures up in the British mind all that is good, honest and decent in politics.

Although Lomas kept up a pretence of fighting on a broad political front, immigration was the only issue which really interested him. His journal, the *Viewpoint and Islington Advertiser*, a semi-literate sheet notably similar to British National Party propaganda, deals almost exclusively with immigration, rats, dysentery, overcrowding, and the 'Defence of England'. Describing the people of Islington in their overcrowded houses, it jibes: 'Perhaps if they were not English, the Labour Council would help.'

The New Liberals put up three candidates for the Greater London Council elections in April 1964 – all polling well – and Lomas himself stood as New Liberal candidate for East Islington in the 1964 General Election, polling just over 2,000 votes in a low poll, and coming near to beating the official Liberal candidate. In the political vacuum that is East Islington (the near-Stalinist bureaucracy of the local Labour Party is almost a joke), the anti-immigrant hysteria of Lomas could spread alarmingly. Already, by May 1965, the New Liberals had nominated a candidate for Islington North.

London and the Midlands are the main centres of organized anti-immigrant activity, but in Bradford, normally a 'show' area for race relations, the seeds of an organization with characteristics similar to those of its London and Midland Big Brothers were planted in 1964. A nation-wide petition calling for a ban on im-migration was instigated in the spring by a 'group of Bradford businessmen', as they were described in the Press. The group was, in fact, formed by Mr G. Smith, a Bradford painter and decorator, and some 25,000 signatures were collected under its auspices, for presentation to Mr Henry Brooke shortly before the 1964 General Election.

Mr Smith was interviewed in July by Mr Maurice Spiers for the Institute of Race Relations. He did not give much away about his organization, but he did say that 200–300 people were willing to help him with petition work. His closest associates were a mill-worker, two clerks, a housewife and a school-teacher. Smith emphasized to Spiers that his was not a political movement of any kind – and had no extremist or political leanings. It simply wanted to stop the arrival of any more immigrants.

Bashful though Mr Smith is about his operations, he can ob-viously rely upon considerable support. The group's middle-class leadership and 'non-political' aims correspond with those of the Birmingham Immigration Control Association and the Southall Residents' Association. Though Smith has as yet no established public organization, he has obviously been in touch with the other Associations through his work over the 1964 petition. Should a break appear in the general political calm which has dominated race relations in Bradford over the years, Mr Smith's embryo could grow into as powerful a creature as John Sanders or Albert Cooney.

Outside London, Birmingham and Bradford there is as yet no evidence that any such organizations are taking shape. The other main areas affected by immigration – such as Bristol and Nottingham – are at present free from such activity. Yet it can only be a matter of time before the S.R.A., the Birmingham Immigration Control Association, Mr Smith of Bradford and their ilk come together and form a national organization. From the evidence available in the two areas, the political significance of such an organization would be enormous.

The common features of the organizations which already exist and of their history reveal the potential danger. They are formed in the main by middle-class people whose political activity without the immigrant issue would be confined to the ballot box and the occasional letter to the local Press. Out of their new organizations they derive great power and prestige. The objective of the organizations is simple – to keep out the immigrants. They are not in the least concerned with the easy assimilation of immigrants already here. Further, the slightest sign of friendliness or cooperation with the immigrants themselves will, for the public and the reservoir of potential support, blur the line between the control organization and the committees formed in most immigrant areas to combat racialism and help the immigrants. Thus suggestions of cooperation from within the control organization are ruthlessly resisted, and all propaganda is directed against the immigrant and the immigration process. Such propaganda inevitably slips, even if inadvertently, into racialism, and is enormously assisted, not by the Fascist and extremist *parties* themselves, but by their insidious *ideas*.

The effect of such organizations on the attitudes of voters and politicians is furthered by the simplicity of their propaganda. The scapegoat which they select for the problems of working-class people – in housing, health, education, wages – is obvious to all. He is black, he is strange, above all he is there for everyone to see. He is not some intangible 'government' or 'council' or civil servant. He is someone close at hand upon whom it is easy to vent bitterness and anger.

There is always some evidence, however slight, for what is presented as the general truth. It is possible – has always been in any community anywhere – to find immigrant dope-pedlars, immigrant brothel-keepers, immigrant criminals, immigrants who jump the housing queue through redevelopment. The propaganda of both the non-party anti-immigrant organizations and the extremist right-wing parties usually singles out one such example and erects it into an absolute.

The very nature of the parliamentary structure, moreover, makes politicians highly sensitive to organized propaganda in their areas. However principled these politicians may be, their principles are often rationalized away by the allurement of power. 'If I cannot get in, I can do nothing' is a typical argument of a politician who gives way against his better judgement before the pressure of an anti-immigrant organization. If the politician's party vacillates on the issue, leaving it to 'local initiative', the politician's tendency to collapse is facilitated.

Yet the anti-immigrant organizations have deep, inherent weaknesses. They are riven by factions and Fuehrer complexes. Every decision is watched closely, for its effect not only on the organization but also on the standing of each individual leader. There is the attraction of the extremist parties with their strange rituals and organized, dedicated following. Above all, there is the embarrassment which so many people feel when faced with anti-immigrant propaganda. Where there is no opposition, where the organization is allowed to sort out its factions and ride roughshod over the general embarrassment caused by its policy, it will grow in influence and power. That is why local organizations dedicated to multi-racial harmony are crucially important.

10. 'Multi-Racial' Organizations

Bowing under the weight of Labour pressure, the Home Secretary, Mr R. A. Butler, established a Commonwealth Immigrants Advisory Council shortly after the Immigration Act was passed in 1962. This was the first Government organization set up to deal exclusively with the problems created by immigration, and it was an unpaid part-time body, which 'advised' the Home Secretary on actions which would be helpful to the immigrants and their neighbours. In its first report, issued almost a year after its establishment, the council came to the conclusion that:

We do not wish to recommend any legislation giving new powers to local authorities. We have been assured that our efforts would not be assisted by the granting of new powers.

In that first report the council dealt with housing and in its further two reports – of February 1964 and September 1964 – with education and employment. In its second report it suggested that some coordination of the areas where immigrants were settled was necessary, and so, finally, some fourteen years after significant immigration began, a National Committee for Commonwealth Immigration was set up, on a non-official basis, to direct liaison and coordination work.

The National Committee consisted of assorted worthies who had shown an interest in immigration, but a full-time advisory officer was appointed – Miss Nadine Peppard. Miss Peppard had been working for seven years with the London Council for Social Service, spending half of her time exclusively with immigrant problems. She probably knew more about the various social problems involved in trying to settle West Indians, Indians and Pakistanis than anyone else in the country.

Miss Peppard took over the job on 1 April 1964, nearly two years after the Advisory Council's formation, and immediately applied her mind to the various multi-racial coordinating committees scattered throughout the country. As a founder member of the Willesden International Friendship Council, she had some idea of the importance and value of such committees, and her aim was to coordinate the existing committees, while establishing new ones on an intelligent basis.

The situation which Miss Peppard found was appalling. There were only fifteen such committees – two of them large regional committees (the London C.S.S. and the West Midlands Commonwealth Welfare Council) – and of these only eight had been formed in the fifties. Only four received any regular financial contribution from the local authority. All the others depended on voluntary contributions and fund-raising activity. Only one – the Southall International Friendship Committee – could rely on funds from trade unions. Only four of the committee executives met as often as once a month. In a couple of cases, they met only once a year. Above all the distribution of the committees was quite arbitrary. In Bristol, a city with an estimated 6,000 immigrants, there was no effective committee, while in Hayes and Harlington where there were no more than 300 Indians and Pakistanis, a Friendship Council had been formed the year before. Between these various councils and committees, all with different names and purposes, there was no coordination and little communication. The whole was a mere skeleton for some national coordinating organization, but with all its bones disconnected and deformed. It was a creature of twelve years' Conservative *laissez-faire*.

Miss Peppard toured the country encouraging local authorities and other interested parties to set up more committees and strengthen the ones which already existed. In a single year she assisted with the formation of committees in Gravesend, Halifax, Bradford, West Yorkshire, Keighley, Croydon, Leicester, Oxford, Slough, Southwark, Camden, Wolverhampton and Smethwick. By the end of that first year, thirteen of the committees, compared with only five before she took over, were staffed by full-time officers, financed either by the local authority or the Council of Social Service. Then, in April 1965, Miss Peppard called representatives of the thirty-one committees to London for the first centrally-organized conference of local committees dealing with immigration problems. She had every reason to look back on her year's work with some pleasure. There were still great gaps where no organization existed; Sheffield, Bristol and Ipswich were obvious, serious examples, as were some of the more heavily affected Midland towns such as West Bromwich, Walsall and Dudley. Still, the fact that so much had been done in one year demonstrated not so much Miss Peppard's own devotion to her job, as the potential which could have been realized many years previously had the Government stirred itself out of its cynical indifference.

These coordinating committees and Friendship Councils have three main tasks. They must find out about the immigrants in their area. What type of people are they? What habits most annoy or please their new neighbours? How many of them are there, and in what areas? Surveys promoted by such councils have produced valuable information on local immigrant problems unrevealed by the sketchy national surveys, and, generally, disregarded by the Government. In the survey which the Willesden I.F.C. conducted after the council's formation in 1959, it was found, for instance, that ten per cent of the indigenous Willesden population were highly prejudiced. As a result the I.F.C. set out to lessen the political and social effect of this ten per cent, isolating them and exposing their propaganda for what it was. They organized a number of interviews with those belonging to this ten per cent to see whether some form of psychological pattern could be established among them.

The second main area of activity is welfare – helping the immigrants with problems of sanitation and hygiene, of living and language. The Southall I.F.C., for instance, has for several years run informal English classes for women who cannot get to the official ones, and in Paddington the Overseas Students and Workers Committee runs a mothers' club where lessons are given, in an informal way, on how to run a house in British conditions. The Nottingham Commonwealth Citizens Consultative Committee, one of the oldest and probably the most successful, sponsors a Housing Association for immigrants, as does the Leeds International Council. In Willesden, in Hackney and in Wood Green, the committees have produced leaflets describing public facilities in the area, and explaining the process of buying a house, while the Commonwealth Welfare Council for the West Midlands produces safety-in-the-home leaflets in Urdu and Bengali.

Quite apart from these outward signs of welfare, many of the committee officials do invaluable work in simply visiting homes, explaining, helping, sorting out arguments with neighbours and the like. The most 'difficult' people to integrate are the Indian and Pakistani women, many of whom do not dare even to leave their cramped homes for fear of losing their way. These are the people whom the racialist propagandists describe as 'not wanting to integrate'. The local multi-racial committees have found, however, that overt friendliness and assistance from the community makes a substantial difference to the attitudes of these women.

The third field of activity is loosely described as 'community and race relations', with the objective to demonstrate publicly and successfully that common activity outside factories and mills between white and black people, between Asians and Europeans, is possible, productive and pleasant. The main stumbling block to success in such ventures is the 'tea and buns' approach. All too often, a local authority or Church group decides to sponsor a multi-racial committee, and provides a hall for the purpose. There is an opening party. Invitations are sent out to all known West Indians or to all the 'Singhs' on the electoral roll. The Mayor attends, together with other civic dignitaries, as do a band of West Indian students and a few middle-class Indians. There are a couple of speeches, a few cups of tea, everyone applauds and goes home, and soon afterwards the project collapses. On the other hand, many organizations, particularly the Willesden one which in the early 1960s made all the running in these matters, have established successful youth clubs and organized well-attended social occasions. Both the social clubs in Willesden – the International Social Club and the International Unity Association – thrived in the early sixties, though both subsequently waned. Their secret was, most probably, that much of the initiative in organizing the club activities was left to the members themselves.

The executive members of the Willesden I.F.C. in 1960–61 applied their minds to the whole issue of integration. Forming clubs was clearly no more than a first move. What mattered was to discover an area of activity which was in itself 'integrated' and enjoyed by everyone who took part. Drama groups, which were tried, appeared likely to succeed with West Indians. Sport seemed an obviously integrated field of activity.

Willesden's own particularly brilliant contribution was the formation of a Jazz Ballet Group in 1961. From a gathering of seven dancers in Cricklewood, the group has risen to considerable fame and success. According to a former president of the I.F.C., now M.P. for Willesden East, Mr Reginald Freeson, 'The people regard themselves as a jazz ballet group – not in the least as an essay in good race relations.'

The political role of these organizations has, until recently, been strictly non-party and non-sectarian. Although Freeson was always associated with the Labour Party, he insisted that the Friendship Council in Willesden should include Conservatives, Liberals and Communists. In Southall, where the council sprang from the trade-union movement, employers are welcomed on the committee. The instance of Smethwick in 1962 and 1963 where Mr Peter Griffiths led the Conservative councillors in opposing grants to the regional committee and refusing to be associated with the town's multi-racial committee is an exception. In almost every case the local Tories have associated themselves with the committees, and, as in Southall, taken an active part in projects to further integration.

What changed in this respect during the last months of 1964 was the increasing militancy – corresponding to the increase in discrimination and incitement – of various groups throughout the country opposed to racial prejudice. The growth of the American civil rights movement has inspired people to 'direct action' projects which have often shocked the dignified worthies on the multi-racial committees. One example of the difficulties experienced by the committees exists in Leicester where there are strong differences of opinion between the Council for Social Service – a 'respectable', multi-racial committee – and the militant Campaign for Racial Equality.

The comparatively peaceful, hard-working life of the committees has been shattered by this new blast of militancy. As in all political organizations, considerable hostility can arise between those vigorously, if carefully, pursuing the work of persuasion, and those demanding militant action to expose the racialist pub-owner or restaurateur.

These theoretical differences – ironically similar to the 'political' disputes which so often split the immigration control organizations – came to a head early in 1965 with the formation of C.A.R.D., the National Committee Against Racial Discrimination. C.A.R.D. was established explicitly as a political body, to expose cases of discrimination and to demand political action to cope with them. The gathering of information, welfare, practical inter-racial activity appear nowhere on C.A.R.D.'s agenda.

Only one of the thirty coordinating committees accordingly affiliated to C.A.R.D. – the Willesden I.F.C. – as a result of increasing militancy in the W.I.F.C. itself. Mr Oswald Murray, the liaison officer employed by Willesden Borough Council, had written in an article shortly before affiliation that the 'educated' immigrants of Britain associated themselves with the civil rights struggle in America – a highly questionable proposition, particularly as it referred to Indians and Pakistanis as well as to West Indians. Although one or two committees could not make up their minds, the overwhelming view among the committee members was that, while in most cases they approved of C.A.R.D.'s activities, their role was totally different and likely to be weakened by affiliation with so obviously militant a body.

The truth is that there is room for two entirely separate organizations, and that a merger can only lead to a general depression in activity. At Leicester, for instance, the 'respectable' committee exists side by side with a militant Campaign Committee and it is possible to be a member of both. The same man can 'sit down' in a pub as a member of C.A.R.D., and slog round on a 'noisy party conciliation committee' as a member of his local Friendship Association. He damages both organizations if he insists on a merger between the two. There are a number of people in this country prepared to engage in constructive 'multi-racial' activity, who do not want to be associated in any way with political moves against discrimination and nothing is gained by driving them away.

The considerable success achieved by the multi-racial groups in removing a great deal of prejudice *and* discrimination should deter those who talk as though the immigrant problem in Britain is already indistinguishable from the racial situation in the United States. It is emphatically *not* the case in Britain, as it is in the U.S.A., that militant non-violent action is the only effective route to progress.

Despite their essentially non-party approach, these thirty committees do have, and have had, considerable political effect. Through their non-party approach, they encompass the Conservative Party, and local Conservatives, anxious to win votes through anti-immigrant propaganda, are faced with the alternative either of refusing an invitation to join a multi-racial organization, as did Peter Griffiths at Smethwick, or of joining and keeping silence. Where effective local committees flourish it is extremely difficult for the local Conservatives to beat the racial drum. It is no accident that when the Smethwick Tories proposed a Council of Social Service, one of whose functions would be to help immigrants, the most militant campaigners against immigration, including Councillor Finney, refused against the majority of their Party associates to support the move. Furthermore, these committees provide a vital counterweight to anti-immigrant propaganda. The areas where anti-immigrant organizations have the greatest effect are those without multi-racial committees. The Birmingham Co-ordinating Committee against Racial Discrimination is no more than a militant anti-discrimination body, representing in the main the Churches and the Left. Similarly the city's committee for work among commonwealth immigrants is poorly financed and only meets once every two months. The way, to a large extent, is left open for the Immigration Control Associations.

Similarly in London, the Fascists and their friends steer clear of areas where these committees flourish. Right-wing extremists thrive in Brixton, Islington, St Pancras and Ealing, but they seldom do well in Willesden, Wood Green and Hackney. This is largely, though not of course solely, because local committees flourish in these latter areas, and are almost non-existent in the former ones.

In Southall a powerful anti-immigrant organization lines up against an excellent multi-racial committee. The Residents' Association and the British National Party make a great deal of headway in the town, but they can never shake off the pursuit of the Friendship Council. Every violent letter that gets into the Press is always coolly, reasonably answered. The Southall Friendship Council, unfortunately, started too late, but it does much to blunt the edge of the S.R.A. Its trade-union basis is its greatest asset. It is no accident that the first effective strike in a British factory dominated by Asian workers took place at a Southall rubber firm in November 1964. Without the Friendship Council, race relations in Southall would be much worse than they are.

Despite the riots there in 1958, Nottingham has one of the best race relations records in Britain. It was one of the first cities where a multi-racial committee was set up – in 1958 – and, alone among British cities, it acquired an atmosphere friendly enough to allow the appointment of a West Indian magistrate. Much of the credit for this situation must go to the Nottingham Commonwealth Citizens Advisory Committee.

The multi-racial committees affect British politics in three major respects. They associate all three main political parties with multi-racialism, and therefore deter any official candidate from grubbing around for racist votes. They make anti-immigrant propaganda less acceptable by helping the immigrant in simple matters of welfare and living habits. They provide an effective counterweight to the propaganda of Fascists and anti-immigrant organizations. For these three reasons their existence, strength and growth are indispensable.

11. Conclusions

Dr E. S. Bogardus of the University of South California has devised a 'race relations cycle' of reactions to immigration by the host community. The cycle emerges from the University's studies of reactions to Mexican, Filipino, Chinese and Japanese immigration into California, and the stages, whose headings are self-explanatory, are as follows: (1) curiosity; (2) economic welcome; (3) industrial and social antagonism; (4) legislative antagonism; (5) fair-play tendencies; (6) quiescence; and (7) second-generation difficulties.

The 'Bogardus cycle' is helpful to the British experience without exactly fitting it. The stages hardly correspond with the immigration of Jews (little economic welcome and few second-generation difficulties) or Irish (no legislative antagonism). Yet in both instances initial antagonisms have faded into quiescence. The first four stages (curiosity, economic welcome, social and legislative antagonism) fit the process of Commonwealth immigration exactly. Unhappily, however, there is less sign of 'quiescence' after fifteen years of Commonwealth immigration than there was after fifteen years of Irish or Jewish immigration. All the signs point gloomily towards increased antagonism.

The first reason for this is colour. The similarities in the reactions to Jews, Irish and coloured Commonwealth citizens over the first sixty-five years of the twentieth century are worth stressing over and over again. They show that anti-immigrant propaganda on grounds of inherent propensity to disease, crime, dirt and immorality has been proved nonsense: they show that, once the immigrants break out of housing squalor and second-class citizenship, they are no more dirty or diseased than their 'hosts'. Yet there are several signs that reactions to coloured immigration in Britain are qualitatively different.

Many British race experts, including Mrs Sheila Patterson, who lived for five years in Brixton during the early years of immigration while writing her excellent book, *Dark Strangers*, dismiss the colour element as comparatively irrelevant. Mrs Patterson feels that the problems are those of immigration, not of colour; that, as in the case of the Jews and the Irish, the odds are heavily on assimilation, at any rate for the West Indians, within two or three generations.

There are, however, various disturbing trends which indicate that colour is crucially relevant. Resentment against the Irish and the Jews was based to a large extent on insecurity about employment. The practice frequently followed by employers of recruiting labour abroad specifically to break strikes or embryonic trade-union organizations naturally infuriated the working class, to whom the Irish or the Jews or the Dutch appeared a further threat to jobs already jeopardized by recurrent slumps. Much of the rioting and discrimination against immigrants before the last war are directly attributable to job insecurity.

Today there is little such insecurity. Only in the depth of a recession, in underemployed regions like Scotland or the North-East, do British workers find themselves on the defensive, fighting to retain jobs, conditions and wages already won. In the areas to which the immigrants have been attracted, jobs are assumed. Thus, this enormous area of potential resentment has been removed by the relatively stable economics of post-war capitalism. Of course, the shortage of social services still exists, as it always has done, to excite prejudice. But the new job security should, on any reckoning, have lessened the incidence of prejudice by a considerable margin. Unhappily there is little evidence that this has taken place.

Current resentment and propaganda is directed almost exclusively against the *coloured* immigrant. At the Conservative Party conference of 1961, Mr R. A. Butler disclosed that some 50,000 immigrants had entered Britain since 1954 from the 'white' Commonwealth, from Australia, New Zealand, Canada, and, at that time, South Africa. He had to admit that the figure was very vague, since the Home Office, interestingly enough, had only made estimates for coloured immigration figures. There is, however, no evidence at all of any resentment against these white Commonwealth immigrants. During the years 1954–64, some 160,000 white alien immigrants have entered Britain to stay, and immigration from Ireland has averaged some 40,000 a year. Yet except in areas such as Bedford, which has received a large complement of Italians to work in the town's brickworks, there has been no hostility towards aliens comparable with that shown towards coloured immigrants.

The figures for immigration since the Act came into force are even more significant. As the numbers of coloured immigrants have been kept down, in 1963 and 1964, so the figures for immigration from the white Commonwealth, from Ireland and from Western Europe have risen sharply. Yet in spite of this rapid increase since the Act, in white immigrant workers, many of them as unskilled as the coloured immigrant workers, all the propaganda has been directed against *coloured* immigration. When Mr Peter Thorneycroft calls for a drastic reduction in immigration, he does not mean cuts in alien or white immigration. He and the propagandists behind him do not want to antagonize employers in London and the Midlands by denying them a free flow of workers. They want to keep Commonwealth immigrants out because most of these are black.

Mr Norman Pannell, reviving after his 1964 electoral defeat in Liverpool by more than 4,000 votes, has summed up this attitude crudely:

They [the Jews, Irish, Huguenots, etc. . . .] have been able to adapt themselves to the British social pattern and have gained full acceptance in the community because, to put it baldly, their skins are white.*

In comparing the long-term effects of Irish and Jewish with coloured immigration, we cannot escape the experience of the United States. There several million Irishmen and Jews have been assimilated. Yet 20 million Negroes, their ancestors shipped to the country by slavers, are still living in ghettoes as second-class citizens, despite civil rights legislation and Human Rights Commissions far more forceful than anything the British have yet devised. The tendency of anti-immigrant propaganda over the last three years indicates that colour is establishing itself as a crucial feature of British politics.

The reasons are not hard to find. Colour identifies an immigrant far more clearly than an Irish accent or a foreign language. Coloured immigrants cannot mix silently in a crowd and lose their

* *Immigration: What is the Answer?*, Routledge and Kegan Paul, London, 1965.

identity. They are conspicuous scapegoats for the frustrations and fears of their neighbours.

Further, they are symbols to the British not only of strangeness but also of failure. Throughout industrial history the British workers have been comforted with the grandeur of their imperial destiny. Their anger and bitterness at unemployment, illiteracy and poverty were assiduously drugged with stories of conquest in foreign lands. The subjects of this conquest were coloured. All great men, they were led to believe, were white men, and all uncivilized, weak, backward peoples were black. The long, grisly process of imperialism was inextricably intertwined with colour. Political independence for the colonial countries was cruel enough for those imaginations nourished on their country's singular glory, and the stream of former subjects into the Mother Country as equals before the law and the Welfare State was a final insult. As Donald Finney put it in the *Smethwick Telephone*: 'They fought for their freedom, and we should not deny them the right to go and enjoy it.'

The magic with which Joseph Chamberlain had bewitched the Midlands working class into Conservatism has been inherited, in another guise but with even more dangerous consequences, by his Conservative successors.

Despite the crucial relevance of colour, however, the process of Commonwealth immigration into Britain could well have been accepted by the British people were it not for the second factor which has arisen to obstruct the Bogardus cycle and prevent 'quiescence': the exploitation of the immigration issue for party political advantage.

On no other issue are the attitudes struck by politicians more crucial. In the choice of economic priorities, the level of social services, the character of defence, the politicians play a minor role. The big decisions are made for them by civil servants, managing directors and the international rate of exchange. So irrational is race and colour propaganda that its exploitation by politicians has an effect proportionately far wider than political propaganda on other matters. The available evidence from all over the world suggests that nothing is more dangerous than such exploitation. Even conditions of substantial unemployment and poverty, though capable of provoking race resentment and antagonism, are unlikely to do as much permanent damage to race relations as the ignorant, prejudiced rantings of unscrupulous politicians. In Brazil, where tens of millions live in appalling poverty, race is not yet a major political issue, despite the number of races and colours which comprise the population. In next-door British Guiana, on the other hand, racial divisions, ruthlessly exploited by politicians for party advantage, corrode the entire society.

More relevant still is the racial situation in the United States. The persecution of the Southern Negroes is not, as commonly supposed, merely a historical hangover from slavery. After the Civil War had smashed the structure of Southern slavery, equal rights were granted to the Negroes who mixed freely with whites in restaurants, law courts and legislatures, to a degree unmatched, indeed, even in the traditional home of abolitionism – New England. The 'white supremacists' were reduced to an impotent rump, and many 'poor whites' joined with Negroes under the flag of Populism, which political philosophy rejected all forms of discrimination and racialism.

Conservative politicians from both Republican and Democratic Parties were terrified by this new, revolutionary political alliance. Spurred on by the silence of the Northern liberals, who were for economic reasons anxious to achieve a reconciliation with traditional white power in the South, they unleashed a stream of racist propaganda and succeeded in turning the poor white into the most savage enemy of the Negro. Using techniques like the 'white primary' and the poll tax, they effectively robbed the Negro of his voting rights and his equality, till the period of racial cooperation disappeared from memory altogether. Yet it was not the 'inherent racialism' of the poor whites which inspired the anti-Negro movement. On the contrary, left to themselves they might well have forged an indissoluble association between white and black Americans. It was conservative racist propaganda from the politicians of the traditional ruling class with the connivance of the liberal opposition in the North, which created segregation as it is known today in the Southern States.

Commonwealth immigrants in Britain, before they became playthings of party politics, and despite a total lack of Government concern or planning, were greeted with general friendliness and hospitality. Of course there was a colour bar in some pubs. Of course there was antagonism in some factories and bus garages. But these were exceptions. Overall the reaction was kind, even helpful. A considerate and coordinated effort by politicians to assist assimilation, to isolate and punish the racialist minority would have been decisive.

Instead there has since 1962 been a steady, consistent retreat on the issue by politicians of all major parties towards the views of their right-wing extremists. Indeed, during the six months in which this short account has been written, the situation has deteriorated dramatically. Crude anti-immigrant statements, which before the General Election of 1964 would have provoked an outcry of indignation from Labour politicians and liberal newspapers, are commonly accepted on the bogus pretext of 'realism'. This process has been remarkably sudden. For no intellectual or economic reason, leading politicians are cheerfully giving voice to sentiments which they themselves, only six months previously, would have dismissed as reactionary and dangerous. It is like some fearful auction, with the Conservatives relentlessly raising the racialist bids, and the Labour and Liberal Parties fruitlessly trying to secure the lot on the same terms. Ironically, none of this might have happened had Labour lost the 1964 Election. Anger and militancy on the race issue from Labour in opposition could well have kept the Tory militants in check. Unhappily for British race relations Labour in power and Labour in opposition are totally different political phenomena.

In March 1965 a group of young Labour M.P.s, led by Mr Roy Hattersley and Mr Ivor Richard (Barons Court) attempted to 'take immigration out of party politics'. A permanent all-party committee was set up under the chairmanship of a Conservative – Sir Godfrey Nicholson – to discuss immigration and to persuade as many people as possible not to raise the matter for party advantage. But only a few Tories have associated themselves with this move, and the move itself was sharply rebuked by that redoubtable anti-immigration campaigner, Mr Harold Gurden. In a revealing letter to the *Daily Telegraph* on 18 March, Mr Gurden wrote:

You report that an all-party committee is to be set up for a bipartisan approach to the immigration problem.

In fact there is no more than a mere handful of Conservatives so willing to oblige the Socialists. One has only to read the past debates on immigration to see that this must be a political move by the Socialists to avoid disadvantage at the next General Election.

It will be interesting to see if these Conservatives attack the problem of over-concentration. Dispersal of immigrants into their own constituencies would be a real contribution.

The case for taking immigration out of party politics rests on the hope that the men who are making a party issue of it will leave the matter alone. Obviously, however, Mr Gurden and his friends will not be influenced to drop the immigration issue by a plea for 'contracting out' from the Labour and Liberal back benches. The plain fact is that the attempt to remove the immigration issue from party politics is an act of political funk. It stems from the fear of attacking the Tory anti-immigrant lobby in a forthright and principled way. And it has the added disadvantage of futility.

I have referred in this book to the 'knife edge' of race relations in Britain. In the predominantly working-class areas where the immigrants have settled they have encountered two contradictory reactions – on the one hand decency, hospitality and solidarity; on the other, resentment and xenophobia. Politics can drive the knife home or remove its menace. Political propaganda which proclaims the criminal habits, promiscuity or disease of the immigrants can stampede the ignorant and fearful into permanent bitterness and hatred, while sustained political activity to educate and integrate can lead to permanent understanding. All that has happened since the Smethwick result of October 1964 indicates that the former course has been taken, for the basest of party political motives – and has continued almost unopposed. No one can underestimate the danger of that choice. The tiger of racialism, once unleashed, knows no master. It devours its liberators and its prey with equal ferocity.

In spite of the racial landslide to the right, there are, however, several structural safeguards in the British situation which hold out some hope for the development of a peaceful multi-racial society. The first is citizenship. Commonwealth immigrants, unlike aliens, are automatically enfranchised and automatically enjoy equal privileges before the law and the welfare state. No leading politician has yet dared to suggest that these rights should be removed or diminished. Sir Alec Douglas Home and other Conservative leaders have repeatedly stressed that immigrants should be treated 'like everyone else'. Largely as a result of this equal citizenship, there are few signs of a racial situation such as the one which plagues the North of the United States. The talk about housing ghettoes, for instance, is grossly exaggerated. There is nothing in any of the British 'ghettoes', except possibly Listerhills in Bradford and Moss Side in Manchester, comparable with the ghettoes of New York or Chicago. The crucial difference is that the British ghettoes are not 'closed'. Stepney in East London and Chapletown in Leeds have, in the past, served as ghettoes for Jewish immigrants just as today they house thousands of coloured Commonwealth ones.

If the Commonwealth immigrants manage to break out of the ghettoes, they will stand a good chance of surmounting the most stubborn obstacle to their progress – their class inferiority. What hampers them more than any other single disability is their formation into a sub-proletariat, working in jobs at the bottom of the wage scale, without proper trade-union organization, in appalling conditions for long hours of overtime. As a sub-proletariat, they incur the worst forms of snobbery from their neighbours. When the Aga Khan lives in Britain, he doubtless finds his neighbours courteous and helpful. But the Pakistani mill-worker is regarded as the *cause*, not the effect, of the inevitable drop in the street's property values. The rights of citizenship and the generally progressive attitude of most trade-union leaders offers some hope that the Commonwealth immigrant can break out of his ghetto and climb from the lowest rung on the social ladder.

None of this is possible, however, unless the politicians act fast to remedy the dangerous situation that they have themselves been largely responsible for creating.

The first priority for political action is to get hold of the proper and essential information about immigrants in Britain. In an article on Pakistani wives in Bradford, Miss Zaynab Dahya has written that:

In Britain it is widely but erroneously believed that Pakistanis speak Urdu, but in fact it has no roots in any popular form of Pakistani speech

Urdu, as any immigrant will tell you, is a *Kitabi boli* (i.e. literary language) and is not part of their folk culture.
April, 1965   *Race*

Yet for some ten years of Indian and Pakistani immigration, enthusiastic election candidates have been distributing election addresses in Urdu, while local authorities have been erecting street notices in Urdu, and even instructing teachers in Urdu and Bengali. The trouble is, apparently, that most Pakistani and Indian immigrants understand these languages no better than native Bradfordians do.

This and many other absurdities arise from ignorance: ignorance about the history, culture and living habits of the immigrants; ignorance even about the numbers actually in Britain, the work they do, the lives they lead, the way they vote. Significantly, the only real effort to find out more about such matters is being made by the Institute of Race Relations in a five-year survey, financed entirely by the Nuffield Foundation. The British Government has left research on a problem which threatens to undermine the entire social structure to the initiative of a philanthropic foundation.

If the politicians had the necessary facts, they could then mount an effective propaganda counter-attack against the dark myths of racialism, and, above all, their implications. Very few people in Britain today will openly admit to being racialist or colour-prejudiced. Yet while the *statement* that a man's rights and treatment should not in any way be affected by his colour or his racial origin commands general respect, the *fact* of such discrimination is widely tolerated. Thus 'it is not a colour bar' to refuse the sale of houses to coloured people; or, as at Smethwick, to build a block of council flats for sale to whites only. 'It is not a colour bar', as at Mildenhall, to turn down a London overspill plan on the grounds that coloured workers are involved or to insist on no further employment of coloured workers. Yet, as long as the English language means anything, all these actions involve and promote a colour bar.

The text of political propagandists on this issue could well be drawn from the celebrated U.N.E.S.C.O. conference on the scientific and social aspects of race. Time and again such conferences have found no scientific justification for a belief in the inherent differences between races, and have dismissed the views of racialists as intellectual fantasy. Such judgements, subscribed by some of the world's greatest scientists and biologists, are not just words. When Sir Cyril Osborne talks about a 'white man's country', when Mr Angus Maude says it is 'reasonable' for white people to want to stay white, when Mr Peter Griffiths supports a plan to sell houses to white people only (without corresponding arrangements for black people), they are reflecting that colour prejudice which U.N.E.S.C.O. has exposed as without any rational foundation.

Even from the statistics at present available, it is possible to nail many of the lies currently circulated about Commonwealth immigrants. Time and again Home Office spokesmen in the House of Commons have denied that immigrants are more prone to crime or ill-health than the rest of the community. Although Mr Norman Pannell has, after long research, produced figures which show a higher incidence of certain types of crime (living off immoral earnings, dope-peddling) among immigrants, it is hard to find a Chief Constable in Britain who will blame immigrants in his area for a disproportionate amount of crime. Under the Immigration Act, the courts have power, subject to ratification by the Home Secretary, to deport convicted immigrant criminals. The figures for deportation, since the Act was passed in June 1962 to May 1965, are as follows:

Irish	452
West Indians	193
Maltese	28
Cypriots	18
Canadians	10
Pakistanis	9
Indians	6

One wonders whether Mr Pannell would draw from those figures the conclusion that Canadian immigration is more dangerous to a law-abiding Britain than Indian or Pakistani immigration, or that it is seventy-five times more important to stop immigration from Ireland than it is to stop it from India.

What of the other allegations that are made against the coloured immigrants: that they are diseased, dirty, cheap labour, that they sponge off the National Assistance, get council houses before their turn and are mainly responsible for the housing shortage?

Tuberculosis and venereal disease are the two immigrant ill-nesses most popular with the anti-immigrant propagandists. The tuberculosis rate among West Indians and the venereal disease rate among Asians are no higher than the indigenous British rates. But it is true that the Asian tuberculosis rate is much higher than the U.K. national average (although the national average is ex-tremely low), and this is due in the main to lack of acquired physical resistance in Asians. They come from countries where poor diets and near-starvation are the norm. Bad housing con-ditions, hard manual labour with many hours of overtime, and in-adequate food in British weather conditions do the rest. Similarly, the venereal disease rate is higher among West Indians, who, with their free-and-easy attitude towards sex, are less inhibited about prostitutes than the indigenous population. Both problems are largely relieved when the immigrant males are joined by their families. In her deeply disturbing description of housing conditions around Notting Dale*, Miss Pearl Jephcott pays tribute to the general cleanliness, against appalling odds, of the immigrant housewives. The answer to immigrant health prob-lems lies in better housing conditions, more health inspection and hospitalization, greater encouragement, and facilities for families to join their husbands.

There is not the slightest evidence that immigrants come to Britain to live off National Assistance. On the contrary, as was made clear in Smethwick, their reaction to unemployment is to move to other places where jobs are available, often without col-lecting unemployment pay or National Assistance benefits. This labour mobility is of considerable value to an economy plagued by the understandable reluctance of workers to leave their homes. In boom years, like 1964, more than ninety-eight per cent of immi-grant workers are employed, and even in periods of recession more than nine out of ten hang on to their jobs. They come to Britain for one purpose only – to work as hard as possible and to make the maximum amount of money.

Not content with castigating immigrants as slackers, their enemies accuse them next of providing a fund of cheap labour which lowers the standards of the indigenous working class. This

* *A Troubled Area*, Faber & Faber, London, 1964.

curious argument, of course, altogether ignores the fact that immigration into industry has been going on for two hundred years. Sometimes the immigration has been from countryside to town, sometimes from country to country. Always the recent immigrants have been prepared to work for less than the workers they joined. The opposition to the cheap labour of immigrants today would have applied just as well to the immigration of workers from the countryside to the town at the very beginning of the industrial revolution. The 'control' addicts of that era were anxious to halt the whole process of industrialization.

Those trade unionists who argue that the immigrants are damaging working-class interests should look more closely at their movement's inability to organize the majority of British workers. The question of cheap labour does not arise in the transport services, engineering shops and mills where the immigrant workers are organized into the relevant trade unions and join in the struggle for better working conditions. If the trade-union movement could organize those areas of British employment which have never seen a trade-union official, it would itself eliminate some of the worst exploitation of immigrants in the smaller factories and workshops. It is hardly for the trade unions to complain if the immigrants gravitate to unorganized factories. It is the business of the unions to welcome and help them wherever possible – on the single condition that they join a trade union and work for union rates and conditions.

The attack by some Conservative politicians and right-wing extremists on cheap labour – a subject in which they take little interest outside of the immigration issue – is interesting in view of the fact that the British economy depends to a significant degree on the cheap labour of women. The average industrial wage of women workers is half that of male ones, and those disturbed about cheap labour could well direct their attention to the low wages of some 8 million women workers. But this, of course, is of little concern to the protectors of the British working class in the anti-immigrant lobby.

Perhaps the most vicious of all the arguments used by the anti-immigrant propagandists holds that immigration is responsible in some way for the housing shortage. The Milner Holland Report on London housing is quite specific on this point. Though it found terrible housing conditions among immigrants, and although twenty-seven per cent of landlords interviewed admitted to imposing a colour bar, the report declared that immigrants in London were economically inevitable, and that they were in no way responsible for the housing shortage.

Housing conditions in Britain are, and always have been, a social disgrace. The Milner Holland Report found a million people in London alone living in sub-standard housing conditions. There are a number of reasons for this situation, not least of which is the bad or haphazard distribution of resources, both within and outside the building industry, and an unplanned industrial location policy which packs people from all over Britain into already congested industrially favoured areas.

Almost all of the immigrants are working; almost all of them are contributing taxes and rates towards the general fund from which council houses are built. Many of them are working in the building industry, actually constructing the houses for whose shortage they are blamed. The others are filling crucial labour gaps, which, if left alone, could damage the general economic effort, and so, inevitably, the housing one. To suggest that the immigrants *cause* the housing shortage is patent nonsense. Some of the worst housing in Britain is in the city of Glasgow, which has *lost* population over the last decade. If the leaders of the anti-immigrant lobby want to check their theories against reality they should take a walk through the streets of Bridgeton, Anderston or Townhead in Glasgow. They will not find more than a handful of coloured immigrants, but housing conditions among the worst in industrial Europe.

More people have left Britain since the war than have arrived to settle in the country. In 1964 emigration, indeed, increased by twenty-five per cent on the previous year. And these emigrants are leaving houses behind them. Of course many are middle class, and the immigrants pushed into the lowest echelons of the working class cannot afford their houses. This is the consequence of the class system which the leading opponents of immigration have themselves fought hard to sustain.

The available economic evidence suggests that population growth increases not only the overall national income, but also income per head. Such evidence can easily be found in the comparative experiences of Germany, Japan, the United States and particularly of Britain, where shortage of labour has accentuated the stop-go economic cycle since the end of the war. Those who seek to show that large-scale immigration is an economic burden should bear in mind not only this, but also other facts which show that the immigrants enjoy less than their proportionate share of the extra wealth which they make possible.

The Immigrant In-put

(1) Because most immigrants arrive in Britain as adults, they spend a larger proportion of their lives in employment there than do the indigenous people.

(2) Because some of them (in fact a large number) are unaccompanied by their dependants, at any rate for a significant period, a higher proportion of immigrants than of the indigenous population is economically productive.

(3) The immigrants not only pay their due share of progressive taxation, like income tax, but also of purchase tax, excise duties, insurance contributions and rates, taxes which bear most heavily on the poor. They can also, as a body, point to the extra receipts from company taxation which derive directly from the higher rate of industrial expansion caused by their contribution to the supply of labour.

(4) Because of residential qualifications, the immigrants are allotted a less than proportionate share of subsidized council housing, and have therefore to depend on a more than proportionate share of private housing. Thus they probably bear more than the 'proper' economic cost of the appalling housing conditions in which they are forced to live.

The Immigrant Out-take

(1) Even when the children of immigrants arrive, they take a considerable time to work their way to secondary education, and to this extent immigrants are paying disproportionately for the education services, especially the more expensive ones. Because of language difficulties a whole generation may be penalized, its already relatively small share of the more advanced educational services even further reduced.

(2) As long as immigration continues, the ratio of contributions for old-age pensions to benefits received among the immigrant community must always tend to be higher than among the indigenous population.

(3) The extra unemployment benefits and National Assistance payments drawn by immigrants are very small even in times of economic recession.

Such evidence as exists thus indicates that the immigrants 'take out' considerably less than they 'put in' to the economy, and very much less than their proper share in relation to the extra economic expansion that their presence creates. The contention that immigrants are 'sucking the blood' of the British welfare state is inspired at best by economic illiteracy, at worst by malicious prejudice.

Propaganda to refute the damaging arguments of the anti-immigrant lobby is vitally important, but it is futile unless it leads to action from the authorities. Racial prejudice is itself not simply an outcrop of ignorance. As Dr Michael Banton has written:

The cause of prejudice is in the subject, not the object of prejudice. It is an irrational, pathological phenomenon, rising from the individual's own inadequacies, and resulting in displaced aggression.

And Professor Robb has described race prejudice as the 'fulfilment of a human need'.

It is not difficult to find such 'human needs' and 'inadequacies' in the Britain of the sixties. Housing shortages, overcrowded schools, inadequate hospitals, irregular transport, a bullying bureaucracy at work, insufficient time for leisure, all these problems and many others besides are all too easily blamed on the immigrant. The main task of government is to remove the root causes of this 'displaced aggression', to end the shortages which so cramp the lives of working people.

Against the background of general social reform, there are also problems relating specifically to immigration which need urgent Government attention. From the moment that the immigrants arrive they are open to exploitation of the most cruel and destructive kind. Government action could range from relatively simple projects, like meeting the immigrants when they arrive and help-

243

ing them reach their destination, to more sweeping reform like the municipilization of multi-occupied housing. There are areas for particular pressing reforms in education, health and language teaching. Clearly, for instance, a national scheme is needed to recruit teachers who speak the languages of the immigrants; to employ sanitary inspectors, clerks, policemen, local authority officials, who are either immigrants themselves or trained in the cultural background of the immigrants.

Government policy on integration should take two basic forms: general reform in the broad field of social services, which would remove much, if not all, of the antagonism against the immigrant, and specific reforms to treat the peculiar problems of immigrants. The overall aim would be to welcome the immigrants to an atmosphere of fairness, to encourage them not to submerge themselves in a foreign culture or isolate themselves in their own, but to live as equals and make their own cultural contribution to their new environment.

This is clearly not a job which can be left to Miss Nadine Peppard, the Institute of Race Relations, the Nuffield Foundation, and, in his spare time, Mr Maurice Foley. Nor is the Home Office, obsessed as it is with control, geared to constructive activity. None of the other Ministries, moreover, can deal with all the problems arising from immigration. What is needed is a new Department of Social Affairs, with a separate branch for immigration.

Of all the many issues concerning immigration in British politics, control is the least important. It is irrelevant to the plain *fact* of a Britain in which people of different races and colours are now established, irrelevant to the problems which the mingling of different cultures in Britain creates. Yet it is the one on which the most constant political emphasis is placed.

The main forms of immigration control are three in number: health restrictions, the deportation of criminals, and general control. The first two forms usually commend themselves to politicians more readily than the third; yet they are, if anything, the least acceptable. Deportation of criminals, for instance, places the immigrants in an inferior position before the law compared with that of the indigenous population, directly contradicting Sir Alec Douglas Home's own argument that immigrants should be treated 'exactly like everyone else'. Demands for the deportation of criminals are inspired by the worst form of anti-immigrant propaganda, and are quite unacceptable in a country where everyone, black or white, should receive equal treatment from the law.

The process whereby immigrants are inspected on arrival at a British port, and deported if found to be suffering from a contagious disease, is palpably cruel, if not dangerous. The whole proposition that immigrants should be tested *at source* is prompted by the idea that disease is all right provided that it is kept out of Britain. If an immigrant decides to come to Britain, and is found to be ill, he should be hospitalized on entry and, when recovered, allowed to stay. Of course there should be more health *checks*, to discover the state of health – not only for immigrants but for everyone. But health *restrictions* are grossly inhumane.

The main argument for general control is that it stops 'unmanageable floods' of immigrants from entering the country. But this control exists without legislation. All the available evidence points to a correlation between unemployment figures in the 'host' country and the figures for immigration.

The right of free immigration from the Commonwealth and colonies has existed 'ever since our forbears ventured across the seas'. Yet in the twenties and thirties, when Britain suffered from chronic unemployment, very few took advantage of this right. Large-scale immigration started only when Britain was hungry for large numbers of new workers. Throughout the 1950s the figures for job vacancies in Britain corresponded, taking a short time-lag into account, with figures of uncontrolled Commonwealth immigration. As the number of vacancies went up, so did the number of immigrants. This pattern was distorted by control legislation, which provoked too many people to come before the Act, and allowed too few to come after it. The only immigration uncontrolled by the Immigration Act – that from Ireland – has, as in the past, corresponded throughout almost precisely with the rise and fall in job opportunities. The applications for vouchers to enter Britain from the Commonwealth since the Act was passed bear no relation to what immigration might have been without control, as the proportion of used to issued vouchers, together with the rush of applications so soon after the Act, amply demonstrates. This correspondence between spontaneous immigration and job opportunities in the host country is not only a British experience. In an article for *International Migration*, the Canadian Assistant Regional Superintendent, European Region, Mr G. D. McQuade, has shown how applications for immigration into Canada correspond, again taking a short time-lag into account, with the employment situation there.

The feudal apathy in much of the underdeveloped world which supplies immigrants to Britain acts as a further brake on immigration. Politicians like Sir Cyril Osborne who suggest, with apparent seriousness, that 400 million Indians might, if allowed, arrive to settle in Britain, demonstrate no more than their own ignorance. The general economic and social state of India and Pakistan indicate that only a vibrant, comparatively prosperous minority even examines the prospect of emigration.

The second argument for control is that the fewer people who come, the easier they are to assimilate. This theory was expressed by Sir Alec Douglas Home in the 1964 election campaign, when he declared that the immigrants were less persecuted, that prejudice was less intense, because of control. This is, of course, impossible finally to disprove, because what would have happened without control, or agitation for it, is hypothetical. Yet what can be established is that after both 1905 and 1961, after the furore over control legislation, prejudice against the immigrant significantly increased. The anti-immigrant lobby in the Conservative Party and the extremist right-wing parties gained strength, not lost it, after the introduction of control. Sir Cyril Osborne was not isolated after his demands were met in 1961. On the contrary, he has risen hugely in stature and can now lead his party's leaders into the lobbies to support a motion more reactionary than any they had opposed before control. The British National Party and the Union Movement can claim control legislation as the consequence of their own efforts and can ask for more pressure of the 1961 type to 'get the blacks out altogether'. Although the Birmingham Immigration Control Association suspended activities after the Act, it was back in the field with renewed vigour less than three years later, and the Southall Residents Association was formed some fourteen months after control was introduced. All the evidence suggests that the association of the main political parties with the views of their extremists only increases the prestige and power of prejudice. The extremists become more important public figures. Their views become respectable. They take command of the pace, and political leaders, anxious to shelve the immigration issue altogether and 'get on with other things', stumble after them with further concessions.

The prejudice and resentment which followed the control Acts of 1905, 1919 and 1961 have been out of all proportion to the figures for immigration. After 1919, for instance, there was a net *emigration* of aliens from Britain, but the anti-alien fury, fed by some Tory politicians, never lost its force. Similarly, from 1962–5, the figures for immigration from the coloured Commonwealth dropped well below their pre-1961 peak, but the baying of racialists has risen to a crescendo. It is more than likely that the incidence of resentment and prejudice actually increases with acceptance of control by leading politicians.

A third argument for control is that the emigration of skilled workers from the underdeveloped countries deprives such societies of the very resources that they most need. The argument, whose logical conclusion is that Britain should accept only unskilled workers from underdeveloped countries, omits the considerable value to the underdeveloped countries of remittances from working emigrants. In 1962, for instance, Pakistan earned a total of £30 million in foreign exchange from remittances by emigrants – her second largest source of foreign exchange.

This does, however, raise a vital aspect of the control discussion. While there is little case for keeping the skilled workers out, there is a considerable case for taking in as many unskilled workers as possible. Until 1961, the West Indian economies were considerably assisted by the emigration of unskilled workers at least in equal proportions to the emigration of the skilled. One of the more cynical aspects of the Immigration Act is its acceptance of the skilled cream from the Commonwealth countries and its rejection of the unskilled workers, who, if anything, need the benefits of migration more than the skilled workers do.

There are two fundamental arguments against immigration control. The first is that control legislation prohibits the Jamaican, the Pakistani, the Italian or the Indian from moving to Britain if he so wishes. Such a restriction on the freedom to move is only justified if some direct or indirect benefit to the individual so affected can be shown to result from restriction. Control legislation, however, is exercised *only* in the interests of the 'host' country. It is nationalist legislation *par excellence*.

Secondly, even more important, control solves none of the problems which allegedly inspire it. It merely sets out to hide them from view, behind a makeshift barrier of prejudice. Control cannot build houses for the immigrants or the hosts; it cannot curb the unscrupulous landlord, break up the ghettoes, or prohibit the formation of a sub-proletariat. There is something grimly absurd about the logic of control propaganda. 'There is rubbish in their yards,' runs the argument, 'and their cooking smells. Give us stricter control.' It is as though control provisions from the Home Office can clear up rubbish or change an Indian's taste for curry.

Immigration and race problems in Britain and other industrial countries derive from the fact that modern affluent capitalism has not provided the necessary social services for its workers. Keynesian economics have to a considerable extent smoothed out the slump–boom cycle of pre-war years, but the benefits of full employment and scientific advance have not provided decent housing, adequate hospitals, properly staffed schools and regular transport for the people who produce them. This is as savage an indictment on the present system of production and distribution as was unemployment before the war. Its effect in this context is to create constant shortages which turn people against each other on irrelevant grounds of race and colour.

Increasingly, a crucial line between politicians on this issue divides those who seek to provide enough social services for all working people from those who seek to exaggerate tensions between them. The arguments for immigration control are started, almost always, by the latter group. They have nothing to do with the realities of international migration. There has never been, is not, and in the foreseeable future will not be an economic case for restricting immigration. The so-called 'social arguments' are founded on the weird fantasies of race and the xenophobic traditions of the British people. They distract attention from relevant and realistic political demands. That is why the Labour Party was right in 1905, 1919 and 1961 to oppose control. That is why a bold, progressive Government should introduce new legislation dealing with immigrants of all nationalities, sweeping aside the restrictions both on entry and on immigrants once they have arrived, and setting up new machinery for dealing with the real problems which give rise to racial resentment. Such a Government, for the first time in British history, would be looking at immigration problems the right way round.

Yet it is in the wider political context that this matter must finally be judged. The industrial world slips year by year into the quagmire of 'planned' bureaucracy – bureaucracy under which governments and politics are separated altogether from the people, under which the electoral processes of parliamentary or presidential democracies become personalized glamour festivals. Such bureaucracies can be 'enlightened', like President Kennedy's intellectual junta; 'dynamic', as in Khrushchev's Russia; 'efficient', as in Adenauer's Germany; or 'sterile' as in Sir Alec Douglas Home's Britain. Yet their basic characteristics are the same – essentially, in the true meaning of the word, undemocratic.

Side by side with these bureaucracies, the 'underdeveloped' world stagnates in the aftermath of imperialism. Political independence is small compensation for the robbery of the 'terms of trade', and the economic gap between the rich and the poor countries grows wider year by year. Race and colour are superimposed over the whole ugly pattern. The developed world is white, and the undeveloped world is yellow and black. Several million people, driven once by slavers and now by unemployment, have moved from the black world to the white. Their exploitation and persecution in the developed world symbolizes the violence of imperialism.

The political rationale for all this is summed up in the words 'national interest'. For the conventional politician today, every unpopular move, every sacrifice is in the 'national interest'. Wages, production priorities, education, defence, foreign affairs, all are judged on the single criterion of the 'national interest'. The rhetoric which accompanies this political theory rings a curiously old-fashioned note in what is supposed to be a modern age.

Mr Harold Wilson, symbol of the 'New Britain', has called for the 'spirit of Dunkirk'. Sentimental intellectuals propose this or that political policy because they 'love Britain'. The language would have been more appropriate before the walls of Harfleur. 'God for Harry, England and St George' is the up-to-date political slogan of the scientific revolution. The justifications for bureaucracy, for the gap between developed and undeveloped countries, for immigration control all tend to be framed in the same 'patriotic' terminology. Unhappily, there is no clear line between patriotism and chauvinism.

In these political circumstances, internationalism is left to the clichés. The international interest is acceptable only if it does not affect the national interest. Everyone wants to opt out of the rat-race between nations, provided that none of the other rats benefit. Everyone wants to help the 'underdeveloped' countries, provided that 'the nation' can afford it. Thus 'aid' to these countries is 'tied' more and more to the national economy, to the national interest.

Mr Philip Mason, Director of the Institute of Race Relations, said in a television discussion on 8 March 1965 that immigration control was 'implicit in nationalism'. He was absolutely right. Control is implicit in nationalism, and consequently has nothing to do with internationalism. The genuine internationalist, for whom the British are no more important than the people of any other nation, for whom typhoid in Karachi is just as evil as typhoid in London or Bradford, for whom the only rational system of society must be founded on an international basis, reacts violently to any suggestion which implies further separation of nation from nation, of white from coloured. Every call for immigration control, every appeal to the virtues of 'British stock', strengthens the barriers between nations and stiffens the bureaucracies which govern the industrial nations. This is the crucial criterion by which the twentieth century British politician's treatment of the foreigner must be judged.

Epilogue

Almost all the political development in the six weeks since I completed this book have followed the patterns written into it. The subject of race and immigration has taken hold even more firmly of the British imagination, and it is hard nowadays to open a newspaper without some reference to it.

The local elections at Smethwick in May 1965 confirmed the tendency, established throughout the 1960s, of Conservative gains. Indeed the Conservatives won seven of the eight seats, and the eighth – the former Labour stronghold of Victoria – was won by Labour by twenty votes. The Conservative cause was, no doubt, assisted by an outbreak of interest in the immigration problem among the Tory majority on the council shortly before election time. Councillor Gould, chairman of the Housing Committee, who a few months earlier had said that coloured immigrants would be rehoused as was their due, took it upon himself to announce that two new housing blocks would not, for the time being, be let to coloured immigrants. (Naturally, this was 'not a colour bar'.)

Meanwhile, Mr Peter Griffiths has climbed still further up the ladder of Tory respectability. He moved all the major Opposition amendments in the Committee stage of the Race Relations Bill.

The Labour Government has all but confirmed reports that it will introduce tighter immigration control. The Mountbatten mission to the Commonwealth was a hopeless failure – Mountbatten being told in no uncertain manner that the Commonwealth countries were not going to solve Britain's problems for her. On 23 June, the London *Evening Standard* carried on its front page one of those 'inspired leaks' by which the Labour Government seeks to probe public opinion. It told of a 'Tighter Curb on Immigrants' and specified a 'fixed quota' of 10,000 immigrant workers from the Commonwealth every year, 6,000 of them for transport and hospitals, and 4,000 highly skilled technicians. Mr Robert Carvel, who wrote the article, intimated tighter checks on dependants, and 'language tests' for prospective immigrants, particularly from Asia.

Perhaps as a sop to left-wing resentment against such manoeuvres (which are not at the time of writing confirmed), the Government have also been suggesting various methods of integration which are far more progressive than anything hitherto mentioned in this field. The recruitment of coloured policemen is the most widely-rumoured suggestion. While this latter tendency is encouraging, there still remains the possibility that the Labour Government will climb down over its progressive proposals (as it has done, disastrously, over the Race Bill) while maintaining a tough line on its reactionary measures.

On the same day that Carvel leaked the Government proposals for further control, the *Birmingham Post* carried three separate items on its main Midland News page (page 5) each with some bearing on the subject:

(1) *Town has 100 vacant jobs:* Darlaston Employment Exchange has been notified of more than 100 vacant jobs with local firms, but there is no labour available to satisfy the demands. The number of unemployed was very low at 22 (0·1% of the insured population).

(2) *Mill's shortage of labour:* Mr Frederick Watts, manager of Hurcot Paper Mills Ltd, near Kidderminster, said at a sitting of a lands tribunal at Dudley last night that the firm had, for its size, one of the biggest export programmes in the business but could not fulfil it because of labour shortage.

(3) *Mechanics crisis may hit public services:* Meriden Rural Council's staff of mechanics, with 31 vehicles to maintain, has dwindled to two . . . Councillor White said that . . . public services would suffer if vehicles were sent back to the manufacturers.

Thus, with her industries straining for more workers and her Government desperately keeping out the blacks, does the Dynamic New Britain forge ahead into the Modern Age.

Appendixes

APPENDIX 1

Ministry of Labour Vouchers for Commonwealth Immigrants

	Applications for vouchers received	Vouchers issued	Voucher-holders admitted to U.K.
FROM INDIA:			
July–Dec., 1962	20,915	12,061	646
1963	145,693	10,692	8,366
1964	33,829	6,084	3,828
FROM PAKISTAN:			
July–Dec., 1962	15,610	3,887	391
1963	122,485	17,055	13,526
1964	25,975	4,158	3,296
FROM WEST INDIES:			
July–Dec., 1962	5,094	3,074	1,600
1963	6,179	3,148	2,077
1964	10,550	3,830	2,635
FROM WHOLE COMMONWEALTH:			
July–Dec., 1962	50,121	25,390	5,121
1963	296,727	41,101	30,125
1964	97,415	20,824	14,705

Totals from July 1962 to December 1964
From:

India	200,437	28,837	12,840
Pakistan	164,060	25,090	17,107
West Indies	21,823	10,052	6,312
Whole Commonwealth	444,263	87,315	49,951

Author's note

The actual vouchers issued by the Ministry do not indicate whether they are 'A', 'B' or 'C' vouchers. As a result it is impossible to know

how many 'C' voucher-holders have been admitted. The only classi-
fication of voucher-holders entering is by country of origin. This is a
serious gap in the statistics available. It is impossible even to estimate
how many of the 'C' voucher applications were real, and how many
were in effect not really serious. Such an estimate is, of course, crucial
for any calculation of the 'economic regulator' after control.

APPENDIX 2

*Immigrant Workers (Permanent and Seasonal) Entering and
Leaving European Countries: 1961–63*

	1961	1962	1963
TO:			
Germany	360,500	396,600	377,500
France	175,900	208,200	216,800
Belgium	5,200	15,400	26,300
Holland	11,300	13,200	16,800
Switzerland	369,200	399,300	386,900
United Kingdom	58,400	55,300	52,500
FROM:			
Italy	526,800	525,100	452,300
Spain	189,700	244,800	256,800
Greece	37,500	52,100	63,800
Turkey	7,200	15,600	34,400
Portugal	9,100	15,500	29,000
Yugoslavia	300	600	500
Others	199,600	208,500	218,200

Source: '*Migrations intra-européennes et action sociale*': pamphlet produced by: *Études sociales nord africaines*, Paris, 1964.

APPENDIX 3

	1963	1964
Entry to Britain of Commonwealth workers (mostly coloured)	30,125	14,705
Entry to Britain of alien workers (all white)	39,683	42,554

The only SMETHWICK Candidate who has ALWAYS called FOR THE STRICTEST CONTROL OF IMMIGRATION

is

PETER GRIFFITHS

REMEMBER THIS WHEN YOU CAST YOUR

VOTE

Printed by Smethwick Telephone Co, Ltd., 24 Hume Street, Smethwick, 40.
Published by C. E. A. Dickens, Election Agent, 68 Edgbaston Road, Smethwick, 41.

Sheila Patterson

The General Election of 1964 made it obvious that immigration is the most explosive question behind the scenery of English politics today.

Dark Strangers presents a remarkable and very detailed survey of the relationships between West Indian migrants and the local population of the Brixton area of London. Sheila Patterson analyses these relationships in terms of the concept of 'accommodation', which she defines as 'an early phase of adaptation and acceptance in which migrants and local people achieve a minimum *modus vivendi*'. She concentrates her inquiry on three main areas of association – employment, housing, and social and cultural activities – and, despite the inevitable difficulties of the future, her findings to suggest that eventually the migrants will be accepted and at least partially absorbed into the local population.

'It is admirably free from the jargon which disfigures so many sociological studies, and it throws so much light on racial problems in general that it deserves a much wider audience than a purely academic one' – Goronwy Rees in the *Sunday Telegraph*.